MID-LIFE CYCLES

About the Author

Marion Ferguson is stretching her middle years as far as she can. She was raised in the City of Detroit suburbs until she married at a young age and moved to the country with her husband. She has raised four boys mostly on her own since her divorce, remarrying once more. She led a homemaker's life until she went to work as a rural mail carrier for the Brighton, Michigan post office in 1966.

It opened a new world for her. She was involved in many facets of postal life and it in turn led to needing more out of life.

She always had a curiosity about nature and loved most outdoor activities. Taking the boys on nature hikes when they were young; canoeing, skiing, snowmobiling, hunting and camping in out-of-the-way places. After the children were grown there seemed to be something missing and it started the activities you will read about in this book.

As time went on so did the many journals sitting in a drawer. She was encouraged to put them together for her family. One thing led to another and it found its way into these covers. Not having any real writing experiences, she read everything she could find on writing and attended English and writing classes to hone her skills. She has written articles for several small newspapers. She has ideas for other books and is looking forward to retirement when the hustle and bustle of work will not be in the way. But, she says, there might not be enough time when she retires. Grandchildren are in the picture now and she is wishing they would grow just a little faster so they can begin to see the things she enjoys, too.

There are just so many things to do and places to explore and not enough time to do them all. She won't be ready for the rocking chair for a long time.

MID-LIFE CYCLES

Or

What Am I Doing Here?

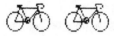

By

MARION FERGUSON

Library of Congress Catalog Card Number 91-066446
ISBN: 0-923568-22-0

Cover design and artwork by Marion Ferguson

PUBLISHED BY

Wilderness Adventure Books
320 Garden Lane
P.O. Box 968
Fowlerville MI 48836

Manufactured in the United States of America

Dedicated to

MOM

who waits patiently for
her daughter to grow up

Mid-Life Cycles
OR
WHAT AM I DOING HERE?

Adventure #1

Mid-Life on a Two-Wheeler

Chapter 1 The Age of Reason

With Newberry behind me, I leaned over the handlebars of my black and red 15 speed bicycle, pushing on the pedals easily as I whizzed by the rolling countryside this glorious morning. Not many cars or trucks were on the road yet, so I didn't feel them as they made their usual air wake. The sun perched between the many pine trees of this northern Michigan region. This would be a good day to ride. I kept my eyes on the road ahead feeling the extra weight of my loaded packs as I encountered the first hill of the day.

Effortlessly, I clicked the gear shift into a lower gear. It was a clue I would be working harder to make it to the top. Already I felt the sweat on my forehead as I tried standing in the pedals for the last stretch, muscles straining. My hands gripped the lower part of the curved handlebars. I padded them with extra padding found on the road the day before. Wrapping them in bandanas absorbed the road bumps and sweat, adding colorful red to my conversation piece. Arms supporting my shoulders and back gained in muscle mass as much as my legs had over this summer. My legs pumped up, down, up, down, keeping their rhythm as I broke over the hill, clicking the gears back into their high position.

I relaxed back onto the small hard seat that had been a part of me for the past few years. I comfortably edged myself down the hill in the typical bent-over position. The wind caught my short hair under my helmet cooling the sweat that was accumulating. I reached down for my water bottle taking a good, long drag to replenish fluids I might have lost already. What a way to start the day!

Ahead of me lay the unknown. I had not traveled this road before by bicycle. It made this just another adventure to add to many over the last 8 years or so. Since I was traveling alone this time, I hadn't anyone to talk to unless I stopped along the way at a restaurant or park. This was a good time to reflect on many topics; a time to solve all the problems of the world according to me; a time to think back on my life...................

When I was a little kid living in Detroit, my world evolved around my parents and my older brother. As far as I can remember, we had a very happy life together. In summer, I would ride my brothers' 3-wheeled bicycle. It made a few scorching moments of the usual hitting and pushing that siblings fall prey. My bicycle riding world at the age of four amounted to going up and down the double strip of driveway and flat expanse of cement leading to our garage.

When I was seven, my father said I had reached the *age of reason*, and he gave me a regular size 2-wheeler. He would push me up and down our sidewalk waiting for me to find my balance. So often I'd yell to him that he could let go. So often he let go, with me falling off. I must have been the "Band-Aid princess" that summer. With diligence, I mastered the art. I would weave in and out trying to stay on the sidewalk. "I can do it myself, Daddy," I'd tell him. Dad would look after me with that proud look fathers have when their young one accomplishes something, but also the look of knowing I wouldn't be his little girl much longer.

Sometimes, if dad was away, mom would push me to get started. "I'm going to let go now, Marion," she'd say as she ran next to me panting. I wonder if they realized back then, they were launching me into an adventure filled world. With that uncertain look most parents get, they kept pushing me on that bike anyway, pushing me into the world ahead.

So often they told me, "Don't go on the road. Stay on the sidewalk." I must have circled our block a million times that summer. I knew every crack in the sidewalk, every overhanging bush that would get in my face, every dog that would come running after me. The new-found freedom brought much happiness into my young life.

As time passed, permission was given to enjoy the pleasure of long distance riding if I went with my best friend, Rosemary. It amounted to six blocks to a church corner to have our lunch, carried in a brown paper bag clutched ever so tightly between our hands and the handlebars.

"My mother said I could go to the church on Monte Vista at Outer Drive. Will your mother let you go with me? Rosemary asked. "She said I could go only if you could go"

"Let's go ask her. Why don't we take a lunch and have a picnic?" I suggested as we ran across the street to my house.

"Mom, Rosemary's mom said she could go for a bike ride and a picnic. Can I go?" I asked her as she was doing the morning dishes.

She didn't look like she was going to let me. But she turned around and asked, "I don't know. Where are you going?" We told her and she relented if we promised to be real careful.

They made us some sandwiches. Mom making peanut butter and jelly for me and Rosemary had tuna fish. I liked mine better and so did she so we shared mine first. An apple and cookies helped to round out our lunch. We didn't have a way to carry anything to drink so we didn't take any. Thermos bottles were too big to handle.

The farthest I ever went on that bicycle later was to her friends house several miles away. By this time, I was gaining an interest in the opposite sex and found bicycle riding a little kids' pleasure, no longer something an awkward pre-teen would be caught dead on. Boys were supposed to ride them, not girls.

It wasn't long before my transportation changed to automobiles. During my teen-age days the bicycle was living its rusty life in the garage waiting for my younger brother to grow big enough to ride it. It had no longer been my freedom friend. No more did I paint it ever so carefully or polish the chrome or oil the chain. No more did I weave crepe paper in the spokes or put long streamers on the handlebars for a parade. No longer did I find playing cards to clip to the frame with a clothespin so they would hit the spokes to make a motor sound.

Years later, I pushed my son on his first 2-wheeler with the same wistful sight I remember seeing in my fathers' eyes. He started out with the new-fangled training wheels. Every so often I would raise them a little farther. It saved a lot of running next to him panting the way my parents did. It wasn't long before I was sending him off with his little hands gripping the handlebars with white knuckles, the front wheel wobbling back and forth in erratic gestures. All too soon he was on his way.

I went through three more of training wheel days before all my sons had mastered this growing-up experience and reaching their *ages of reason*.

I never knew back when my father launched me in this mode that it would become my exercise, entertainment and transportation. As a middle-aged adult I found the joy of riding a more sophisticated bicycle that would carry me over some 16,000 miles by the time I was fifty years old.

I started my second childhood when I bought my youngest son who was now twelve and myself new Shwinns. I wanted to ride the roads but not alone. We would ride together on the paved country roads with our bodies leaning over the low handlebars. We thought we were big time racers at an unknown speed of probably twelve miles an hour. We carried them to the south one winter, finding new horizons in the warmer Florida sunshine.

Larry Hollenbeck, who I'd only known a short time, rode for long distances I had only dreamed of riding. That year he would call me each night after riding all day up the state. He was not riding alone but with several hundred other bicycle fanatics. He made it sound like it was so much fun that I was determined to do it myself. DALMAC was the name of this ride. Dick Allen Lansing to MACkinaw.

I found Shirley Dippold who wanted to try my idea of DALMAC. She was married but her husband was away on business most of the time. Her children, like mine, were all gone and we were both living alone. She worked only part time, making a perfect companion with unlimited time to ride.

We would ride around town practicing our skills, enjoying the open air in preparation for the four day ride across the state with 1500 other riders. We joined a city club that scheduled rides lasting up to 100 miles in a day. We never rode more than 50 miles in a day thinking that was an accomplishment in itself. We must have only ridden 400 miles all summer thinking it was enough. We didn't have the nice computer type odometers that were on the market. It wasn't long before we realized our worst.

We didn't practice for as long as we should have. We did meet many new friends. We learned some of the ropes of group riding, heard talk of the right equipment importance. We paid attention to some.

4

Chapter 2   DALMAC

When the day of the ride arrived, we were very excited. We could have packed a tent and have a truck haul our gear around to our next overnight stay as the others did but we didn't really have any gear. My mother volunteered to be our procurer of motel rooms for the duration. She would ride around worrying till our day was over and drive us to a good nights' sleep on a nice soft bed in a comfortable room. At the end of the tour we would just ride on home rather than taking the optional bus back to the beginning like most of the riders.

The tour itself was supposed to take us four days and almost 350 miles north from Lansing to St. Ignace, Michigan. We would cross the Mackinaw bridge that connected the upper to the lower peninsulas of the state. Our average miles per day should be 85 miles. We were to ride each day to a school the tour group selected. We would be served breakfast and dinner. The rest was up to us. They would provide water and some fruit along the way occasionally. But the big thrill was to ride across the bridge. It was only for auto traffic and we needed to be escorted along its five mile distance.

We found the place in the capital park where we were to meet the rest of the group. People dressed in those funny tight pants, shirts in a multitude of colors, helmets or little caps with upturned visors. They were busy packing their gear from the night before. Some were just getting out of their tents or milling around moving bicycles, making last minute repairs, putting long flags on their bikes or standing in what we found would be one of our biggest headache, long lines.

"I'll stay here by the car if you want to see where you're supposed to go, Marion," Mom volunteered. We wandered over to the lines and saw that the only way we were going to go anywhere, was to register. Forms were given to us to fill out, signing our life away. In turn they sent us down the line of tables to receive a packet of stuff, a t-shirt and a flag. Looking in the packet we found a piece of weather resistant paper with a number on it.

"Hey, I feel like we are going to be in a race with this." I said.

5

"I saw them wearing them in other bike rides," explained Shirley uncertainly. "They're called *fanny patches* because you wear them there," she laughed as she pointed to another rider.

"Let's see what else we've got. There is at least a map so we won't get lost and here is a map for Mom so she won't get lost," I said as we rummaged through the stuff they gave us. We also found a decorative patch, and the best of all, an information book.

We walked away reading our booklet, carrying our flag in one arm and hanging on to the rest of the equipment. Getting back to the car, we found Mom standing there in amazement while she surveyed the sea of bicyclists.

"I suppose we'd better at least get our bikes off the back of the car and get to the start point. I wouldn't want to be late," I offered.

"No, maybe it would be better if we just left them there and pretended we were riding with this tour." Shirley looked at me hoping I was just kidding. I was so bewildered and excited at the same time, getting the bikes off the car became a struggle. Shirley helped, this becoming one of our first attempts to collaborate in the packing-unpacking dilemma.

We still had to put the flag on the bikes It was bright orange on a very long flexible pole. We were having a little difficulty doing this when one of the riders offered to help. We could see he was much more experienced than we were and before long we were set to continue. Since we had never ridden for such a distance it was a little scary. Grabbing our helmets, putting on our riding gloves and checking for last minute items, we instructed Mom where she was to meet us that evening. It would only be about seventy five miles away and it seemed so easy. All of us were starting from the state capital building so she walked the couple blocks to the building with us.

We thought we had seen the bulk of the riders in the park. Here, there was a flood of people and bicycles, mostly riders, all standing around holding up their bikes, flags waving in the breeze or sitting on the ground laughing, eating, or renewing old acquaintances. A police motorcade was to lead us out of town. The flashing red-blue lights revolving on top of the squad cars made the atmosphere more colorful. Bringing our bulky cameras along was one of the dumbest things we had thought to do. After the four days were over we never took them again.

We never had to pack light before. This was going to be a trying situation, if we had only known. In our little bags on the fronts of our bikes we packed in all the "emergency" things we could think of. The cameras would document that we actually rode some 400 miles to our destination. They were rather cumbersome. Researching for information for this book, I could not find any good pictures. Food was not on the top of our list but changes of clothes were. We didn't want to get caught without rain gear and cold weather would be a disaster, so we didn't leave much room for extra water or any food. This was going to be a good place to lose a little weight. Good, pure exercise!

A speech was given by a government official and the head organizer for the tour. That over, we all lined up in a couple of rows to start our escort out of town. Somehow we fanangled a place in the first few rows. It was beginning to look more like a race than a tour. The others around us all seemed to know each other, talking excitedly as we just kept watching and listening. Our own excitement was building rapidly when the motorcycle police joined our escort. It wasn't long before they started their sirens, motors rumbling, when we were given the go ahead sign to begin.

Mom stood on the corner with others who were observing this phenomena, taking pictures. She must have some photos salted away somewhere. I think she wanted to know what her daughter looked liked before she was to go off and never return. Did she remember those days when I had reached the *age of reason?* She could have been thinking of that statement at this very moment! Is there such an age? She was using her new Polaroid camera so we would be able to see her photos that evening if we saw her again.

Off we started in a flash! The thrill of it all began as everyone yelled with excitement. Some trying to get in front of others even though they were told to stay in lines until we were out of town. We began slowly, riding through red traffic lights. Cross traffic was held back by the police cars with their flashing red-blue lights. I didn't know how long it would take them to wait for all 1500 of us to clear their street crossing. It was exhilarating to know they were watching just us. Some gave us the thumbs up sign, some clapping. There were also those just trying to get to where they were going, impatient with us for interrupting their morning. The sun in our eyes for the first few blocks promised us a good day for riding.

Suddenly, pumping my pedals became a most difficult thing to do. I felt as if someone was holding me back. I kept going, losing sight of Shirley as she was swallowed up by the faster riders. The sweat was pouring down my face even though it was still a mild morning in early autumn. I didn't remember having to pedal this hard all summer. If this was the way to start a fun ride I was beginning to have my doubts.

Shirley slowed a bit and yelled, "What's the matter?"

"I don't know, but keep in line, I'll be all right," I yelled over the chatter of the others. The motorcade took us several miles before we were left to ride on our own at the city limits. The rush was on! Finding a grassy corner in the shade, I stopped my bike and fell to the ground with Shirley just ahead of me, stopping also.

7

"I don't know, Shirley, I'm really beat. I feel like all the wind has been knocked out of me. I will never be able to finish today let alone four days," I panted. I sat on the grass trying to get my breath back while she stood holding onto her bike watching me.

Sitting there, looking at the bike lying on the ground, I saw what must have been my problem. "Hey, look at my flag. It's messed up my brake pad somehow." I jumped up filled with some new energy. Sure enough, the help we were given was as much help as we, ourselves, could have done. The pole of the flag was pressing my brake pad making me ride with the brakes engaged. With a few twists and adjustments it looked like it would at least last till the end of the day. We were off again in the middle of the pack. So much for the help we got.

Now the riders were easing into a more relaxed pace. There were the ever present speeders from the Wolverines of Detroit. Someone informed us, they always raced in team formation even though this was a tour. They would start late, finish early in the day, riding in a single file, heads down. There were those, like us, who were there just to enjoy the camaraderie of other bicyclists just riding at a nice, even pace. A few young riders made the group more rounded. Since it was supposed to be quite a vicious ride there were not any very young unless they were pulled behind by a parent in a child carrier called a 'bugger'.

Feeling more comfortable since the flag was fixed we joined the ever lengthening group. Faster riders far forward, us slow ones in back. With many spaces between riders all riding close to the edge of the road we really began our tour. I recalled my parents telling me not to ride in the street.

After some distance I said to Shirley, "I hope we are still friends after this trip." She agreed with a little apprehension. I made this statement every day after that.

Our first break was pleasant. There were a group of riders milling around a car parked along a shady section offering homemade cookies, bananas and juices. The ever present water jug for those who needed it was sitting in the trunk. The tour provided this nicely at different points along the whole four day tour. This was going to be a great way to start a diet!

We came to our first of many small towns. Dewitt. Bikers were parked everywhere, mostly at breakfast places, bars or small grocery stores. This became the regular sight for any town or store or place to eat or watering hole for the rest of the tour. It would remind me of a movie I saw about a locust epidemic; once it passed through an area there was nothing left. After we passed through a town there was not a bit of food to eat. We would stop to rest at many of these places. We refrained from eating too much since we thought we could diet and still enjoy the ride.

A regular lunch stop was set up for us at the half way point in a VFW hall in Perrington. The members sold us a variety of nutritious lunch items and we joined the others, listening to the tales from the front of other rides in other places. Some had ridden this tour before, telling us about some of the fun ahead. Everyone seemed to be wearing a t-shirt from some ride they had been on. It was good advertisement.

We didn't linger long at lunch even if we wanted to. We still had the rest of the distance and we had never ridden 75 miles in one day before. We didn't want to be late for the dinner that the tour provided. We heard from the other riders that they sometimes ran out.

With a little reluctance but still enthusiastic, we jumped back on the bikes heading north. We found we didn't need the map they gave us today as everyone was close enough together so we couldn't possibly get lost. The bright orange flags helped when we spread out on today's straight flat terrain. We could see a rider or two off in the distance either in front or behind us.

After lunch we seemed to need to stop more often to rest. We stopped every ten miles or so and then every five or less. At about the 60 mile mark we thought we would never see the end of the day. It became much hotter and humid, making us feel more tired than we thought we should be. Our seats were becoming a bit uncomfortable. We were still unaware how those tight funny looking pants helped our seats but were beginning to find out the hard way.

Once in awhile we encountered a resident who left their hose running by the side of the road for us to fill our water bottles, one asking us if we would like to be sprayed as we pedaled by. It was refreshing and I looked forward to the nicety on other days, in other places.

Just a few more miles to go. It seemed like hundreds. A rise in the road over the highway crossing on an ordinary day would mean nothing. Now it looked and felt like a mountain. It took all I could muster to shift my gears to get over it. At the top we could see the stadium of Central Michigan University where we were destined. Why, for heavens' sake, we looked like we might have been the last to arrive. It was 6:00 and there were a thousand tents set up already. How did they do it so fast? Riders were reveling as the day waned down. Many were just walking around, or going in or out of the school building for showers. They all looked so fresh!

Since we didn't know if we could even make it, we made arrangements for Mom to come look for us if we weren't there by 6:00. Sure enough, there she was waiting a little nervously. We weren't the last ones as more were coming in, riding like they had just started out.

"How come everyone looks so rested? It looks like they've been here for most of the day," I said flatly and rather confused.

"Look at the riders coming in behind us, Marion. They act like they're just out for a stroll around the park. How disgusting!"

It felt so good not to have to ride that bike to get to any place. We were so exhausted. After an all too brief rest we attached them to the back of the car. Standing outside the cafeteria building, a line of the same people we saw all day were wrapped around the whole courtyard. We learned that to get fed supper we had to wait. We were almost too tired to stand that long but food had been on our mind for many miles. We sat on the ground like some of the others. But even that position felt pain. Getting up was worse. The next best thing would have been a long, hot shower and a soft bed. Mom had found us a room a couple miles away.

The line took forever, it seemed. It was well worth the wait. The university had a fast crew and lots of food with quite a variety to choose from. We took some of everything. Hang the diet!

We admired the others who were lounging around the tents and would be sleeping in them all week. Sure wish I knew what we did with those pictures of the field of tents!

We headed for the car to be driven to the motel.

"I'm glad your mother is getting us rooms every night."

"At least we should get a good night's sleep and not have to wait in line for a cold shower."

"Yea, and we won't have to pack up a wet tent in the morning."

Chapter 3   It Gets Worse Before It Gets Better

That night I never knew a bed could feel so good. I thanked myself for not having equipment to sleep on the ground like the rest of the riders. By morning every bone and muscle cried out in anguish as I tried to lift my head from the pillow. I didn't have enough guts to ask Shirley if she felt the same way. Watching her get up I knew I didn't have to ask. I could see it in her eyes. Mom just looked at us and felt sorry. This was supposed to be fun.

Getting up late, didn't help the situation. We kept the bikes in the room with us. We put them back on the car. Had we been more experienced we could have ridden them back to the school. What would an extra mile or so be! We needed to return to stand in another breakfast line. Since we were late the line wasn't as long as the line for dinner. The hall had the unaccustomed odor of Ben Gay and a few other liniments.

Mom left us with the same instructions. If she didn't see us by 6 p.m. she should start checking the hospital wards.

Breakfast was indeed a big pick-me-up. If nothing else, we would enjoy the food. We now could recognize some new-found friends from time to time, they being concerned about our soreness. We got needed advice on positioning and conditioning.

"You know, they say the second day is the worst day." someone offered. We didn't need to hear that!

A little late but we tried to adjust. Riding today was not going to feel good. Once we were into the saddles again it didn't feel too bad until several miles were under our belts or should I say under our seats! Many stops for rests and water breaks where bananas were a staple, helped our ego.

"On your left" or "Good Morning" came some of the greetings as we rolled along. "Morning" we'd reply. We decided no matter how good the morning was we just couldn't say "Good morning" yet.

The terrain was still rather flat but we heard of the hills yet to come. Since they weren't there, the wind decided to do its best to make us miserable. It blew from the side for most of the day. We had very few breaks from it as we were mostly in open farm land.

With our sore muscles we could hardly engage our gears in anything but third and fourth which is less than half on a ten speed bike. Someone telling us the second day was the worse made us look forward to the third day. But it wasn't all bad. I can say that now that I am looking back.

We rode with other people who sympathized with us as having been there before. It did take our minds off our pain when we talked to someone else other than ourselves.

"Are we still friends?" I asked as I pushed the pedals around, squirming on my seat to find a more comfortable place. I received a slightly positive answer back. This was the day that the total mileage was off just a little but an extra mile was too much to be off at all if it added to a larger total. The wind kept beating at us making our bikes ride on a slant, flags waving frantically. Luckily, we were not heading into it. The sun was hot, humidity stuck to our skin, dripping down our backs. There were the beginnings of sunburn on those who hadn't seen much sun this past summer. Finding the school in West Branch tonight was going to be a welcome reprieve.

We could hardly wait to get off the bike seats. Hands were cramped into one position, shoulders ached and feet didn't want to come out of the stirrups but knowing we had to stand in line again, we didn't linger. Using the bathroom facilities wasn't any easier. Another line. A smaller school, less to offer also meant less food, too. At least it hadn't been as far to ride as the day before nor was it after 6 p.m. again. Supper wasn't served till 7 p.m. giving us several hours to wait.

We headed off to the motel this time to wash up first and relax before supper. Hopefully we wouldn't fall asleep and miss it! Mom said she'd wake us up if we did, so we relaxed in pure air-conditioned luxury.

Much later, we learned to go for walks after a full day of riding to stretch the leg muscles. But this knowledge was not etched in our memory banks yet.

The clock was ticking away in our room, oblivious to the snores of two tired riders. One of the snorers woke and opened a crusted-over eye to see if it was time to get up.

"Shirley, it's late. Get up."

"Oh! darn it. I was sleeping so good. I layed there half the night before I could get to sleep. Are you sure it is?"

I rolled out of bed to look behind the curtains to see how the weather was going to determine what we would wear. It looked normal. Cloudy. Windy. Dull.

"We will be late for breakfast. Hurry up. I'll put the bikes on the car while you get washed, " I offered.

12

We were late but not last. We must have been close to the tail of the riders. At a check point along the way someone indicated that.

Some of the soreness had come out of our necks from our seemingly heavy helmets. The rest of our bodies wanted us to know they were still there. Our hind ends screeched as we slid them onto the vinyl mens' seats that weren't made for women. We learned this the hard way, too. This definitely became a learning experience, not just an adventure.

But today had an added feature. Not only did we have the wind back but we also had intermittent rain with a temperature drop. As mornings were pretty cool and hands got stiff in the cold, Mom bought us some canvas gloves that came in handy. This was also a good day to test rain gear. Shirley had a nice poncho that kept her dry from the top but let in a lot of cold air from the bottom as well as water. Her legs were spattered with road dirt and water until she put on some leg warmers. My poncho was too long and kept getting caught in the wheels. Its cold, wet plastic would whip against my legs taunting them to ache a little more. My legs were spattered with road dirt and water, too. Water would splash up from the wheels as we tried to avoid puddles with little success. Shoes were soaked through with the first sprinkle. They squished on the down side of the pedaling.

The other riders were mostly in good spirits making small talk or trying to make a good thing out of it. It did help us underneath it all. We laughed in spite of ourselves.

"If Mom meets us somewhere along the way today lets put the bikes on the car and ride a little further up, Shirley." I suggested.

"Sounds good to me. I don't like being in the back, it makes me feel like I have to hurry and I don't think I can." she answered.

"Are we still friends?" I asked.

"I don't think I want to talk about it," she grumbled.

Just as I said this about Mom, out of a side street she appeared. I was never so happy to see that white car as I was then. It perked us up a bit and when we rolled up behind it, achingly hung the bikes on the rack and slowly sat in the car, Mom didn't say a thing. We just said "On James". About 20 miles down the road she stopped, we got out, took the bikes off the rack and carefully got back on. It was noted by other riders we passed. They commented on our cheating when they caught up with us on the bikes.

"We saw you riding up the road in the car," they taunted good-naturedly. They were just jealous, we decided.

Later that day when the rain stopped and we were really getting tired, someone very nicely said they made a misprint on the maps and we had another 20 miles to go before we would get to the end of this day. That really made us feel good. I think it played on our minds so much, it slowed us to a crawl. At least the rain stopped.

We skipped the lunch spot opting to diet. But weakness crept in seriously. About three quarters into the ride our water ran out. There looked like nothing between us and the end and we thought we were dying. Nausea was beginning to enter our systems. Legs and thighs were so painful it was a chore to raise them in the circle the pedals needed to push on. Our shoulders ached from the unaccustomed weight of the helmets for such long periods. Someone offered to give us something to nibble on but we still refused it. Where was the banana lady now? Where was the water man, this time? Where was the ambulance? We laid down on the side of the road debating whether to walk up to a house we spotted on a lake. Just as we were making up our minds someone yelled there was a party store up the road. We didn't have the energy to walk to the house so we went to the store replenishing ourselves with Moon Pies and chocolate bars. It helped somewhat for the next few hills.

The scenery was pleasant but the hills were so bad. I rode so slow that I could literally count the stones mixed in the concrete road. With hands in the down tubes and oftentimes standing in the stirrups, no more gears to shift to, we would just barely make it up the hills without walking. Push that pedal down. Push the other one. Others were either walking themselves, or some smart-alec kid would make a dash past like we were standing still. Most rode slowly.

With only 10 miles to go, out of the blue again there was the beautiful white car. Back onto the rack the bikes went and she drove us into the next school for the night. We would be in an elementary school in Vanderbilt.

As we passed many of the riders we could see they weren't pedaling. They were all going down hill! We said we didn't care but underneath we were seething that we didn't go a little further to ride down hill, too.

We told Mom about the 6 mile down hill we rode just a few miles back. It took all the strength we had to get to the top, stopping many times to get our strength. Sometimes we even walked our bikes up short, steep hills, but oh! the feeling to go down for 6 miles without pedaling. We would bend as far forward over the handlebars as we could, rising up off the unforgiving seat and hang on for dear life as our bicycle carried us down about 30 mph or more. We needed many more of those hills but only on the downgrade. We were headed north. I realized on this tour that when it is said "up north" it means literally "up".

Tonight all we could think of was---one more day.

This school was the smallest of the schools we boarded. Vanderbilt was small, there were nothing for anyone to do here but rest and relax. Mom took us to the only motel she could find. We almost wished we could have stayed at school, perhaps sleeping on the bare ground. Little cardboard units were no doubt used only for hunters. The bed looked glorious.   Shirley had brought her sleeping bag. Seeing how we couldn't possibly all fit in the double bed it was going to come in handy. Bringing our bikes into the room left little room to maneuver so she had to lay her bed under the bathroom sink.   Our bones creaked as we hauled in our stuff thinking no one in their right mind would have stolen our bikes if we left them on the car. The thought crossed our minds that we wouldn't have minded if they did.

The hot water was not turned on till after we arrived so we had to wait for our showers. But it was better than what the rest of the group were getting back at the school. Riding by the shower room we could hear squeals and shrieks from the women as they tried to wash in a cold-only shower. Here they didn't even have a hot water faucet! We didn't complain.

The ride the last day started out pretty good. We headed into a tail wind for quite a few miles. Some groups had bunched together to draft each other making much better time. We gave Mom the cameras we hadn't time to use and the extra clothing so we wouldn't have to carry any more than we needed. A few hours later it turned out to be the one thing we shouldn't have done.

The weather turned sour on us in the most beautiful resort areas on the whole tour. We stopped on the Lake Michigan shoreline at Harbor Springs not to look off into the open water to see the many luxury boats anchored in the bay, but to lie on the grass. We hoped to make our backs straighten out, feeling more like beached whales than beach beauties. Around the corner a bike shop set up some drinks and watermelon. Naturally, we stopped to rest again as the sun hid behind the clouds. We spent as much time as possible looking at bicycling gear and equipment wondering if any would have helped. Too late now!

Negotiating a steep hill, the temperature dropped and the rain that only started as a soft pitter-pat turned to a downpour. Mom had the rain gear. At one point we found shelter in a garage. It was a good excuse to get off those hard seats that were wearing blisters on our bottom sides, but as more and more riders rode by, we felt a little ashamed we weren't punishing ourselves like they were and enjoying it still. The lady who owned the garage donated some garbage bags and we donned them for rain coats. They worked pretty well.

We had hills half of the day and our feet, legs and any other part of our anatomy did not like a one of them. We had to walk a couple of them as we just lost all our strength. A television station set up a camera on the biggest hill for a feature story. We smiled unhappily. Our personal agony must have shown through as we pushed our bikes up. He turned the camera off as we approached. "Thank you, we know we look bad!"

After the day without food we made sure we had something to munch on today but, even that didn't help on the hills.

"Are we still friends, Shirley?" I hollered back of me.

"Marion, if I ever say I will do this again, just kick me in my seat so I will remember what I've gone through," she said somberly. Others rode by saying the usual "On your left" or "How ya doin?" We weren't doing. Our hands hurt, everything hurt and we were miserable. But we could still laugh at ourselves.

We had the rest of the day to get through. The rain lasted all morning. We were looking forward to going over the longest span of bridge in the U.S. The Big Mac. We had to be there by a certain time or we would have to wait for another escort.

From Harbor Springs it was supposed to be pretty and flat. First, we had to get up the hill out of town. We walked. How flat it really was going to be we had no way of knowing. There were some rolling hills, then into a scenic area along Lake Michigan lined with trees. We could see the grayness of the water from the road as we entered this long, winding area. There were many white caps out there revealing the true nature of the rain storm. We picked up a little speed as we pushed our pedals around and around. It still seemed to take forever to get to the half way point.

By the time we arrived at Cross Village we were soaked just like everybody else. Here, we were told by some of our new friends, everybody partied down before they got to the bridge. There was only one small bar and we would have lunch here if we could get it. The bar was uniquely made of logs and everything inside made from the same. It was full of people.

Mom felt how cold it was getting from inside her heated car and met us with a change of clothes. Only we didn't see her for a long time. We waited inside the air conditioned bar shivering with hundreds of others, our bikes parked outside stacked up with all the other look alikes, each with their orange flags waving. She waited in her car for us, not wanting to go into the bar. Finally, I went out and there was that white car with dry towels and clothes. I hailed her down and went to get Shirley who had finally got our ordered lunch. Someone else held our place at one crowded table while we changed into something dry and warm. Thank God for mothers! We decided now to wear our ponchos for wind breakers.

Back inside, riders were getting a little drunk. They were there for quite some time. This was their last chance to party before going over the bridge. Some were even dancing on the tables laughing and causing quite a raucous. Some motorcycle people dressed in black leathers couldn't understand us and some left in disgust, but then we couldn't understand them, so the feeling was mutual.

16

While we had lunch, Mom went ahead to wait for us at the bridge. Inside, the news spread around that it quit raining and sure enough, everyone started to clear out to head for the bridge. It was still a long way away for us and those were probably the most agonizing miles we had to go. At one point I could see the spires of the 5 mile long span through the trees as we rounded the lake but it still seemed so very far away.   Most of the hills had disappeared.

Shirley was riding with someone else for a good part of the day so I didn't see her reaction when she went up the last short, steep hill. I'm sure she was cursing me under her breath. I was. The bike just didn't want to go up any more. The pedals would not turn, the wheels felt like they were square and my butt felt like there were open sores on it after riding in wet clothes for so long. The bike seat must be a 2 x 4. But one thing going for us was the warmth. The sun came out for the rest of the day as if it was forgiving us for our endurance.

We found each other at the entrance of the bridge. Several hundred bikers were standing in line getting ready to cross the bridge. If we could hurry now we could go across with them instead of waiting a couple hours for the next group. We pleaded our bodies into one more push to make it. All we wanted to do was get this over. The thrill of riding across the bridge would be the culmination of this whole tour. It was like a reward for doing a good job and we were finally here to do it!

The excitement accelerated. Bikers were whooping it up as they slowly began to go up the ramp. We had to have a small ticket and awarded a green ribbon with something printed on it. We were almost in the tail as we reached the end of the line. We grabbed both, putting them in our teeth as we rode along not wanting to fall back and they stayed there most of the whole five miles across the bridge.

Up we went in our turn, behind two rows of bikes with orange flags waving in the brisk breeze as far as the eye could see, winding our way up the ramp to the apex of the long bridge. Traffic was halted in our lane but sped by us in the left lane, waving at us with smiles, windows rolled down watching this phenomena. Bikers all around were yelling and carrying on while all we could do was hang on to our bikes without falling off. We were going at such a slow pace we were grateful. It was uphill.

On either side there was danger. If we looked to the right we got dizzy seeing the water so far below and no mother earth. The other side had cars going by so close we could almost touch them if we could let loose of our handlebars. Below through the iron mesh was the blue water of the Staits of Mackinaw. But we white-knuckled it all the way. Once every few minutes someone up front would holler "breaking" or "stopping". That was the signal to be on the alert to stop. There would be the screech of brake pads on metal as the line would almost come to a stop, then start up again. At all the expansion joints there were staff laying down planking for us to ride over or if they had none would help us off the bikes, walking us across. We didn't need to get our wheels caught in them to go hurtling into traffic or over the side.

Old time riders who have ridden many times rode up next to us, putting their hands on our backs to help push us up the hill. It felt so good to have help. Every once in awhile along the ride they would do this, it was very welcome but they couldn't do that the whole four days! We still had our rain ponchos on to shield us from the cool air. But the wind would whip my long tails up, smacking me in the face or getting caught in the wheels. I'd grab them up as best I could without losing my balance with the ribbons still in my clenched teeth.

Mom planned to wait for us on the other side to take our pictures. As we started our down grade I could see bikes in front and in my mirror, bikes in back. I looked for her as we neared the end of this very long bridge but didn't see her until too late, she not seeing us. The pictures were never taken. But it didn't matter.

We will never forget the feeling we had as we rode to the end of that bridge no matter how many pictures we might have to jog our memories. So many people lined the end of the roadway many rows deep, shouting to us, "Good job!"

"You're looking great!"

"Hooray!"

"Wonderful!" with thumbs up, clapping and shouting. We felt we just won a race and we were the only winners. We were winners. They were praising us! Goosebumps ran up and down my back as I finally realized I just conquered something I never knew I could do, and no matter how much it hurt, I did it. I thought I had a friend who was feeling the very same way. We almost fell off our bikes when we came to a clearing at the end of that bridge hugging each other with tears in our eyes knowing the anguish we had just endured in the name of having fun.

"Are we still friends?"

"I'll let you know if and when I heal," she laughed in her tears.

One last time we laid our bikes on the car rack for the final journey to the school a couple miles away in St. Ignace. There was just no way we were going to ride up the last hill on the bikes, just to go to one more school. But we had to say some fond farewells to some of the people we met who kept encouraging us on our way. We'd have our last meal with them all and enjoy the unified feeling of being together for one last time, at least till next time, if there would be a next time.

On the four hour return, we stopped somewhere for a light supper. We could hardly get out of the car, or sit on padded seats in the restaurant. Every move we made was sheer torture. Our bodies didn't have a decent place to feel good. Mom had sympathy for us but I don't think she could really understand the pain we felt or the exhilaration that was still with us.

We understood what was said when you were supposed to stretch your muscles before and after exercise. We realized it a little too late.

All the rest of the way home we said we would never do this again, once was enough. We'd hang up our bikes and let them rust before we'd ride them again. We were too old to do this kind of stuff. What were we old ladies doing here anyway? At least we did what we started out to do and finished.

Chapter 4   Piece of Cake, Mom

Funny, how plans can change so easily. Just one word or comment to test your vulnerability and zappo, you've done it again!

My then, 17 year old son, who I started riding with just a few years before listened to our story when we arrived back home. He hadn't ridden for a couple years himself. Listening intently to our tales of woe, how we endured such pressure and pain, he only laughed, "Piece of cake, Mom. I could do that without any training. Anyone can ride 350 miles or better, you're just getting old." Open mouth, insert foot.

Shirley looked at him aghast! "Don, how can you say that?"

"Well, I'll tell you what, Don," I argued, "if you think it's a piece of cake, how about challenging you to a match? I'll put up the ante. I'll pay for your tour ticket if you finish this ride next year. One hitch, though."

What's that?" he laughed.

"You can't practice ride first, no training."

"I could do it without training"

"Actually, I think I'll give you one day of training and I get to pick the day. I want to know if you at least have riding skills before you start a four day ride."

"No problem."

His grandmother chided in. "You will never make it, Don, no way! I'll even lay a bet on it. $10."

"Piece of cake, Gram."

As it was, I found that my son had outgrown his old Schwinn, and I had to buy him a new one plus a helmet. He would have to repay if he couldn't make it. I picked the day for training. One week before the four day ride he would go with a group on a Century Ride. That is 100 miles in one day. If that didn't break him nothing would! It didn't! Gramma upped the bet a few more dollars as the next year went on.

I bought a lighter 15 speed Schwinn; he had a clunker. I trained for over 2,000 miles that next summer. I rode every sanctioned ride and every day between. I was going to be able to ride it without pain, and he was going to fail. Mom was going to win her bet and Don would lose. I would be repaid some $300. Shirley and I both invested in womens' seats, those funny biking pants and read every helpful article written.

She forgot all about our idea of hanging up the bikes and never using them again. She trained much better, too, and we added Julie, another young gal to our twosome, along with the camping gear so we could sleep in the school grounds with the rest of the riders.

We rode that ride. Don got through the one day 100 mile ride with no trouble. I was beginning to think he was right. I was old.

At the end of the first day on DALMAC, he didn't want to move from the ground he fell on. He didn't have much strength to put up the tent or to roll out his sleeping bag. I'm surprised he could even make it to the shower. He did manage to find food lines. I thought I had it made the very first day out!

On the last day before the ride across the bridge, his grandmother was waiting for him. She didn't tag along every day but met us at the end of the tour. He held out his hand with his palm up and she slipped him the higher ante of twenty dollars. He didn't do much sitting on that last day but he made it to the end. We just all swore it was because he had youth on his side and we never challenged him again!

Since that time, Shirley and I have ridden many tours, pedaling our butts over many miles still not knowing what the *age of reason* is and always wondering what we were doing there. I guess we are still friends. Reflecting back it was the best 8 years of my life. We laugh sometimes when we reminisce of that pain but always wonder if we will continue to be good sports in the future. We rode that tour again another year with her daughter, husband, another tour with her two grandchildren, and across Iowa with her daughter and husband and 17,000 other riders. But that's another story in itself.

...................I rode on, heading home thinking about other good times I had. We would camp out up north on occasion, dragging our bikes with us sometimes or just enjoyed the outdoors.

I tried my hand at fishing. Every time she thought the fish were biting I would lather the mosquito repellant on and grab my tackle box with all its new items she helped me purchase. I bought two poles, one for light fishing and one for salmon. Then I had to add the tip-up rigging for ice fishing.

Rarely did we catch the big catch of the day. I got a lot of mosquito bites. She caught some blue gills. Our biggest catch of the small fish was a day on the ice. We spent all afternoon on it and came away with enough to fry. I called them fish chips, they were so small.

Our best effort at salmon fishing was a heavy brown trout another fisherman gave us. He didn't want to ice down just one fish. We gladly took it. I got her into the salmon fishing after I learned to

21

do the sport from a friend during the snagging season. It wasn't hard to snag them. They were running into the river outlet and were vulnerable. The law changed. Snagging wasn't allowed any more. Using bait never yielded anything more than sore arms. It was not as much fun any more. I must have jinxed the sport.

I rode on in the morning sunshine still thinking of other times we had together. I had nothing better to do while riding home. It would be a week alone with just my thoughts.

Riding around the upper peninsula was something I wanted to do and the following years were going to be a big help in teaching me the self-reliance and confidence. Riding a bicycle was not the only thing I did during those years. Some thought I was crazy. Some thought I had a lot of guts. Some were envious that I would do it. Shirley was a big part of the overall adventure. We became a good team. What one didn't think up, the other did.

ADVENTURE # 2

SHOOTING THE RAPIDS

Chapter 1   Something New

How I found myself on the Colorado River "shooting the rapids" as they say, is beyond me. I don't really know why I would do such a thing. Perhaps my sense of adventure or my quest to do something different was stimulated.

One October, Shirley and her daughter Sheri, found tickets for a raft trip through Shirleys' husband. This was something I had wanted to do for a long time, not thinking the opportunity would ever surface. I made a few phone calls to the river runner company "OARS" where they got their tickets and was able to find another opening in this daring undertaking. After getting the ticket I wondered why I was doing this.

I was not a water person.

I didn't fancy boats.

I didn't much care to get wet.

I didn't care for fishing.

OARS sent us the particulars for packing essentials. We tried to put as many things as we could in small day packs and a huge duffle bag to find the right combination for weeks. We were on our way to a brand new adventure of hiking and rafting the river. We packed and unpacked the few items allowed so often we wore them out without using them.

Our itinerary called for jetting to Las Vegas, and hopping a smaller plane to Grand Canyon City. Hiking down to the Colorado River, we would raft, hike some more and return in less than two weeks time.

23

We were excited as we jumped on the plane carrying day packs and checking in an assortment of other carry-alls. A large duffle would be carried down the river trail on a mule. We felt a little conspicuous at Metro airport carrying small backpacks and hauling around the duffle bag. We acted like three teen-agers out on their first date or something, giggling, laughing and full of anticipation.

Our flight called for two plane changes, Milwaukee and Dallas-Fort Worth. At the latter we needed to run to our next gate to make the departure time. With all these changes we worried about our bags being properly sent on the right plane.

Flying into Vegas, as many people call it, after dark was interesting to say the least. From the plane window we could see nothing but the wing lights. Suddenly as we approached our destination, billions of lights exploded in a huge starburst on the ground. As we approached they began to glitter and sparkle, spreading larger and larger.

"Look, isn't that pretty?" Once we landed the lights became daylight. So this was the city that never sleeps.

None of us were ever here before. This could be a good place to see if we wanted to call off the raft trip and just gamble away our money.

We took a cab to the main part of town. Walking around with all this stuff wasn't my idea of fun until we decided on a hotel that wasn't the Taj Mahal. I suppose the cab driver saw his share of oddballs like us.

"Look, you guys stay here, I'll register and then you can come up to "my" room," I said. They stayed outside with the bags as I registered for one person. It looked like shift change was coming on. While we waited for the changing of the guard I inspected "my" room and made a few attempts to haul in the bags myself while trying to evade the clerk. When all was clear, the girls brought in the rest of the stuff and relaxed for a few minutes before going out on the town.

"Nothing cheap about us," one of them uttered as we left.

We walked around looking at the various spots, tried a couple "one armed bandits" without much luck and admired the gaudiness. When we wanted to see a special showing it was either just over or wouldn't be back for hours. We spent a few more dollars, bought a few souvenirs and headed for bed. It already was a long day.

We found a place for breakfast in the morning and looked through the phone book for transportation to Grand Canyon City. There was an air service providing the scenic look. Ideal. We took it. Piling all the stuff in a cab trunk we were off. Vegas didn't look as nice in the daylight. A few small mountains could be seen from town.

We waited a short time and boarded the prop plane of Scenic Airlines with a handful of others. The view was breathtaking. Our cameras had been clicking away. Whenever the pilot indicated a point of interest it was always on the wrong side.

We flew over Hoover Dam and all along the river itself. Small rivers looked like trails. Most were dried up, it being October. The sides of the canyon were colorful and rugged. We flew above the flat mesas frightening a herd of mule deer. The Colorado River was a muddy green, rapids were small white lace ruffles. Colors were at a minimum below. Mostly muted greys with tinges of muted violet.

Landing, we still needed to get from the small airport to Grand Canyon City. We were advised to take the bus. Inquiring, it seemed nobody quite knew what they were doing or where anything could be found. We finally got the information we needed. They would deliver our bags to the park lodge and we drove off through the lush countryside. The short pine trees gave us the notion we were in northern Michigan. We inhaled the wonderful clean air. So exhilarating!

Our next effort was to find a place to stay for the night. We had an appointment with the river at 3 p.m. the next day.

The adventure so far was exciting. None of us had traveled like this before. The uncertainty didn't seem to bother us. Time was our biggest factor. There were several lodges where we could have stayed and a few motels. We were told of a hostel somewhere down the road. We could board the bus that ran continuously in a circle around all the tourists' attractions till we found it. We must have ridden the circuit two or three times before we spotted the place we wanted.

It was a rough hewn dormitory cabin with a locked door. The sign outside said they wouldn't be open for some time. The day was sunny but a bit cool. We decided to wait it out. The paved road in front of the hostel was warm with little traffic. We lay down on it in our jeans and sweat shirts to absorb some heat and rest. "Anyone seeing us out here would really wonder what the hell we were doing, you know!" I said. It didn't seem to matter. We carried a couple snack foods and began feeding the chipmunks skittering about.

Later the doors opened and we were informed the place was full!

"Now what do you want to do?"

"Well, we have to have the duffle bag down to the mule livery for transport tonight. Let's take it down there now," suggested Sheri, "at least it will be out of the way." Back on the circuit bus to the lodge for our bags and down to the livery.

The lodge was a log building operated by the park service. Basic information was given here. It housed a cafeteria, post office, gift shop and contained lodgings.

25

All our bags were not there. I was missing my bag with all my essentials. We looked all over. The man behind the desk made a call to the airport with little success. Another bus driver came in and said they were all here.

I said to him with a little dismay, "How can a small airline lose my bag? They are not all here. The large airlines always lose them. I didn't think a small one could, too. I've got to have that bag before 6 a.m. tomorrow. What am I going to do for the next 9 days on the river without it?"

He understood where I was coming from. He felt a little bad but there was not a bag left at the airport the last time he made the circuit. He would be back in an hour.

We dragged the large duffle and the other smaller ones to the livery. It smelled of leather and manure. A couple rough looking mule handlers milled around doing whatever mule handlers do with mules.

Free of our biggest baggage we hiked back to the lodge to make calls to the motels in the area till we found one with a vacancy. Since it was getting close to the hour for the bus driver to return we waited around the lodge talking to a few of the hikers coming and going.

Backpacking looked like something we could handle some other time. A young woman from Germany just came out of the canyon wearing corduroy shorts, t-shirt with heavy hiking boots, wool socks and backpack. A couple Chinese students came here just to do the hike into the canyon. They all lauded the beauty.

The bus driver returned with nothing. Back to the phone booth. I called Vegas where the airline was based. They had nothing, no knowledge and would not admit they may have lost it.

Everyone was alerted in the area for this bag. My name tag was on it but I hadn't any reservations about it being returned to me especially by morning. It was going to be a miserable week staying in my jeans, with no sleeping pad and bathing supplies. I could see my companions shunning me by pulling me behind the rafts after a couple days.

We jumped another bus and found our motel. The clerk behind the desk asked if I had lost something. How did she know? Did it show that bad? There behind the desk was my bag. I was so elated, I looked through it and found it was all there. "The bus driver brought it over here this morning. They said it came on another flight and didn't have an owner on the same plane. They decided to leave it here," she said. "We didn't have you listed for a reservation but thought maybe you had told him to drop it off here anyway."

I was so relieved I couldn't sit still.

26

After depositing our bags in the room, we walked around the area some more, eating out of the cafeteria and hiking down a part of the Bright Angel Trail we would be hiking in the morning. It was going to be a beautiful hike. I just knew it. The air here was so clean. The view from the top led us to believe we had come to the right place for an adventure. How could it be otherwise when it looked like you could see forever. The canyon beckoned us.

Chapter 2　　　　　　　　　　A Mile Down

The next morning we were up before dawn to start our trek to the river. We had not slept a wink. It was only 32 degrees, with frost. We had to dress warm enough for morning. We wore our shorts under our jeans so our packs were a bit lighter.

We were told the water was undrinkable on the trail so we carried our bike water bottles and a few things to make a lunch.

We needed a flashlight to see where were going in the near dark. Vaguely the October sky was just visible in the distance. Shortly the dawn started appearing on the horizon. Looking down from our high vantage point we could not see the river. All we saw were walls of dark limestone rock, some trees here and there tucked away in them. How could they grow in such little soil? Why, they looked like they were growing in the rock. Their formations were so windswept. They reminded us of those little Japanese gardens.

The canyon had the look of mystery. The dirt trail ahead lured us down into its' depths, winding its' way along the rock walls.

With the sky turning a hazy blue as the sun rose, the shadows of the canyon turned to ruddy reds and browns as we walked. When the sun crept into our canyon it licked the tips of the rock walls just enough to set them apart from the rest, turning them to gold as the haze left. If I hadn't known better I would have thought they were cathedral domes. This was surely Gods' domain. He lives here.

Every turn in the trail brought new views, so breathtaking. As the hike went on, we were mostly in shadows but the other side was in brilliant sunlight, exposing the craggy contours in reds, purples, browns and greens with now a royal blue sky. We startled a small herd of mule deer munching on the short pinion trees with a ground cover of Prickly Pear cacti.

Mules also had gone the way we traveled and at every turn in the trail we had to detour slightly. They added their contribution at each change of direction.

By noon the sun was upon us. Canyon walls changed color as the sun entered deeper into each crevasse. Off came the wools, and jeans. We looked back to where we had started at dawn still seeing the notch in the canyon wall 3,000 feet above. Such a long

28

way up and we were not even half way down. We still could not see the river.

Passing a major bend we met other hikers coming up. The temperatures at the river were in their eighties they said. A couple ladies in their seventies carrying well used backpacks hailed us. We knew if they enjoyed this trail this much coming up, we should do so going down. Our bodies were not hurting yet but we expected they would have their sore spots by morning.

We looked down the steep trail looking over the snaky switchbacks. The trail narrowed to about five feet in places crossing a smaller river far below in our sights. It was such a well traveled trail we had nothing to worry about.

We came onto a camp area after several hours. It was in the shadow of cottonwood trees and gave us a chance to get some much needed water and a bit of a rest. We finally saw the river. A tributary was running along the trail. A shelter on the other side beckoned us. We tried crossing the water without getting our shoes wet. Little did we know that those same shoes would be wet for the next week.

I ran out of water. There were signs all over the trail warning of contaminated water. I started to feel nauseous. My feet were getting sore from the constant downward pressures. Our shins ached from the unfamiliar down grade. I felt blisters had formed.

We didn't know were to go when we got to the river. There wasn't anyone there. A foot bridge crossed it taking us to the other side where Phantom Ranch was located. We found a general store but know one knew anything about the guides we were supposed to meet. I was getting sicker by the minute. It was almost time to make our connections. The other two were getting a little worried. I let them worry. I didn't care any more. I just followed them.

Back to the river. Some rafters were there when we returned. I sat letting the women handle the situation.

Apparently this was our group. Some people were ending their trip here and would be walking up the canyon from here and others would be going with us. They set up a table for lunch and were adjusting and replenishing the rafts.

Bruce Helin was the head guide. He and Mike Boyle showed us how to pack our waterproof bags. So much had to fit in those bags we were amazed every morning. I couldn't comprehend what they were saying by this time. We were given instructions on what to do if we fell out of the raft. That did it. I turned over and just barely got up in time to rid myself of my daily intake of calories.

Mike looked at me saying, "You didn't drink enough water coming down, did you?"

"No, I suppose not."

"You're suffering from hyperthermia." I heard him but didn't pay much attention. I was hot but not sweating. I felt delirious and nauseous. What was I doin' here?

"Here, come over here and drink some lemonade, a lot of it, you're dehydrated." I looked in the green bucket where they had mixed pink lemonade. Since I couldn't even locate my Sierra cup someone loaned me theirs. The sight of the pink and green was enough to start me up again but they encouraged me to drink all I could.

Chapter 3   Learning the Ropes

I guess everyone was introduced as I sat off in the shade of a cottonwood tree on the white sugar sand drinking that awful stuff.

We had more guides than passengers. This was the final trip of the season. Since there were extra seats other guides came along for the fun of it. Two were in training. We thought that great. We may need extra help if we go over the side.

We had a mixed bag of personalities. A couple guides were just adventurers following the seasons on the river. I suppose you could call them real river rats. They would go to Peru and other countries for untamed rivers. We have since read articles of their adventures in publications. They wore short shorts and flip-flop sandals with bandanas around their necks and yellow OARS caps. One was a writer and expert on biology, they all had knowledge of geology and natural history.

A passenger, Andy, was a retired Air Force pilot, having flown Air Force One. John and Sandy were guides from Maine learning Colorado ways.

I felt much better.

We finally packed ourselves into our rubber rain suits to protect us from the 50 degree water, donned our wool socks or neopreme, stowed our gear and shoved off. We were shown how to tie down our personal ammo can that would hold our valuables like our cameras and keep them dry. Hopping over the softness of the big raft and into the wet bottom I remembered how we tried to keep our feet dry coming down the trail. One or two passengers to a big yellow raft made a very individual ride.

This part of the river seemed so fast to us but were informed it was just slow. I worried about being sick some more as we bounced along through the first small Granite Rapids. The guides manned the long oars skillfully. I had the feeling we were in good hands watching them maneuver. I started out with Bruce. We would change rafts every day so were able to get more acquainted with each of the guides.

In only an hour or so we were at our campsite for the night. They always picked sand banks. As we set up our tent and laid out our wet shoes and socks, the guides set up our kitchen. We were also

31

instructed in kitchen etiquette. They cooked everything. We had the best food out here in the middle of nowhere. We didn't eat this good at home. Appetizers every night before dinner. Fresh fruit and salads. Boiled coffee, strained, at every hot meal. Beer and wine flowed quite freely.

All garbage and paper trash was taken with us. We were to leave nothing here that wasn't here before we came. A latrine was set up the farthest away from camp as possible. Near camp a raft cushion was placed. One carried it to the latrine as a signal it was occupied. They carried all the contents of it and the garbage on a raft. We were instructed only to put solid waste in the latrine. Liquid would have to be in wet sand or the river. Easy for the men to do!

Don Usner had a hot recipe for salsa which he prepared. One night was Mexican food night. I remember taking a large sample of it that should have burned the roof of my mouth and sent a stream of fire out two feet. It was delicious! After that it was salsa with everything. It was one of my favorite foods. Since some nights would be dark after dinner was served we were taught how to wash our own dishes. A trail of plastic bailing buckets sat in the sand in the direction of the water. The first was for scraps, second for a rinse, a soapy, hot rinse and a cold rinse. It was always set up in the same direction so you didn't dump your garbage in the final rinse in the dark. Worked well.

I was feeling better by supper and ate some of it but mostly got acquainted with our group. Every night if there was light we played horseshoes. We had a hard time believing they carried these heavy items in rubber rafts. They cooked in iron pots and pans. Dry ice kept the perishables good and the beer cold.

Sleeping under the blanket of sparkling starlight with a full moon made for a very pleasant atmosphere. We didn't need flashlights in the evening. We had moonlight. We still couldn't sleep. We wanted to savor all the experience. They did doze off, and I lay watching the moon still overhead through the tent door. It wanted to follow the river on its east-west course. No matter how steep the walls were it could be seen all night. Its big yellow globe a beacon in the night.

The rest of the trip was varied. We could tell a rapid was coming up by the sound of it. Smaller ones sounded as if heavy rain, the largest, a freight train approaching. When we came to a rapids, we were all told to get out of the rafts before them. The guides all gathered to discuss the direction for sliding through them while we wandered around. The first raft through would be the test raft. If it worked for them then the others would follow.

At Crystal Rapids, Shirley and Sheri were picked to go first with Lester Bleifuss. I photographed them after saying good-bye. I stood on the six foot boulder strewn shore as I snapped photos of their raft flipping up here and there in the white water very close to the rock wall on the other side. "Oh, no, they're going to flip it!" I hollered to no one in particular. It sure looked like they weren't going to make it. They screamed as they flowed through it. I was scared to death when it then became my turn. I was with Bruce. I felt I must be safe enough. He told me the first day not to hang on with the rope wrapped around my hand. We glided through the rapids with the water careening over the bow where I sat. I couldn't see where I was going from there. Water flung itself into the raft over my head as we rocked up and down in the flexible raft. Wow! What an experience! I could do that again!

We slid out into the calmer water, the women looking back to see that I had made it safely. Now I was taught how to bail out the water with the buckets tied to the ropes. The water was always in the bottoms of the rafts. Dry shoes were a luxury. No wonder they all wore flip-flops. They must be used to the cold water as well. They hardly ever wore anything like rain suits. We all wore life jackets.

We floated with everyone immersed in their own raft conversation. Occasionally the guides yelled back and forth to each other, their voices echoing off the walls. Otherwise the air was filled with a splendid quietness. Occasionally we could hear bird cries. We saw blue heron, hawks and ravens. Mostly we just watched the scenery float by in the deep vertical canyons with flat horizontal water. The sunlight played many colors on the water. It in turn looked flat but in places you could see it roiling beneath the surface as it slid over boulders deep below.

Different times of the day the sun played on the canyon walls changing the colors at any given moment. The walls were so craggy. Deep shadows contrasted the light.

At another rapid we did the same thing. I waited as Don took Cynthia through the Bass Rapids. They disappeared into the hole of the rapids and then shot up like a blast from a shotgun. "Oh, my God, we have to do this again!" was all I heard from the others. Our emotions were always mixed with exhilaration and anxiety.

After a few days on the river we had the opportunity to give "oaring" a try. Sheri tried and didn't do too bad. When I tried I found it was quite a heavy pull on those oars to get them to mind. I let her have them back. We never oared through rapids. Randy did once a on little one. His ambition was to oar for one whole day. He seemed to have a knack for it.

At lunch time the crew brought out their tables and set up small meals that weren't cooked. Usually sandwiches with a salad and always cookies with lemonade. Water was provided by the river for everything.

In camp, the guides were seen most often with a toothbrush stuck in their mouths. They were very fastidious about their dental cleanliness.

Most days we had chances to hike into the side canyons to explore. The guides knew where each trail went. They walked around on those little flip-flops like mountain goats. We saw falls where we elected to wash our hair in its cold waters. One trail had to be hiked by climbing up two rope ladders adjacent to a falls, hopping over rivers and gaps. We saw four-legged mountain goats in the higher elevations and many varmint tracks around our tents in the morning. Someone caught a fish for dinner. We laughed, had a great time and snapped many photos.

Sheri jumped one creek only to do some damage to ligaments in a knee. It bothered her for some years later until surgery repaired it.

Two of our rafters hiked out on the second day. They were to catch a ride or had parked their car near that point. A female guide hiked out with them to make an appointment with a doctor and then hiked back to meet us on one of our remaining days. It instilled a greater love for future adventures in our blood.

Some hikes John and I refused to make. He had a fear of heights to get over from a fall he had taken on a mountain. He gamefully tried most. I had foot surgery just that year and was unsure of myself in sticky situations. An inner ear problem limited my ability to balance giving me a fear of heights with him.

We hiked one trail constantly on an upgrade over boulders, some as big as houses. Coming to a crevasse, the trail led alongside of it. It was only about a foot wide. To pass here you hugged the wall as best you could with your fingertips and dug your toes in along the dirt trail.

"Look, I'll hang unto the wall and you just hang unto me from behind. We'll get you past this tight edge," suggested Giggs.

It didn't take me long to decide this was not the trail I wanted to hike. It was a deep crevasse and very tight. I could see myself falling into it and trapped midway down. No, thanks.

Mike Boyle was dropped off on the other side of the river to explore another would-be trail. A raft was tied where he was supposed to come back out. I could see him across the river as just a yellow and blue speck against the dark shadowy rock. I wandered back down the trail to watch his escapade while the others went on ahead. Bruce was fishing, but never caught anything. Sandy read.

Every guide could explain the variations in the canyons wall geology, the history of the dam system. We watched kayakers ride over some rapids and camped one night with a crew of boaters.

Every day was warm with blue skies. Every night we could see the moon rise and fall from one end of the canyon to the other. The night air dried our wet clothes.

I talked my companions into sleeping outside the tent after the three of us crammed into our little three man tent once too often. That night we had a slight wind blow up. It blew sand into every crevice of our sleeping bags, hair, eyes and anything else it could get into. That was the last night they slept out. I did so the rest of the trip with no problem.

Hiking into Havasau Falls was shear delight. We packed lunches at breakfast making sandwiches and combining our own kind of snacks. All the guides were adept at preparing meals for us. I don't know how far we hiked but were led by Bruce into a canyon wading through the creek at least a dozen times almost to our waist in places. At Beaver Falls, it turned into a fairyland of lush green tamarisks and hanging travertine with emerald waters flowing off terraces of limestone formations. It was a beautiful place for lunch. We ambled around the area, wading into the water, some opting to swim around a rock outcropping to see what was on the other side. We were informed it was the trail to the Havasau Indians land where there were horses with pastures and only a trail in or out. Emergencies were handled with helicopters. We were left on our own to find our way out. We missed the trail once crossing the river but eventually found it. Tied up to flat rock formation without benefit of a sand beach we climbed from one raft to another to reach the one we were assigned to for the day.

That night while we lay on the sand, Andy Radel, the pilot gave us a quick course on the stars.

Chapter 4   Sound of Trains

One day was the best kept secret of the trip. The guides wouldn't tell us till we got there. After the usual good-natured kidding around little things started to eke out about it. By mid-morning we just about all knew we were in for the biggest rapids of the river. I'm sure everyone had their own thoughts about the adventure ranging from confidence to sheer fright when we could hear the "freight train" noises from a long way off.

At breakfast, Giggs had said it was the deepest rapids if we hit it at the wrong time of day. They said they timed our arrival to the safest hour. The dam let out water periodically to keep the levels artificially where they wanted them. If we hit it at the wrong time it would take some real oarsmanship to get us through them. It was a long walk around.

Lava Falls! Just the name said it was more than just a rapids. There were volcano eruptions that created these incredible falls.

The "train" came closer and closer. We all sat in the rafts with dire expectations. Around a bend we could just see the source. Water sprayed slightly at the surface of this discontent. Since we were at water level now above the falls all we could see was the upper part. We were all ordered to get out of the raft on the rock shore. A helicopter was perched on the opposite bank in the shadows. They stayed long enough to see if we would make it. We could not talk to them for the noise of the water. We could hardly hear ourselves.

"Sheri, this is no rapids," I yelled as we walked through the rocks to the source. "This is a falls!"

"We are going to raft through this?"

"Oh, my God!"

How deadly this looked. Many boats and rafts spilled here, they said. The sound was more like a 747 jet. The waves leaped twenty feet into the air. Water dropped 37 feet in only 150 yards.

The water was hurtling itself over a rock strewn barrier from the extinct volcano, rushing into a sea of boiling, churning white water that we were expected to flow through without spilling. "Oh, my God!" I shrieked again when I was the chosen one to go first. I was scared to death. I hated water. This wasn't my kind of place. Why was I doing this? What was I doing here? I was with Mike. I knew he was good, but did I really want to trust myself with his expertise? But did I have any recourse? No!

If I ever prayed it was now as I picked my way along the rocks back to the raft. Some others boarded their rafts. Others stayed on the point of rocks. All nine guides had combined their knowledge of the river and made the decision to get through the falls safely. I hoped they were right. I knew I would panic if I dumped out of the raft. There was only a small rope to hang onto. I had wanted to twist it around my arm for security but I knew I would be told not to in case I really did get dumped. I would lose a hand that way.

Slowly we edged to the parapet. Water could be seen rushing over the rocks on one side where I thought we would go. It looked like a huge water slide. Mike guided the raft over to the white gurgling water where it looked like we would be churned up for sure and then we were caught up in the flow and were off into the unknown, hurtled into the abyss of no return. I hung onto the rope for dear life. The front of the raft went down, water filling it, filling my suspendered rain pants. I gasped for air but water filled my mouth.

Up went the raft, shot into the air as though spat out of a grape skin, twisting and turning. The noise of the water resounding like thunder in my ears. I yelled. It was better than a roller coaster ride. Mike yelled a big "ya-hoo" and down we would go again turning backward to the river, swirling around like the"Whip." A few more jostles, bumps and twists and turns and we were in the clear headed for the shore. "Oh, Gez!" I gasped. "That wasn't near as bad as I thought." I really envisioned myself trying to get my feet to go first as I slid down the river to never-never land somewhere all the while swallowing most of the river.

Mike oared over to the shore with little difficulty. As soon as we were secure I jumped at him with the biggest hug of his life. He just laughed and hugged back.

We no sooner stopped when the next raft came down. It was Shirley with Bruce and then the others. Sheri, Randy and Lester almost flipped out at one point.

While I was busy with my camera Mike had opened up a bottle of champagne. "It's tradition," he said, "that when you go through these falls without dumping, you celebrate." I was not going to refuse this. We all celebrated for the rest of the day and night.

"Tradition" seemed to enter our conversations for the remainder of the trip.

I don't know where all the beer and wine was stashed. It seemed impossible to have as much as we drank in these eight days all stored on just five rafts. Wine was carried in silver packets with pour spouts. We found one from some other outfit floating on the water.

That night we had appetizers of oysters, sardines and crackers. Clam chowder for dinner and lots of beer to wash it down.

The walls of rock were getting shorter. Gone were the tall expanse of sheer rock face. More iron oxide showed in the formations making shiny black surfaces. Piles of fencepost lava littered some areas. As the sun set on the tallest of the Kiabab sandstone, they all seemed to turn to beautiful gold domes at the top like we saw on our hike down into the canyon that wonderful day a little more than a week ago. We knew our time here was nearing an end. We didn't want it to end yet. We still had just two nights out here of camaraderie unsurpassed. It was not only the beauty of the land but our fellow companions we would miss.

Chapter 5   Where Next?

On the last night in camp we played the championship game of horseshoes. I don't remember who won anymore. I suppose we all did.

For dinner that night Mike and Lester dressed up. Wearing a white dress shirt and shorts was Mikes' contribution and a Hawaiin floral was Lesters'. With his baseball cap he reminded us of Magnum P.I. television character.

Dinner consisted of pineapple ham, cranberries, sweet potatoes, green beans, salad without onions for a change and wonders of all wonders-blueberry and blackberries on freshly made cheese cake. We sat around the campfire later than usual tonight passing on stories and talking about our past weeks' experiences.

Before arriving at the take out point a small plane came into the canyon. Just in time he pulled up. He just missed a cable crossing. A platform on the cable carried two people doing a silt sampling of the river. It is illegal to fly that low into the river canyon. The helicopter was illegal at the falls.

A bus and truck had arrived at our take-out, Peach Creek Canyon, and supplied us with a banquet of hors d'oeuvres and sandwiches with the likes I've only seen at high class banquets. We all helped to empty the rafts of cargo and air, pack them into a truck and were bussed out to a motel where we cleaned up for the flight home.

Mike drove the truck up the dusty dirt path passing us as best he could. He was in a hurry to get the remainders of our garbage scow emptied so he could have time to see us before we flew home. We all hugged and laughed but were almost tearful in our final farewells. These fellas had become part of our family.

Some of us were left at the motel to mostly fend for ourselves. We had to get back to Vegas somehow. The motel was out in nowhere. It was closed. They had only rented two rooms for us to shower. A gas station was not far away. The attendant was of no help. We were told to go over a fence to a field. There should be a patch of a landing strip and a couple of small planes would pick us up.

We carried our stuff over there. Randy, John, Sandy and ourselves. Didn't look like much of a landing strip. A little gravel. We sat on our bags for an hour or more wondering if the guys were just playing a trick on us. Should we set up camp? Then off in the distance we spotted the two six and nine seater planes and we were off to finish our flight home from Vegas.

We had said most of our good-byes at the motel. We promised to keep in touch. The crew was all going back to Flagstaff. We played one last "one-armed-bandit" before entering the plane.

We were to see Sandy again in two years where they lived in Maine. We have never seen the others. We maintained a writing relationship with Giggs and Lester for awhile but that faded as well.

John and Sandy went the following year at the same time and found themselves in the water more than out. The weather was cold and rainy making their second trip uncomfortable.

I felt I learned a lot on this experience. All the stories and pictures I saw in books over the years came to life and became reality. That same self-reliance and confidence became stronger and stronger. Granted we had guides to show the way but it was the getting there and acquiring new skills.

On the way home on the plane we talked all the way about our wonderful trip. "How are we going to top this one?" I asked. "I don't know," said Shirley.

We had ridden on bike tours for a couple years now and camped out here and there. We were all lost in our thoughts for a long time.

"Why don't we get a couple motorcycles and travel around the country?" she offered.

Little did she know on the plane then she had just launched a whole new ball game.

Adventure # 3

SOLO BY HONDA

Chapter 1   **"You Wouldn't GO
Alone, Would You?"**

I have often wondered what it would be like to be an explorer; treading into places where I'd never been before. As a child I studied geography in school and could tell you where just about anything was on a map. As I grew into adulthood reading pastimes were consumed with adventures of explorers, travelers. I never paid much attention to history itself but rather as stories told. I had a love for the west but never saw it.

Later, I began to piece together scraps of information as a quilter would a quilt. Certainly our own United States looked like a badly cut quilt. The lines in colors representing roads became the sewn design. Often I would dream of traveling those quilt designs. The designs had many directions to chose. One could follow the wide ones if in any hurry, or the blue ones if not. Travel in my age could be by many modes. I wouldn't be burdened with dependance on canoe or horse.

Most of todays' modes cost money. I had not enough to travel by motorhome or travel to motels every night. Little did I have. Flying, I would not see the countryside. The adventure would be over all too quickly. I preferred the slow pace. Riding a bicycle, walking, canoeing all would fit that bill.

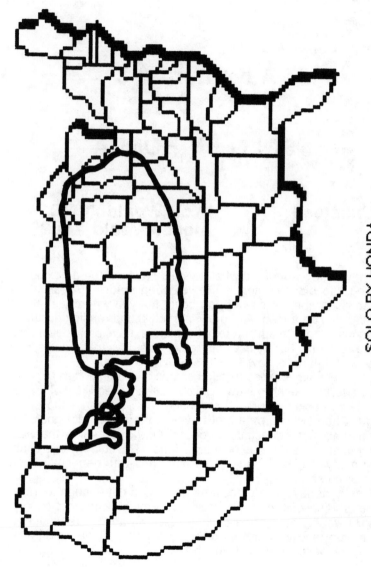

SOLO BY HONDA

I studied maps. During my younger years my travels were limited for lack of funds and a family. But we managed to paddle a few rivers and backpack a few trails.

Bicycling was in its beginning stages but moving up right along. I dreamed of a cross country ski escapade that has yet to be tried.

After finishing the white-water rafting on the Colorado River with Shirley, touring the states together burned holes in my mind. My children were grown, I was single again with little to keep me from dabbling in sought-after quests. I worked for a living, tying me down to schedules.

The difference of this trip was the mode. By motorcycle.

With the whole winter ahead we had plenty of time to ponder this. Shirley and I had both ridden motorcycles before. She still owned a couple small ones but I had sold mine.

I purchased two with my husband, riding them to the east coast and to Florida one year. They were strictly bare bones bikes with little comforts. Chain driven, no fairings. When we parted ways we parted taking our bikes with us. Without a riding partner I found I owned a riderless motorcycle in the garage. It was sold.

After muddling through the travel brochures all winter, refreshing my mind on distant wild areas to explore in spring, I suggested, "Let's go down to the Honda dealer and try on a couple bikes."

She gamefully entered the store with me, looking at all the styles. They exuded power as they were all lined up on the showroom floor. Chrome shining. Sporty and touring. We were allowed to sit on a couple and get the feel. These didn't feel like the one I used to ride. She had never ridden such large ones before. We felt like we could handle these.

Honda built Silver Wings for a few years. These were cut down versions of their larger line of Gold Wings. They just happened to have a couple for us to try out on the road. Now they were shaft driven for a smoother ride. The Silver Wing had front faring and saddle bags, even a trunk. Bill, the sales agent, rolled one out to the parking lot. "All you do with these babies is pull the choke, open the gas valve and turn the key."

The bike started after the first couple tries. It hummed while Bill explained the shifting pattern by using the clutch on the left hand grip and pushing or pulling the lever at the foot petal. Braking was on the right handle bar grip and foot pedal. Turn signals and light dimmers on the grips. "Nothing more than just drive out," he explained. "Go for it, I'm sure you can do it."

"Do you trust me on this thing?"

"If I want to sell you one, I best trust you, hadn't I?" he asked.

42

Strapping on my own old helmet, I started out on the street uncertainly. I wanted to try it but felt a little unsure I could handle it. I was excited. Gee, it felt good to be back on a bike. It had been a couple years since I had ridden. Turning into traffic I became very conscious of the shifting. I didn't want to screw up the bike. It all came back in a short time. I perched on that seat like I owned the world. I went down the road wanting to wave at everyone. I turned back, reluctantly.

I didn't go far, just far enough to know this was what I wanted. Perhaps you never forget how to ride or the feel of power under you. Shirley took it for a ride and felt the same way. She never rode a bike this size before.

"Go ahead, write it up," I said to Bill. Shirley hesitated. She had to contend with a husband and wasn't sure he would allow it. Well, I needn't let that bother me. She could talk him into it if she wanted to. And she wanted to. Since he was frequently away from home she was left to do just about as she pleased.

Looking out the window of home, the bike stood in the drive one sunny day in spring. Snow was piled high where I shoveled the last of winter away. The chrome contrasted so well with the deep maroon fiberglass of the body. The sun made the whole bike gleam as if it begged to be permitted to be taken on the road. I longed for the weather to warm just to ride it around anywhere. I would smile to myself knowing that was my bike out there.

By June I had ridden many miles around town getting used to it. Shirley was looking for a used one. She would come to my house and we would ride double while we checked out ads from the paper. We drove around every once in awhile in search of the perfect fit for her to no avail.

I made the final plans and showed them to her. "I'd like to go to Yellowstone Park and beyond. That will have to be the destination until getting there. I understand tenting isn't the safest thing to do in the park because of the bears so I've made reservations for a lodge cabin. After that I want to go as far west as I can till I know I have to be back to work. I want to see everything there is to see. I feel like a kid in a candy store and this atlas I hold in my hand is the candy. Even if you don't get your bike I'm still going to go," I said to her one day.

"You wouldn't go alone!" she gasped.

"Sure, why not?"

"Your mother would kill you," she returned.

"I'm not going to let that get in my way. It's not like I'm living at home any more, I'm almost 45 years old, for heavens' sake, with grown children.

43

"What about your kids?"

"Hey, they don't tell me what to do either. I suppose they will be concerned, but I'm a big girl now."

My family was concerned. Mom shook her head before I left like I would if I were in her place. Most of the kids rather expected Mom would do something like this and worried much less. I was an independent person and they knew it.

Actually I thought I was entering my second childhood and didn't feel like the 45 year old mother of four.

Mom lived in Florida in the winter and stayed with me in the summer. She was on her way here now. I told her my plans during the winter. It wouldn't be a surprise.

The next obstacle I faced was to get this bike packed with the important things for travel. Clothes weren't much of a problem but the saddle bags on the side hardly held them. I needed to carry a sleeping bag, pad and tent as I would be camping out. Mom, and neighbor Jean, helped me devise a better system. Three waterproof bags were bungied on the back seat. It gave me a nice backrest I knew I would appreciate on the long haul. Some days I planned on riding for 500 miles. That is a long time to sit in one place.

Another neighbor, George, who rode Harleys, suggested a sheepskin seat cover to relieve saddle sores. It proved a god-send. He would have liked to go along but was caring for his invalid wife. He was still a young 75 at this time and still rode his chopper. He was always offering encouragement. I needed that.

My food, cooking and other hard items were placed in the saddlebags.

Something that was really important to my well being was a CB radio. Mom liked the idea so I could get aid if I needed it. I liked it because I could have conversation with someone besides myself. It was fastened to the cover over the speedometer and RPM gauges. I wired a set of ear plugs into my helmet in stereo. The road noises made it difficult to hear otherwise. A second set of plugs could be plugged into a FM radio. Strapped to the gas tank I fashioned my navigation materials. A large road atlas encased in plastic was tied to the gas tank with elastic. I wouldn't have to stop so often to consult a map out of sight. It proved the helpful item.

My plan was to head west. During the winter months I read several historical novels on the discovery and confrontations out there. *The Journal of Lewis and Clark Expedition,* Dee Browns *Bury My Heart at Wounded Knee* was probably the most profound works. *Centennial* by James Mitchner and many others instilled in me the need to see for myself. This would be a perfect time to see what I only read about. I would be gone a month. I made reservations at

Yellowstone Park for the cabin. I tried to plan correctly to be there on time. I hoped to ride no more than 500 miles a day. Some days I went no more than 100 miles.

I packed like I was going west the following week-end when in reality I went to a convention upstate. By trial and error I would have this thing ready to go by June 29.

I changed my cooking source to sterno. It was smaller and readily available. Using a piece of gutter mesh I fashioned a stove to rest my cook set pans over the sterno can. I carried it stuck on my rider foot peg. I added a thermometer and compass.

I had planned to go by way of Chicago to save time.

I hated Chicago.

It would be Friday rush hour traffic time.

I changed it.

I would head north across our Upper Peninsula into Minnesota and ride across the northernmost states.

By June 29, my odometer registered 2000 miles. Shirley didn't find that bike. Mom made me promise to send a post card every day, or she wouldn't let me go.

I was ready.

Mom and Shirley both saw me off in the afternoon after a quick day of working. I had worked at the post office for 16 years as a rural mail carrier. I gave myself the handle of "Pony Express" for my CB call name. It was emblazoned on the back of my helmet. I hugged Shirley good-bye, sorry she wasn't going with me, secretly loving every minute of my lone adventure. Not so sorry that I would postpone the adventure. It was her choice. Mom was almost reduced to tears. She was just going to have to get used to me leaving on unusual treks. I felt I had so much living to do.

I married early and lost my childhood. I also felt more like doing things the male populace was allowed. This definitely was not a feminine practise. I wanted to be a Boy Scout like my brothers when I was a kid because they went camping. I would rather climb trees than play house with my young girl friends. I was definitely the epitome "tomboy."

Sticking the key in the ignition, I turned the engine on. The Honda started better than my car. Gone was the kick start of the old bikes. It made a low rumble, quieter than most cars, while it idled in the drive. Shifting into gear, I smiled my fond farewells, waved my free hand. I revved the engine.

Off into the unknown I was filled with anticipation. A feeling of freedom swept over me on my way north on U.S. 23. Actually this was not the unknown yet. I had traveled throughout Michigan for a long time. Friendly turf would get me used to going alone.

45

I rode with boots, jeans and a leather jacket for the coolest part of my tour. Once in the hot plains things changed.

I thought stopping every fifty miles or so for something would be a good policy to follow. Gasoline was needed every 200 miles or so but that is a long time sitting in one seat. I had a five gallon tank. But a rest was always warranted or a stop for eats or to see an attraction.

Rest areas were easy on the expressway. Met Bob, Don and Suzanne at the first rest stop who were off to Saginaw on this warm sunny afternoon on their cycles. They left shortly after I pulled in.

At a second rest area on U.S. 23 there was a handful of bikers sitting at a table drinking sparkling wine. I was thirsty but didn't much cater to any form of liquor till they invited me. I had some and dallied too long eating some of their snacks as well. Had to remember I wasn't sitting in the saddle of my bicycle now. I didn't have to carbo up for the endurance. I would be a blimp if I kept this up for a month.

Stopping at a rest area in Grayling on I-75 I met John and his other Lions' Club band. They tended a coffee station for drivers. I enjoyed conversation with them and they thought it was great when they found out where I was headed. John would have liked to go along. He must have been 80 years young. Gave me a "thumbs up" signal when I left. These first encounters made me realize I could do it.

The sunny day was turning into clouds and chills when I arrived at Indian River. My first mistake was to think rain was imminent requiring a motel. It never rained, it did get cold. Perhaps it was my way of easing into this being alone thing. It wasn't cold enough to kill off mosquitos yet as I sat outside to write in my daily journal and look over my map for tomorrow. This became the ritual every night.

A couple miles away I found a nice resteraunt where I felt a little conspicuous but I couldn't let it bother me. I would be eating alone for a long time to come.

Didn't take long in the morning to pack up in the 57 degree air. Had a hard time seeing where I was going for awhile. Motorcycles don't come equipped with defrosters and windshield wipers. I'd reach around the windshield to wipe off a spot as the dew accumulated as I drove.

Breakfasted in Mackinaw City, sent off my first post card of a long series to Mom, and then across the five mile Big Mac bridge into the Upper Peninsula. I always thought it another world up here. The air smelled clearer, the traffic thinner.

Three fellows along U.S. 2 decided they wanted to tag along. They tried to talk to me a little over the road noise. They were from Wisconsin and on the return. After seventy miles of that I tired of it and stopped as they went on. Three people on two bikes were stopped at a bridge eating lunch. They looked like just nice folks out for a ride. They were from Green Bay. Five more stopped on motorcycles. They were going the other way. Hey, I could like all this companionship. I never met so many riders at once. So often bikers were given bad names. The new bikers were just nice folks enjoying riding.

The folks from Green Bay were headed for the Porcupine Mountains. We rode together till they had to turn north. Suddenly the lonliness sneaked in. Oh, well, I had to get used to it. I had a long way to go and one way to get there.

Around 6 pm a few wisps of clouds showed in the azure blue sky. I looked at the map on the gas tank seeing I would have to go some distance to the next camp area. "Top of the Morning" campground was ahead.

The owner put me to the back of the tenter area away from most everyone. I was thankful later. I found most people in the camp were not very friendly. They had brought everything they owned with them. It looked like a miniature city. This was not a transient camp.

The shower room needed quarters to get water. Taking a handful I found two was enough. I even had enough water for the needle-like jets to massage my tired shoulders. I walked down a hill after cleaning up, to see the lake. The usual busy camper noises prevailed, down to blasting radios. I hoped it wouldn't continue into the night. I liked peace and quiet.

The sterno heat and gutter mesh worked very well to heat up a little supper. Chipmunks shared some of my meal. I brought a book along when there wasn't much else to do. As the sun began to set I relaxed in my tent and read till I was sleepy, using a headlamp. I discovered this to be very effective for keeping hands free. Guides on the Colorado River used these to enable them to clean up after dinner in the dark and make breakfast before daylight. It was a good day, I decided. I traveled 403 miles.

Chapter 2   Wisconsin, Minnesota and North Dakota

I didn't have many miles to travel through Wisconsin to get to Duluth, Minnesota. I slept so well the night before I could have stayed in the sleeping bag much longer. I finally emerged from my tent into the quietude of this sleeping park. Most of the campers were up most of the evening with their campfires and rowdiness going on for what seemed far too long into the night.

Preparing hot water didn't take much doing. I started the water before I went to the wash room. When I returned, it was ready for my instant coffee and oatmeal, my regular staple. Add some English muffins with peanut butter and it was more than enough to start the day.

I only needed to stop once for gas and had bad feelings at the station. I'm so used to seeing and talking with friendly people I was having difficulty with this. Using a credit card usually prompted conversation once you give the state of your license plate. Not so here.

Arriving in Duluth, the first large city since leaving home, filled me with trepidation. Thank goodness for maps. Studying it, I saw Superior was south of Deluth. It looked like it should be easier to cross the river there. Crossing the Lake Superior bay inlet from Superior to Proctor tried my patience. A wooden drawbridge was selected. The gapping boards were lain the same direction as my travel. I could feel the two wheels of my Honda wanting to sink between them as I negotiated my way across. A bend or two in the bridge was of no help. I was happy it was Sunday morning. No heavy traffic as I slowly maneuvered my way.

Once on terra firma the road wound uphill on the opposite bank. A lovely park and nicely landscaped housing development attracted my attention. I stopped to admire the view across the bay from which I had just crossed. Lake traffic seemed heavy with many shipping terminals at factories on the other shore.

Traveling on U.S. 2 across this state, I missed large cities or towns. The few I encountered were rather nice. Listening to the radio kept me in touch with the weather updates and local happenings and music. If I ran out of radio stations I had a couple of my own tapes to fall back on.

Met June and Dave at a one pump gas station in Floodville. They were trying to locate some folks in the area. We sat on a bench for awhile drinking orange juice talking about the places I planned on seeing and where they had been. Once I left them it was quiet on the road again. Not many were out on this nice day. My surroundings were wooded for a long time. A fishing contest was going on at Leech Lake in Walker. Seeing that I jinxed Shirleys' fishing sucess, I didn't think I should investigate a contest.

Out came the rain gear when the nice weather turned into a little sprinkle. It only lasted for about 50 miles when the sun appearred again.

In Moorehead, I stopped for dinner of spagetti in an Italian resteraunt. It did not sit well for the rest of the evening. I looked through a phone book while there. I had some relatives in the area. Calling, found no answer.

I entered I-94 freeway. The older roads were nice. Traffic was no problem but after many miles it seemed rather lonely not to hear voices on my CB radio. On the freeways the truckers were always keeping a conversation going. I felt I was back into civilization. The territory changed from trees to wide open spaces. There was a gentle up grade as far as Jamestown and then leveled out till Bismark where I found a Motel 6 for the night. The sun was hot and browning my arms and face as I headed into the west all afternoon. As it set on the flat horizon, I would push my helmet down further to shield my eyes. Sunglasses didn't block out enough.

I put on almost 500 miles today. My shoulders felt somewhat achy from the long day. So happy I put the bags on the back seat to lean against.

It was still light and I needed to stretch my legs. A walk would be nice but there wasn't any place for good walking here on the freeway and city. A K-Mart store was next door but was closed, this being Sunday. I walked over and back anyway to catch up on television news.

I was up and out of there early the next morning. Not having to pack up a tent and sleeping bag helped get me out earlier. I washed out some socks and underwear, hanging them to dry in the room. I remembered down the road, they were still hanging there. I needed them and so returned to retreive them.

The sun was behind me now. Visibility was much better. The morning already warm enough to wear only a shirt.

4 9

The truckers who travel all night sounded rather tired. I came on the radio with my well rested voice, wishing them all a "Good Morning!" A couple came back with a response and we talked a little. I'd pull up to pass them on their left and I could see them looking in their big mirrors as I passed and then they'd smile and wave as I went by. They thought I was traveling by car when I talked on the radio. Were they surprised when they'd pull up their rig next to my little bike to pass me and I'd hold up the microphone to prove it was me. That would start a whole new conversation. Many offers of even trades, or why-don't-we-put-that-two-wheeler-in-my-truck-and-you-sit-up-here-with-me. I turned them all down and they all understood. They were also jealous. I could feel it.

I didn't like riding in their wake so I would ease in front of them. I heard if you pull in good and tight behind a rig you could save gas. You rode in a sort of vacuum. That wasn't my style. I'm sure many a trucker thought motorists must be doing just that when they rode their bumpers.

The terrain being unlike my home state, I rode along marveling on the beauty of it. The plains may be flat and look like nothing was out there but that was an expanse that carried its' own splendor. A few buttes, I heard them called, were off in the distance, their flat tops seeming to hold up a blue sky with enormous billows of white clouds. In the distance they looked hazy blue or purple. I expected to see a stand of buffalo feeding off in the distance or an Indian village with teepees set on the side of the road. I longed to see one with authenticity, natives dressed in everyday clothes of deer hides and beads, their black hair shining adorned with feathers. Horses corraled and children playing, cook fires smoking, old women tending them but I saw none in my reverie.

The sun was in its full glory. I found the heat was too much as I sat on the seat to bake. I had not worn my leather jacket even though it offered some protection in case of a fall. Off it came long ago and it was stashed inside the bungie on the back seat.

Theodore Roosevelt Natioal Memorial Park attracted my attention. A good place to enjoy what began to look like badlands. Hundreds of caverns, canyons, crevasses and some flat spaces with grass and trails running through them. Other tourists were stopping here as well. I spotted a buffalo several miles away. He was only a dot on the landscape. I would like to come back here someday to explore.

In the town of Medora, I toured through a museum, read all the memorials on President Roosevelts love of the land. The city park allowed camping and was a lovely place for lunch. It was also on the site of an old butchering operation. Buffalo and cattle were processed here and a shipping rail yard in the same vicinity carried the meats to the city of Chicago years ago. Mendora was an old town, mostly historic. It was the town Roosevelt stayed as a young man trying to find himself, as is said nowadays.

Leaving there after lunch, the wind had picked up steadily. I wore only a tank top shirt with jeans and after hours of riding couldn't tell I was burning from the hot sun or dry air.

Chapter 3   Montana and Wyoming

Crossing over the line into Montana did not change the terrain any. It was definely "Big Sky Country." A road crew had just laid new asphalt paving on the road. The black of the tar had absorbed much of the heat of the sun radiating it upward to me. The wind did little to cool.

Stopping at a shelter from the wind and sun was welcome. There were no others here in the middle of nowhere, just the traffic on the freeway and wind sounds. Then up in the rafters of the shelter I heard a lone bird singing his little heart out. It had a yellow belly with gray back and wings. I thought it a type of warbler by the song it was singing. It was there for some time. When it flew away I got on my cooled Honda and flew away myself.

Later I stopped at a truck stop to rest the bike and myself over a tall iced tea. Good thing I had a water cooled engine. It did want to get warm when I got stalled in traffic of towns. Out here there wasn't much trouble. It was still quite windy and hot.

Met a couple from California. I saw them off and on the rest of the day along the road and rest areas. They were on their way to Billings, and I, to Hardin. We parted by waving after Hardin. Since it was early in the day I made my campsite in Hardin at a KOA campground. It was flat and still windy here with no real shelter from the wind, but there was shelter from rain and sun.

Gone were the treeless plains area. Now it was green again with rolling terrain. Custers' Battlefield was not far away. I read a few books on his escapades over the years. Anxious to get into the historical aspect of this trip I headed there. No wonder the Indians fought for their land. It was worth the fight. After touring the grounds and listening to a native Indian speak of the battle itself it reinforced my thoughts. Looking out over the main battle I could almost visualize what had happened here so long ago.

Back at camp I saw I had neighbors. Novice campers from Wisconsin and their two children. I was invited to dinner. They brought everything here but the kitchen sink. A microwave was brought in case they needed it. But she made hamburgers on a grill that turned out a little burnt and hard but better than opening a can of something like I had planned.

I frolicked with the children in the hot tub for awhile. I thought it was the last thing I needed on a hot day but surprisingly it felt wonderful to emerse in it. The pool was chilly but did cool the body down.

The sun began to set with the clouds forming some gorgeous shapes. The sky turned deep oranges and reds, then purples reminding me again of Montanas' Big Sky.

Mosquitos were thick after the sun set. In the tent I hid from them, reading until after dark. The wind had died down.

I wasn't up too early this day as I wanted to go back to the battlefield. It wasn't open till 8 a.m. I ate a quiet breakfast of coffee and oatmeal. The neighbors arose while I was packing up, inviting me to breakfast. The kids didn't want me to leave yet. But I had places to go and things to see.

At the battlefield again I walked down the famous ravine where the main attack occurred. Archeologists previously dug around where victims supposedly had fallen. In the museum, the night before, I viewed the items that were found. It was an ongoing project. Squares were dug next to crosses with about six inches of soil removed. Marked metal tabs were nailed into the surface to mark where something was found at a few of the squares.

It started to cloud up as I walked. I decided I'd better hit the road. Headed south on 90 into Wyoming. In the distance I could see much higher elevations than I had seen since I left home five days ago. I wanted to go to Sheridan and Buffalo. There were a couple battlefields I wanted to explore. But the weather made it look like I would not enjoy the side trip. It rained some but only enough to wet the pavement.

Jumping off the freeway to state road 343 would head me into the Big Horn Mountains I read so much about. They rose in front of me higher and higher as I approached the pass through them in Ranchester. I would follow the Tongue River. They were in the 10,000 foot elevation status. My first heights on this trip. The road was slick with the rain. I stopped in town. Signs along this road warned of repair work.

Not knowing if I should continue, I stopped into the post office dressed in my red rainsuit. No business was being conducted in this quiet place. I introduced myself to the counter clerk and explained what I was doing there. Asking for advice on the best way to get to Cody I received many suggestions.

"My husband and I ride motorcycles all the time," she said. "That's mine right outside the office. But if you go up this way here you probably will find the road is gravel for a good distance. This other road, Randy skidded off to the side in the rain once."

"Doesn't sound like I have too many choices," I decided. "Neither way looks too great."

"Well, good luck. Wish I was going with you."

I was wishing she would drive over with me too, in case I had any trouble. I went a little farther when I found a storefront with a covered porch. Good place to sit out the rain and build up my courage, I thought. Several cyclists went the way I should be going. Seeing my bike parked out front, they waved as they went on up the mountain road.

I stalled.

After telling myself I could do it, I sat back on the Honda. It started up with its usual confidence.

I wished I had as much.

Putting all my courage in my pocket I headed it out onto the roadway.

The road zigged and zagged in hairpin curves. The rain stopped but it was not dry. Changing gears to maintain at least enough speed to get me up, I kept it at 30-35 mph most of the time. Once I reached the top I was so elated I had to stop at a look out spot. The riders I saw earlier were also there. I parked a distance from them. I could see they were all men. I didn't know if I liked them yet or not. They watched as I took off the rain garb and helmet. Cheering because they saw I was a woman I suppose, and from out of state. I waved. I just went about my business and they, theirs. I didn't want to start something I couldn't finish.

Riding down was a trip in itself. It was harder to maintain proper speed for the turns, slipping into a lower gear was mandatory.

Shell Canyon was beautiful. It reminded me a little of Grand Canyon on a smaller scale. Riding through the canyon with red rock on the side, mountains of higher elevations seen between the canyon wall in front filled me with ecstacy. Shell Creek ran swiftly alongside the road, the water jumping and splashing as it sped down its way to the Big Horn River. This should be the Bighorn Mountains. Just the names of the mountains excited me.

Once I cleared the canyon the terrain became flat and open again. Being void of mountains or trees or buildings, I could see for miles. In the distance on either side were mountains. Bald Mountain at 10,000 feet to the north and Cloud Peak at 13,000 feet to the south. I changed roads and went through Granite Pass since there was construction on Alternate 14. Still west in front of me were the tips of the Rocky Mountains. Snow could still be seen on them this July.

I found a nice KOA park in Cody. There was quite a crowd in town owing to the 4th of July celebration tomorrow. I had barely noticed the wind picking up in this open area till I tried to light my stove to fix a meal. After fashioning a windbreak with a towel and fiberglass saddlebag I was finally enjoying a hot beef stew.

My neighbors were a couple young mothers and their children from nearby Craig, Colorado who spent most of their summer here. They gave me a birds' eye outlook on life in Craig. They hated it as a mining town. Nothing to do, but here in Cody there was plenty to occupy the time the children were out of school. Out across the plain a very large log house sat on a hill. I could see it in a close-up with my long camera lens. They said it belonged to some underworld figure who donated money to the town of Cody.

I drove into town. A small metropolis compared to what they must have in Craig. Even found a car wash where my mechanical steed had its first bath of the trip. I felt good wiping down the beads of water from the warm chrome tail pipes and maroon gas tank. I checked the other vital signs and found everything just like they were when I left only four days before. I was going to like this Honda.

The day had been a good one. I had conquered a fear of the mountain so far, little as they were in comparison to the Rockies I had yet to ride. If the rest of this trip would be like the first I knew I needn't fear anything.

In my excitement to get to the real Rockies I was out of bed at first dawn. I only had to get to Yellowstone Park less than 50 miles away. After a McDonalds' breakfast I visited the Buffalo Bill museum and watched many horses and their riders readying for todays' parade. Massive Budwieser draft horses in brilliant reds and whites pulling huge wooden wagons of supposedly full beer casks. Cowboys were in great supply riding on the road with their horses going to some final destination. I sat outside the museum taking pictures of the large Buffalo Bill sculpture. I was writing in my journal when several ladies on a tour bus stopped, asking what I was doing riding on a motorcycle. They were so thrilled they found others of their group to have pictures taken of themselves with me and my Honda center stage. One wished she were younger so she could do what I was doing. I chided her that she was still young because she still had young thoughts.

Toward the western edge of town I toured the reconstruction of an old time town, Old Trail Town. The buildings were very rustic with many articles in them to bring the real west to life.

As I rode closer to the Rocky Mountains, their monumental beauty struck me again. I had been here once before but in Colorado. Most of them were seen from my feet or the floor of a sports car whose owner made a test track out of the mountain roads. I garnered fears from that one trip I will never forget. I knew I could handle them much better on the back of the Honda now.

I stopped for lunch in the first picnic area within the confines if the park with a young couple and their baby. We sat on a quiet lake with tall lodgepole pines towering toward the sky with huge rock formations beyond. Calendar picture perfect. The Continental Divide lie ahead.

I was too excited to stay long, continuing to find Roosevelt Ranch Lodge where I reserved my cabin for two nights. It being nothing more than what looked like an old miners' shack. Bedsprings of the high double bed creaked in unison with the wooden floor boards. A small hard chair, a cupboard to cook and eat on and woodburner provided the creature comforts. I was given a "Duralog" to burn if necesary. Holes in the ceiling must leave water spots on the bed and floor but I saw none. I had the option of a wagon ride to dinner or breakfast or a tour by horseback there at the ranch. I opted for the horseback for the next day. I wanted to do everything. Watching the wagon coming in from the dinner ride was quaint. It was actually a stage coach with four horses pulling it. Dust billowed behind just as I watched in the movies. Talked awhile to the young lady who directed traffic, she being a college kid making extra money for the summer. The horses in the corral all looked fairly tame as did the wranglers.

Not wanting to waste the day admiring my cabin I hopped on the back of Honda to see the sights some more. Gorgeous! I could've ridden around here all day. I stopped at Inspiration Point to see the falls that just about every painter must have painted at one time or another.

Metting four motorcyclists from Midland, not far from my hometown was delightful. They, too, were surprised to know I was out here alone. Riding around the park without the weight of my baggage made me feel light as air. It was a hot summer day. I donned just a pair of shorts, tennis shoes and t-shirt. Bending into the curves going first to the right then to the left felt like a giant ski slolum should feel. Not being a skier I imagined it.

I stopped along the road near Yellowstone Lake to take pictures. Snowcapped mountains became the backdrop of this enormous lake. Two bicyclists were laying on the ground resting. One had the same bicycle as I had at home. They said they didn't find riding up the mountain very difficult. Much easier going up than down. Going down took a lot more control. Perhaps I would get the chance to try that one day down the road.

As the day wound down, I continued to flick away with my camera. Back at the lodge a beer sounded so good I took my journal with me to the general store. They sold single cans. Sitting on the little porch I met a fine young man, my age.

"What are you doing out here?" I asked. "Well, I'm supposed to be on a religious retreat but that's over for now. Now I'm just enjoying the atmosphere."

"It is rather laid back and relaxing, isn't it?"

"If it weren't for the tourists I could like it better," he said.

"Have you been here often?"

"Often enough to know what I like in the way of rest and relaxation. Tomorrow night the lodge will have a delicious dinner menu. I'm planning on leaving shortly after." I waited for an invitation but didn't receive any.

"Where is a good place to do a little hiking alone?"

"Well, if you take Slouth Creek Trail it should be OK. I wouldn't go alone to too many trails because of the bears around here. But that one is pretty much out of the way for them. I've walked it a few times."

"Good, maybe I'll give it a try before I leave."

He stood up and stretched putting on his small day pack saying, "Perhaps I'll see you tomorrow."

"That would be nice. Good-night now," I returned as I headed for the broad front porch of the lodge searching for a vacant wooden rocking chair to perch in to watch the sun set and finish my journal and write my card to Mom.

The next day was really going to be full. I had so much planned. I was up too early, of course, so fixed some breakfast in my cabin and wandered around until my 8 a.m. appointment.

The early morning horseback ride was so quiet and serene. There were only a couple of us with the guide. My horse was the usual gentle "dude" type. We had only gone up switchbacks on a shady hillside when we rode into a meadow of spring flowers. The sun was lifting into the sky drying the dew on the meadow. A small herd of deer heard or saw us approach. We watched as they fled. I elected a one hour ride but I could have stayed on that horse for two hours. My shins hurt from walking, I suppose from the day before. I didn't need my backside to hurt.

After returning, it was still morning. I wanted to take some photos of a river in the morning light. Back on my mechanical steed. I shot some buffalo, the river, a few falls and Yellowstone Lake with my long lens. They all had different colors to them in the morning light. I buzzed around following the rest of the tourists, some stopping too quickly without warning when they spotted something to see. The maneuverability was welcomed. I could squeeze my Honda between some mighty tight spaces of parked cars on the road.

Crossing the Great Divide provided me with the thought that I could ride with confidence anywhere. Old Faithful became a prime target of my attention. The weather was now becoming more humid. I suppose the added water from all the ground seepage helped. Snow was still melting from above. I walked all the platform walks around the area admiring the colors and temperatures of different pools. The sun was at its' best brilliance, tingling my exposed skin. Using plenty of sun lotion I still had the beginnings of burnt and wind dried arms and face. If only I could get my legs to get as brown as my arms!

Sitting out the blow of Old Faithful gave me time to visit the wonderfully solid log lodge. This building had been the scene in some movie. I want to recall *White Christmas.* A clerk quit restocking one of the shelves in the gift shop as I approached.

"Hi."

"Hi," I returned. Just a young thing probably not wet behind the ears yet.

"Where ya from?" he asked straightforwardly.

"Michigan," I replied.

"No kidding! I was raised in Owosso. Do you know where that is?"

"Sure, it's only about fifty miles from me. What are you doing here?"

"I came out for a little adventure. I graduate next year. My folks thought I would like to do this for a summer before I get serious over any girls or forget college."

"You don't live in Michigan any more, then?"

"No, we moved to Utah when I was ten."

Hadn't you better get back to work before someone sees you?"

"I don't much care if they do. They don't pay enough to hardly keep you here. It's after hours that I enjoy. I sometimes get time enough to see the park."

"Well, I wouldn't want to keep you. Talk while you're working. It'll make the time go faster."

"OK. Listen, my dad visits Owosso in the summer. Would you call him for me when you get back? You are going back this summer, aren't you?"

"Sure, but why don't you call him."

"I don't have that kind of money and don't want to make a collect call. I told him I could take care of myself. I don't want him to think I can't.

"Well, here, write down the number in my journal. I may someday use this to write a book on my travels. Would you mind if I used your name and our conversation?"

"Oh, gee, that would be great."

"Good. I won't even mention our secret about your expenses."

"No, that's OK. My dad doesn't read much anyway."

I watched the steam spurt out of the ground while eating an ice cream cone and drinking a cold pop, shooting with my camera.

Roaming around to see all the sights was so pleasurable. The air smelled so fresh. I stopped at a river some distance from the geysers to see how warm it was. It was just tepid. Sitting down, I slipped off my shoes and socks and splashed my feet in the emerald waters. Oh! How good it felt after walking for several hours!

One of the places visited was a vista with the river running smoothly in a valley. The great mountains were high in the background. The middle ground was loaded with tall, spiraling pines. From the parking area, a lone log cabin sat near the river. The sun was lower in the sky when I came upon this. The sky was still a light blue in color with a few wispy clouds. The mountains held a blue-purple, showing snow in the upper heights. The grassy area around the cabin was wild and green-brown. The trees were dark and forbidding across the river that reflected all the colors in the picture. This was a rendezvous place for Lewis and Clark in their great expedition. They split up to find a better pass through the mountains, returning here with what they found.

While riding through North Dakota and Montana I remembered smelling the fresh mown hay. Here the overpowering odors of pine and water must have multiplied with the altitude. Even that corral smelled good this morning.

Back at the lodge in the evening I met the same fellow I had spoken to last night. He was just finishing his meal.

"Too bad you came in so late. We could have eaten together."

"Well, if I knew we had a dinner date I might have been on time. We didn't, did we?"

"No, I don't think so. You will enjoy their shrimp. If you don't mind I'll stay awhile and talk with you."

"That would be great. How did your day go?"

"It was superb. I hiked a trail on the eastern part of the park. I think it was about sixteen miles. Such beauty here. Especially if you can get away from the tourists and unto the trails. You must do one while you are still here. You aren't going till tomorrow, are you?"

"No. I'll try that trail you told me about. Being on the west end it will be the direction I will exit. I plan on heading back into Montana."

"Well, here is the nicest waitress in the lodge. I will leave you now to your dinner and hope you enjoy. If I don't see you again I wish you a safe journey."

"Why, thank you, and you, too. Maybe we'll meet again someday in our journey through life."

I hated to see him go. He was such a kindly gentleman. Looking at the pricey menu I carefully edged around the shrimp and headed for something I thought I would enjoy.

Returning to my cabin among the several rows I met my next door neighbors.

"Someone saw a bear out there on the other side of the road a little while ago. You want to go with us while we see if we can find it?" she asked.

"Sure, why not. It wasn't too close, was it? Let me get my camera. I'll put the long lens on it in case we see it."

"Hurry. We don't want to miss it," he pleaded.

We never did see one. It could have been anything in the semi-darkness that was befalling the park. We did see a couple deer. Perhaps they did, too, but failed to realize it.

Chapter 4   Montana Again

In the morning I was up and ready to see the sun rise over the mountains. Said farewell to the couple next door and some others in near-by cabins. Sitting on the lodge porch rocking chairs drinking a couple of cups of coffee I mused over how I wished I were younger. I could just come here to work summers and enjoy the park at my leisure like Dan Clark from Owosso.

I knew I wanted to hike at least one short trail before leaving but with thoughts that a bear might still be in the area from last night I changed my mind. When I finally left slowly with the sun on my back I looked very carefully to the sides. I didn't want to miss anything. I wanted it to register in my mind. I might never have the opportunity to see this park again.

When I passed a trail head almost on the outskirts of the park I had second thoughts about leaving. There were a few cars and a horse trailer with the park service logo displayed. I wanted to walk the trail. It beckoned me. My motorcycle was much more exposed to vandalism and theft when everything I owned was laid on top. I took my chances again.

The trail head posted signs gave maps and directions on how to treat bear sightings. "Play dead," it advised. Sure, I thought. If I saw a bear I know I couldn't play dead. Bear would know if I was shaking with fear while he pawed me.

Taking just my camera and extra film I headed down the trail in my early morning blissfulness. Shooing up some short-tailed squirrels bent on their own mischief, I listened to birds singing and slapped at mosquitos aplenty. Larkspur, Forget-Me-Nots and sunflower-like flowers were just about bloomed out already but were in such profusuion they could not be ignored by my camera's eye. Lupins, wild roses and another five petaled flower ranged in colors from light violet to rose-red bloomed everywhere.

A bluebird perched on a high bush. I hadn't seen one of those in ages. The trail zig-zagged down through this meadow till I could hear the rush of a river. There in the distance flowed dark, dark water with white splashes of frothing spray churning along its entire path as it rushed through its narrow channel of rock. It looked so much like the Colorado River in smaller scale. Since I had been on that river just the year before I seemed to judge all rivers by its immense status.

A bridge crossed the river. The roar of the water prevented hearing anything else. It was only a footbridge but it was made of iron. I sat admiring the water. Heading back, I ran into a forest ranger on horseback.

"Good morning," he saluted.

"Good morning," I returned, "isn't this a beautiful day?"

"Yes. You here alone?"

"Yes. Is that all right? I didn't go very far. Probably only a mile from the trailhead. Am I right?" I asked.

"Yea, I'm just returning from the camp at the end. Been gone a week."

"Is that the one that is eighteen miles away?"

"Yea, we usually patrol it. There's been a lot of bears lately. You didn't see any, I take it."

"Naw, if I did you would have known about it by now," I laughed.

"Otherwise is this a good enough trail for me to venture on alone? I'm on my way out of the park and just had to have a last fling."

"Are you going farther?"

"No, just wanted to go to the bridge."

"You'll be OK. I'm going to go on ahead. Maybe I'll see you at the trail head."

"All right. I'm glad I'm being protected. See ya."

When he told me there were 10,000 miles of hiking trails it piqued my attention. Perhaps I could make another trip back to just hike!

Stopping at Mammoth Hot Springs I walked the tourists trails some more. I didn't like this area as much. It was interesting but more like a moonscape. Small bits and pieces of plant growth stuck out of the bleached surface of overflow sulfur as if stuffed in a scare crow. Aquamarine water spewed out of underground fissures creating interesting shapes around them. Trees looked rather mutant and twisted. Everything looked dried up but it was still alive.

"Would you take my picture with my camera?" came a voice behind me.

I turned to look and a pretty young Chinese girl held out her camera toward me. "I will for a price," I answered. "You have to take me with my camera. We did so and went about whatever we were doing.

Once free of the park I headed up 287 toward Virginia City. The name reminded me of several western movies watched over the years. It drew me forward like a magnet. Clouds came over and a few sprinkles made the day a little cooler but not necessarily nasty. Mountains receded into the distance. A few snowcaps remained here and there. The land was again in the barren stage with some tree rows where farming showed.

Riding along the Madison River it became greener and more like home. Fishermen in waders and johnboats were catching whatever they caught in the river. Looked like the kind of river Shirley would have like to spend time on. A tree alongside had a sign on it with a long explanation of why the arrows and ribbons were stuck in it at high levels. I did not snap a picture nor did I write down what it said and now I regret it. It was interesting. Perhaps one day I'll return and find out.

An earthquake rumbled in 1959 in the valley. A tourist station along the road explained what happened and how. A slide show presentation and lecturer gave details of the aftermath. Binoculars would show pinpointed areas to view. It was a good diversion for my day.

Pulling into the only campground in Virginia City I noticed a huge black cloud hovering over the mountains to the west.

"It's not going to rain," announced the owner of the camp. A native of the area, I figured he ought to know. He was taking his time talking to some other folks and myself and had not issued any permits. I was getting edgy. I wanted to set up camp on dry ground so I would have a dry floor and a place to sit out the storm besides with him or in the bath house.

"Are you sure?" I asked.

"You don't believe me?" He was astounded at my perception of him. He felt he knew everything about the weather. I decided he must be right. He lived here. He must know something about how the weather acted.

I hurriedly paid for my permit and sped down to my assigned area of tall grass in a little valley with very little trees. Just as I opened my waterproof bag, laid out the tent, the black clouds that were not supposed to drop their water opened up. I cussed out the owner as I grabbed my still dry tent and exposed belongings and ran for the wash house just a short distance away.

Camping out in a bathroom was not my idea of a good place so I sat outside under the eaves in the lee of the storm waiting for it to stop. Looking up the hill from where I sat were some motor homes. How I wished I could be in one of them now. Just then the door popped open in the nearest one and someone was yelling at me to get out of the rain and come inside.

"Thank you," I gasped as I jumped the step into their crowded home.

"There is no sense you siting out there getting wet. You must be cold," returned the other resident. "Have a cup of tea."

"That sure sounds inviting, but I don't want to put you out any."

"Nonsense. The water is always ready on the stove."

"I sure appreciate it."

"Where ya from?"

"Michigan, not too far from Detroit."

I don't remember where they said they lived. I left my journal on the bike when I ran and forgot to even ask their names. We talked for awhile about the usual things. People like themselves were always inquiring as to the "what," "how," and "why" I did things. They always marveled at the thought of traveling alone on a motorcycle. The female part was certain to be a conversation starter.

"Looks like it will quit now for awhile. I think I'll try to put up my house while I have the opportunity. Thanks again for the dry roof and tea."

As I put the tent up the rain came in little bursts. Not enough to stop me. Everything smelled so fresh now.

Joan and Charles Lee pulled up shortly on a tandem bicycle. They had their camp set up in no time at all. We got acquainted while I conversed over their ideas of condensing everything down to small sizes.

"We are from San Jose, California and like you we have been asked the usual questions. "How long ya been on the road, where ya going, when will ya get there? We will be in Washington D.C. in a few months. We started in Portland, Oregon. We have maps that Bikecentennial provides its members routing us on good roads, scenic roads, tourists sights and even places to camp and eat."

He pulled out his map carrier and gave me a look at the strip maps he was provided. "I sure would like to do that someday," I wished aloud. "Maybe next year. Have you two eaten supper yet?"

"No, we have been eating all day but we only eat enough for energy. You know, you can't pedal on nothing. I like to save a big meal for evening.

"I could take us into town. I haven't been there yet. The owner says it's pretty nice. Just like out of the old west. There is a place to eat, too."

Coming over to my area they inspected my bike. "Sounds like fun but don't you think three on a bike is a bit much?"

"No, problem. Town is only a mile or so. I'll take you one at a time. Much easier than on your bike," I mused. I only had one helmet but we thought we could get away with them wearing their inadequate bicycle helmets.

"OK, sounds like a good deal. We have to change into something more substantial first. How about an hour, after we've cleaned up and stuff?"

"Sure, take your time."

We toured the town. So many places to see. The community had recreated many stores filling them with mannequins, surrounding them with the things of the olden days. Numerous old buildings have stood in the same spot for over a hundred years. Square nails were used on the siding of the time, windows that never were replaced still showed the imperfections and thickness of days gone by. Wood here, we were informed later, took forever to deteriorate because of the dry climate. One small building set back from the street was outfitted as a brothel with customers and ladies of the night dressed in the finery of the day. What a delight to move back in time. One realization we were still in the present was the paved road and cars.

We backtracked to the local pub for a beer and hamburger and conversation.

Back at camp we found our tents were still soaked. A bunch of noisy kids had moved in the area partying till after 4 a.m. keeping all three of us awake.

Charles invited me over for breakfast. I thought it should be my place to offer them breakfast but oatmeal and coffee was all there was in my kitchen. He made pancakes with real butter and syrup. Since they were out of coffee, we shared.

"Where do you put all this stuff?" I asked.

"We buy as we go along. I wanted to get rid of this pancake stuff and you're the vehicle for it. I've carried it too long."

"Yes, I'm getting mighty tired of the same breakfast. Maybe we should have exchanged with your oatmeal," Joan added.

"Now that we've finished off the pancakes, I'm not going to trade you my oatmeal. I'll give you some for a couple breakfasts, if you'd like."

We packed our respective camp and parted ways. Before leaving, Charles came over making an apology. "We lied to you last night about going to D.C. We are really planning on an around the world trip."

"You're kidding!"

"No. We didn't tell you because most people we say that to wouldn't believe us. So we've narrowed it down. We know you are a person who would understand."

"How long are you going to be gone, then?" I asked.

"We figure two and a half years. We put all our things in storage, quit our computer related jobs and said farewell. In that field I can't see why we can't pick up where we left off."

Amazing, the people I met on this trip. These were young enough to still enjoy such a trip. No children yet but it was in the planning stage when they return from their lifelong dream. I heard from them several times later. They made it around by plane, boat, train or anything else that traveled. Europe, a little Africa, India, Japan, Australia and New Zealand, liking the last place the best. Incredible!

I headed back to Virginia City still west and north. I sat on my bike next to the curb when I heard, "Where ya going?"

"I don't know yet. I thought I'd go up this hill to see what's on Boot Hill."

"You weren't going to walk up, were you?"

"I don't think I want to take this monster up, so I guess I'll walk."

"You just wait here," she said, as she aimed her car up the driveway to the house where I was parked. "I have to give this lady some eggs and I'll take you up."

There was no asking. Just telling. Dorothy Bacon had an authoritarian attitude. She didn't take "no" for an answer. I followed her orders and jumped into the car.

"Will my bike be OK there?"

"No problem. Nobody takes anything around here. We have a very law abiding town here. They'd have to answer to me if they did." Somehow I believed her.

Dorothy became a long-time friend after that. She drove up to Boot Hill, showing me her husband's grave. The signs over the infamous gunshooters' graves were replaced periodically because thieves kept stealing them! And I believed her!?

"This used to be a silver mining town. All the overgrown, sloping hills you see around here are the tailings left when it was dug by hand. The town was filled with Chinese coolies and prospectors. When they played out all the silver they left only our town. I think I would like to go up and redig some of those hills. There must be some more silver in there."

"Sounds like a good way to explore. Maybe one day I'll come back and you can show me how to go about doing it."

"That'd be fun but I'm too old to be runnin' around those hills."

"What d'ya mean? You're not too old. You get around better than most people do your age."

She laughed. "Oh, yea, but I'm due to have some hip surgery one of these days. I've been putting it off. I'll be unable to come here for a summer and I love it so much I hate to miss one."

"That's a heck of a reason, but I understand." She gave me the tour of the town and invited me to her house for lunch.

"Get those things in here and we'll throw them in the washer," she said when she found most of my sleeping paraphernalia was wet from the rain. I not only stayed for lunch but dinner and breakfast the next day. She wanted me to stay longer but I had somewhat of a schedule to keep. Students staying with her were met as they came and went about their activities. She said she liked young folks around. It made her feel young. She was around 70 years old. Wintered in Anoka, Minnesota. I've kept in touch with her since and made a return trip on one occasion passing through to another destination.

Chapter 5   Idaho

I wasn't ready to leave Montana yet. I rode up through Twin Bridges. Four rivers passed through here--the Big Hole, Beaverhead, Ruby, and Jefferson, all changing names in town. Heading north to Missoula I lingered. I needed a few things to replenish some supplies or I would be eating out again. Most of the camps required fuel cooking rather than wood fires. My sterno was doing fine for a quick meal. Finding a mail drop box was another necessity or Mom would be calling me back home. I was faithful to my promise so far.

Turning south to Idaho along highway 93, I followed the Bitterroot River. It was just rolling hills for a good distance till then. I could see the larger Rocky Mountains behind me with snow caps still on the tallest peaks. In front I approached the Bitteroot Range. The Continental Divide at Gibbons Pass with an elevation of 7,000 feet brought me back into the taller peaks. Engleman spruce clung to the rock surfaces in their tall splendor, thrusting their spires into the sky, branches up-turned embracing it.

The day was perfect again. Sunny and warm. I just hummed along feeling the vibration under my body. Such a comfort to know mechanical failures were not a problem.

At Lost Trail Pass, a memorial was built to honor Chief Joseph of the Nez Perce tribe. I stopped to view the Big Hole Visitors' Center and follow the trail outlining the last battle he and his band fought. I envied the inner strength he had to keep his band together for such a long time.

It intrigued me enough to want to visit as many battlefields and monuments as possible while here. I'm positive I would have bored anyone else who may have come with me. This was what I called my "Vision Quest" copied from the Indians. It should give me a better understanding of their land we so violently took from them.

Walking back from a creek trail I ran into a fisherman walking my direction carrying his catch for the day.

"Looks like some good eating there," I ventured.

"Ah, yes, I'm going to do myself a favor and devour as many as I can," he returned.

"You live around here, I suppose."

"A few miles away. I like to come here to fish. It's quiet and peaceful on the banks where Chief Joe fished."

"Are you some kind of history buff? I asked.

"No, I'm a builder by trade."

I had seen many large log houses in the mountains in this area. They were new and many different designs. I could live like that. Just give me a try.

"You wouldn't be building any of these log houses I've seen around here, would you?"

"As a matter of fact, I have."

"Wow, they're beautiful. I could live in one of those. I've thought I might want to build one at home."

"They are too expensive to build."

"Why is that? You've got the resources all around here."

"It's not the resources that's expensive. It's the inside finishing. Most people want flat surfaces."

"I want the flat surface, too, but the logs I looked at in the market were "D" shaped. They didn't seem that expensive compared to the traditional house."

He made no further comment. We came to the end of the walking trail to a picnic area.

"Would you care to share some fish with me?"

"Gee, I don't know. How long from line to table would it be? I can't stay too long."

"Not long at all. I already have the fire going, just need to clean the fish."

"In that case, you've talked me into it."

"What's your name?"

"Marion. Yours?

"Chuck."

"How'd ya do, Chuck? I asked holding out my hand. He put everything down on the table, wiped off his hands on his pants and offered his in return.

We talked a little while he cleaned, breaded and cooked the fish in a frying pan over his grill fire.

"What are you doing out here? You're not from around here."

"How do you know that?"

"I know everyone around here. That doesn't take much to know. There aren't many natives here and I build all the new houses in the area so I know the new ones."

"O.K. I'm from the east. Michigan."

"And what does a girl from Michigan do way out here?" he asked.

"See that Honda motorcycle over there with all that stuff on it? That's mine. I'm just bumming around looking at the countryside I've never seen."

"Alone?"

"Alone. Wasn't supposed to be, but I am. Does that bother you?"

"No. I just don't know that I've seen a woman riding a bike before."

"You've seen one now."

"By golly, you're right. I'm glad you decided to share my lunch."

The fish was delicious. Trout. He had a bag of chips to munch on and some pop. I enjoyed the encounter and regretfully said my fond farewells.

"If you ever get out my way, look me up," I said, as I handed him my card, "maybe I'll have you build a house for me."

I took a short jaunt to the east to Wisdom for gas and returned. The road was partially gravel and rock, but navigable. Nothing special here. Perhaps I thought I could find some wisdom in Wisdom.

Passed by a dirt road to River of No Return. I was tempted to investigate but since the name brought on a little of my superstitious self, I passed up the opportunity. I still had a long way to go.

Continuing south I found Salmon River Days as a celebration of a sort. I guess I was in Salmon. I was in the middle of it. Everywhere I saw canoes, rafts and inner tubes carried on trailers or tops of cars and the river. Races were being held and this was the end point. It was very festive. Many canoe and raft liveries along the river. I was tempted to jump one. Inquiring, found there to be a waiting list of a couple days because of the races. Not having the time I continued on.

I did spot a Good Sam Campground nearby. The area required some more exploring. After setting camp, I spent a little time in the recreation hall watching rain falling from a cloudless sky. It didn't last long, but it made everything wet. Back at the campsite, one of my neighbors doing the walk around the grounds trip, stopped while I was writing in my journal keeping up my notes.

"See you're from Michigan," Duane Arnold stated. "Where in Michigan?"

"Brighton. You know where that's at?"

"You're kidding. My wife, Betty and I are from Fenton just a few miles away."

"Oh, my gosh." We're almost neighbors.

"And we're traveling the same way. See those two BMW's next door? Those are ours."

"Congratulations," I said to Betty. I don't see very many women riding out here, especially more in my age group."

"Neither do I. This is my first time. I've always ridden on the back of his. He talked me into doing it myself and you know, I really like it."

We talked about where they've been. Almost the same places I visited. They were on their way north in the morning and I, south. We exchanged addresses and promised to write when we got home and share experiences. After a couple years that, too, faded in time.

The following morning I was up and gone before they were. Their tent was sealed up and all I could hear was a soft snore eminating from inside. I could not say good-bye. It was rather cool at this time of day in the mountains. I needed to wear my leather jacket with a hooded sweatshirt and gloves. The sweatshirt was tied snug around my neck to act as a scarf to keep the cold air from running down my back.

Driving along the Salmon, I stopped at another of a series of picturesque photo spots. It so much reminded me of the Colorado River in miniature I thought of Shirley again. Whenever I see things we have seen together I would do that. She always enjoyed the water so. I wished she were with me. A few wind-whipped trees outlined my photos but the chill in the air made me seek out the sun.

The mountains were to the east and west as I winged south along the valley floor. Farms took the place of rocks and pinnacles. Rounding a curve I narrowly missed striking three cows crossing the road. No fences here to contain them. Horses were in just about every other field or farm corrals. Signs in Montana and Wyoming alerted travelers of open ranges. These were the closest I came to the theory. Relieved I had prevented damage to my traveling companion beneath me I noted the many rough weathered shacks along the way. Most looked like mine shacks, abandoned or occupied.

I stopped at a restaurant finding another gathering place for the local people of Challis. I only stopped for coffee. A street with the same name was on my mail route at home. Associating the two compelled me to stop. It was built of logs. Since there were no such things as sweet rolls, I had a slice of pie with my coffee.

On my map I saw "Craters of the Moon" noted. That sounded interesting. Arriving in the park I saw such a change in terrain it was almost frightening to me. It looked like too much devastation. The black lava from extinct volcanos spread around everywhere. I remember my father stopped here on one of his expeditions. He thought it something to see. The black rock was ugly to me. I didn't go into the park. Going through it was enough.

I stopped at a God forsaken place among some rocks and ate lunch in the sun. No trees, just a couple birds who sang for me while I ate. After Shoshoni it wasn't as much fun.

The wind was strong enough to blow my sunglasses off my face. I wore an open helmet but was surprised I couldn't keep them on. Wearing my leather jacket, to ward off the cool air at least gave me a convenient pocket to stash them.

Arriving at Twin Falls I expected to see twin falls. I crossed the Snake River over a high suspension bridge. I spotted a sign on the other side indicating the falls. Following a short dirt road I came to what I would call a lot of falls but not "twin" falls. I hurriedly took my pictures and left the engine running so I could just jump on and go. I was afraid the wind would blow the bike over if I left it too long on the dirt.

Seeing how this wasn't fun any more, I chose highway 30. The farmers irrigated their potato fields. The wind began to whip up a crosswise path. Some fields were dry. I was either dusted or sprayed for many miles as I worked my way to my next stop for the night. A park called Massacre Rocks sounded inviting. I drove in and around finding nice campsites but not one with a windbreak. I would never pitch my tent in this wind. Even if I did I might not be where I went to bed tonight. I could be in the next county or someplace.

Another couple on a big Harley stopped with the same intention.

"We are going to find a room in Twin Falls. This is just too much," he yelled over the wind.

"I just came from there. I'm not going back," I returned.

"There is a KOA park in Pocatello. We passed the sign on the road. They may have shelters."

"Good, maybe I'll take a look. See, ya."

We split up to find our place for the night. I jumped on the expressway 15, tired of the off-shoot road. I had to get out of this wind. I looked for the sign directing me to the KOA but never found one. Must have missed it somewhere. I didn't care anyway. Behind me the black clouds were building with a vengeance. They didn't look too friendly. If I could stay ahead of them at a good speed I might make it to a town big enough to support a motel. Idaho Falls was just ahead. But then so was Blackfoot. It looked big enough to have one. No such luck. I entered the expressway again to go another 19 miles to Idaho Falls, hoping to find one there.

I kept getting the dirt and irrigation sprays thrown at me from the bare fields. It felt like the water was glueing the dirt to my bare arms and face. Getting off the exit I stopped at the first motel. It had just turned itself into a home for the handicapped. They hadn't changed the sign yet. The second, I couldn't find anybody around. It was early in the afternoon, perhaps they didn't expect anyone so soon. The third had some real live people running it. I hurried to get to my room in the corner to rip my stuff off the bike before I got caught in the storm. The clouds looked so heavy with rain, they were ready to unload any minute. It was dark enough for the mercury vapor lights to light up on the street. It was only 2 p.m.

Right behind me another young fellow on a bike pulled in doing the same thing as I. The air was warm and the room stuffy. I left the door open a little to freshen it up till it started to rain. We said a few words to each other and I invited him to my room before it started to rain but he said he really just wanted to take a shower. He felt the same as I did about the blowing dirt and water. So we respectfully cleaned up and a short time later the rain stopped and the sun came out making it quite humid.

He stepped out the same time I did to find we had a brilliant rainbow over us.

"Must be a good omen," I said. "This ought to tell us something."

"Like what? We're crazy?"

"No, it's going to be a good day tomorrow when we leave."

We used the white motel towels to wipe down the bikes as we shared a cup of instant coffee.

Chapter 6   Return toWyoming

A good night's sleep in a bed did wonders to my physical self. Washed and dried some clothes, caught up on the national news and felt rejuvenated after yesterday's winds. It looked calm out the window as I dressed and packed. After a few words to my motel mate in the next room, wiped the dew off the windshield again and was off to replenish the groceries for the day.

Still heading east along highway 26 and the Snake River, the day was sunny but never warmer than 68 degrees. Out of farm land and into trees and rolling hills gave another twist to the otherwise boring terrain. Before noon I found a sandy beach alongside the river to take a break. I took out my journal and cooking supplies to make a cup of soup. The river water was a gray-green in color, running at a fairly good clip. The sun felt good. A raft full of people could be seen coming down the river. Just then an empty bus arrived on my sandy beach. I surmised they were going to join up and take the rafts out. This was the drop off spot.

The raft used here were about half the size we used on the Colorado holding nine people. They all wore street clothes and life jackets. This river must have been calm without any white water. I didn't see any wet feet or clothes coming off the raft.

Once I reached the Wyoming border I headed north to Grand Teton National Park and Jackson Hole. I didn't find Jackson Hole anything special. Perhaps for the jet set, but this girl is not of that set and never could be. I didn't stay long. The stores were having a sidewalk sale. Lots of tourists milling about. On to the park. I was given a brown map of the park. It wasn't as good as the one I received at Yellowstone. I couldn't read it as well from the distance on my gas tank. The colors blended too well.

Putting that aside I stopped at a roadside pull-out to have a grand view of the Tetons. A telescope was available for me to spot climbers off in the distance. As hard as I tried I couldn't spot any. Perhaps they weren't there at all. The Tetons seemed to jut right out of the ground. There was very little grade. There was flat ground and then the mountain. No foothills. These are supposed to be young mountains and they hadn't eroded enough to do that. Very majestic no matter how you sliced it.

I found a small trail head with a circle tour. I needed to walk. I hadn't done so in days. Being only two miles long in the shadow of the peaks it made for just the right length to find superior photogenic views. I snapped many photos of the mountains and wildflowers. I brought my close-up lens making striking shots of them. I should have studied to be a naturalist or something. I was always spotting something along the trails to stop to investigate or take a picture. Too bad I waited so long to decide these things.

Having enough of that I headed out to a KOA campsite outside the national park. There was still a nice view of the peaks. Since I was on the east of them there would be a good possibility of a great sunset that night. It would go down behind them.

Next to me were a couple from Iowa on a BMW heading for a rally in Missoula, Montana. They were heavy smokers. She looked like a real tough lady. They were going to a bar up the way and invited me for a hamburger. I didn't think I wanted to ride on my bike to the bar I told them. I'd been riding too long now and needed to walk somewhere. I got out of that one.

Walking around the park perimeter, I met a foursome from Rhode Island. One couple lived in the same area I used to live. They traveled in motor homes. I was invited in to meet everyone and we discussed my one time home.

Met two bicyclists traveling the Bikecentennial route. One was from Tallahasee, Fla. The other was from Ann Arbor, Michigan just 20 miles from my home. They hadn't set up camp yet. I said I'd try to visit them later if it didn't get dark too soon. It was dark too soon.

I bought some milk and orange juice for morning. I tied in a mesh bag and put them in the cold river running behind my tent site. Four more bikers came in from Muskegon, Michigan. This was beginning to be "old home week" convention or something. We all had something in common anyway. I was the only one traveling alone and heading east.

Sunset arrived before I was ready. I grabbed my camera and ran to a good place for the picture without having power lines visible. Didn't know I was out of film. Darn. I ran back to my tent while rewinding the film. The rewind handle broke off in my endeavor. I turned the film without it as the sun dipped lower with such speed I was getting exasperated. Finally put the sixth roll of film in the camera while running back to my spot and took the picture. I missed the best shot.

Back at camp new neighbors in a Volkswagen bus were taking care of camp business speaking only German to several children. For the rest of the night and early morning I was to listen to the "whoosh-bang", "whoosh-bang" of that door. It just about drove me to insomnia.

By morning the temperature dipped to a cold 32 degrees. Frost was covering everything. I grabbed my leather jacket to cover my feet during the night and wore extra clothes. This was to be the coldest night. John David, a youngster from one of the sites kept coming over to inspect my Honda. His mother said he loved motorcycles. He was about three or four years old. I put a towel on the seat as it was wet yet and plopped him on. His little eyes just lit up like beacons. As soon as I turned the key to start it up he couldn't get off fast enough.

I retrieved my breakfast from the river. As cold as the air was, it wasn't necessary.

I don't know why it is but in my notes I state I went through Union Pass to cross the Divide. On the map it is called Togwater Pass at an elevation of 9,658 feet. Being above tree line it was cold. So glad I remembered to bring a pair of long underwear. Snow was everywhere but the road surface. I followed the Wind River. I read much about this river and the Wind River area. Ahead was the Wind River Reservation.

At Dubois, I bought some stamps, found a fishing spot along the river and wrote a couple of cards to mail home. The cottonwood trees were shedding. It looked like snow. I had heard it snowed in the upper elevations last night. I suppose so. It was cold enough.

At Riverton I ate lunch in a city park driving north to Shoshoni for no real reason and then back. The area was full of uranium fields. It smelled more like oil. Lots of antelope skittered and fed here.

I headed now for Casper. Leaving Riverton I began having trouble with the faithful companion. It seemed like it wasn't getting any gas but it was losing all electrical power. I had gas. It would go and then falter. I looked around. I passed a sign that said 75 miles to Muddy Gap. A cow out in a field and barren everywhere. No traffic. Even if I wanted to summon help, I could not use the radio and nobody would have heard. It had only a five to ten mile range.

I headed back to Riverton. Perhaps I could get it back to find a dealer there. One thing I noticed on this trip was that every town of any size had a Honda dealer.

Once I turned around the bike kept running. I thought it was telling me something. Perhaps I wasn't supposed to go that way. I found a dealer. For $5.00 he made me feel foolish. Someone like myself traveling alone ought to have figured it out. My battery cable was loose on the post. When I tightened the wires down for the radio I didn't tighten them enough. Whew! I felt better.

7 6

Not giving my gasoline any thought, I turned around and headed toward Casper. Muddy Gap was 100 miles away. Not much was on the map. One town in 75 miles. They should have a station. I could make that. Herds of antelope roamed the vast ranges. I passed dead animals on the highway. Once in awhile I would only see a lone animal feeding on what looked like sparse pickings. A dead Black Angus cow lay on the side blown up ready to burst.

No station at Jeffrey City. It was lucky to have a post office. But they didn't sell gas. What do these people do for gas out here? I continued on hoping a town with a name like Muddy Gap would have some. The miles sped by. I went on reserve. Would I make it? Just what I'd need, to run out of gas!

In the near distance I saw a few low buildings. Muddy Gap. I must have been on fumes. I drove more than my suspected 200 mile range. They had a gas station and a cafe. I would never have made Casper. On leaving the people in the cafe told me to watch for the water dogs in the road. Not wanting to sound like I didn't understand what they were taking about, I assured them I would. Did they mean the antelope?

Relieved I wouldn't have to walk I went on to Devils' Gate on the Sweetwater River. The pioneers stayed the winter here if they couldn't cross the divide before winter set in. If they continued south along this river they would go through South Pass, the lowest point through the mountains this far north. A monument of sorts was designed to explain the area. It showed the Oregon Trail, how they navigated uncharted land by landmarks. In the distance could be seen Split Rock in the otherwise flat terrain. Wagons headed for the split and from there had another landmark to find. Sounded like a scavenger hunt. Only they played with their lives. As people died in this wintering-over ground, they were buried. Not in cemetery fashion but where ever it was convenient. Therefore, the land was off limits to development calling it sacred grounds. The harsh weather did not obliterate the wagon wheel ruts in the ground since that time in the 1860's and before. Very impressive. The pioneers deserved much credit. They, too, were explorers of a sort.

Independence rock was also in the area and a monument for the Pony Express. I looked at the memorial for the Pony Express or I would have never forgiven myself. Nearby, the old trail the Mormons took was still to be seen where it crossed the Platte River. Just like in the book *Centennial.* Long ago the crossing was changed to a safer passage down the river and this spot was abandoned.

I couldn't see the names on Independence Rock as it was getting late. I still had a distance to go to find a place in Casper. No real prospects of a camp according to my map.

77

When I finally arrived, I found not one campground open. A KOA camp was advertised on a road sign. I arrived with a couple in a car from New York. "We've looked all over for a campground. I've got directions but always end up back here," he said perplexed as we compared maps.

"Well, maybe we should camp here anyway. If someone comes along and kicks us out maybe they can show us where to go," I suggested.

"Let me try again."

"All right. I'll follow you." I followed him but he missed a sign that directed us to a park in town. I signaled to him as best I could but he kept on going. Maybe I would see him later. They pulled in a long time after.

The camp was not very good. I got a sort of tent site on what looked like a parking lot. The ground was grassless and was as hard as cement. There would be no staking the tent down here. Relieved I had a place, I took it and hoped for the best. A few doors away some fellows waved and said hello. They were just sitting around their motor home enjoying some beer and getting ready to eat. I walked over.

"Smells good over here."

"You like barbecued pork chops?" asked one of them.

"Sure, is that what I smell?"

"George, here is our official cook. We couldn't eat anything we make, so he does it all."

"How about a beer?"

"Sounds like a good idea. I've had a rather bad day today." I told them about my battery and gas trouble.

"Look, I'll be back for the beer after I get that tent up."

"Here take it with you. You can have another if you get it up."

"What's that supposed to mean? If I get it up. I've put that tent up quite a few times by myself."

"Oh, I don't know, we just all took bets you couldn't do it on this hard ground."

"Fooled you. It's a free standing tent."

"O.K., the bet's on." I hurried over and had the tent up quicker than they could dish up the chops. Surprised myself that I could do it. I threw the rest of my stuff in and went to dinner.

They were the most interesting men I had met on this trip. All were archeologists working for the State of Wyoming. They found some new diggings not far from Casper, digging up things and recording them for a future museum. The local Indian tribe was giving them a problem on ownership. They continued to show me the Indian artifacts they found. Arrowheads, beads, bullets and pottery in zip-lock bags with identifying numbers on them. All this was recorded in a book. They asked if I wanted to spend the day

7 8

with them. I was so tempted. It sounded like something I really wanted to do. Darn, I wished I didn't have a deadline.

I turned them down.

"What should I not miss seeing while I'm here?" I had my map with me and had inked in the route I just traveled. "If I'm heading this way there must be something around here that most typical tourists miss." I inquired.

"There is a lot of stuff you'll miss if you keep going north or south. Did you stop in Buffalo, up here?" one asked pointing to the map to the north.

"No, I just went toward Sheridan but the road was under construction. I was a little scared yet to try that. What's up there?"

"There are two places you should see. Massacre Hill and Ft. Phil Kearney here, and you'll probably want to see Ft. Fetterman. Then on your way north you will look for the little side road, I think there might be a name on it to "Hole In The Wall". That's where Butch Cassidy and the Sundance Kid would go to hide out." He drew a map in my journal.

"Oh, yea? I can hardly wait. Looks like there isn't any road into there on the map."

"That's why not too many people see it. It's just a dirt road with just a little sign," the other said. "We've been there a lot of times. Sometimes we find some good stuff if we poke around some."

We talked until it got dark and I said I'd see them tomorrow.

In my tent I tried to make my bed more comfortable. The ground under was unyeilding. I rolled off the air mattress in the middle of the night to try putting more air in to no avail. Then I tried letting some out. It was humid and hot. I did not have a good night's sleep.

I didn't see the fellas before I left. They were up and gone before I crawled out of my bed. They said the Fort Casper museum was nice. It was not far from camp. They did some diggings for it in previous times. My curiosity needed satiating. The fort itself needed some work but the museum was well done. It was going to be a hot sunny day.

Sure enough, I missed the "Hole In The Wall" like they said. I passed through the "Richest Light Oil Field" in the country, so a sign read. Derricks all over the place pumping. Barren, eroded land. Miles of power lines were strung everywhere for electricity to pump them. Very few personnel around. A few pick-up trucks.

Stopping in Kaycee for gas, I met a nice young black man driving a yellow Volkswagon convertible. I kidded him about getting as dark as he in the hot sun. He was good-natured about it. "It would take two years in this Wyoming sun for you to get this dark," he came back. He was traveling to Casper, disappointed we couldn't ride together. He had a CB, too.

On one of the few street corners, I found a monument to Dull Knife, who surrendered to the Army after a ferocious fight I read about him in *Bury My Heart At Wounded Knee.* Both sides lost many men in that fight.

I arrived in Buffalo in 90 degree heat with no shade to be found. Highway 25 was like an expressway but offered no sheltering trees. I was hoping for some in town with no such luck, only to find a restaurant for a tall glass of iced tea. It was empty save for one or two patrons and owner. The town was the same way. Deserted. There wasn't anything here to write home about. I donned a flannel shirt to escape from the hot sun. All the lotions in the world would not keep me from burning to a crisp.

I headed still north to Ft. Kearney and the Wagon Box Massacre. Rummaging around in the fort I tried to imagine the life here in this almost desolate place. I could feel the heartbeats of the men as they labored at living. I could see the paths the Indians took to attack the fort, I could see the sweat and tears and sound of the guns as the battle was lost. I could see the anguish on the faces of the dying as they were being carried off the field of death. The heat was devastating enough for me now. Was it this bad back then?

I returned to Buffalo for a cold pop in a gas station. There was a little shade in the lee of the building but the heat remained.

It was 68 miles on I-90 to Gillette. The road could be seen for miles as it stretched out in front of me. Two ribbons of black in a beige painting. Azure blue sky. Once in awhile the road was dotted with a car or truck. Two trucks traveling together making conversation on their radios gave me the knowledge I wasn't out here alone. Sixty eight miles with only one rest area between.

It was so hot I felt I was burning up. My lips were burning. I could peel bits of burnt skin off them. I could see skin peeling off my nose as I watched through my sunglasses.

Arriving in Gillette, I rode through the whole town for a camp with a pool to swim. I found one campground that wasn't very inviting, rather dirty and scrubby. No pool. Since it was only 2 p.m. I didn't feel this was the place I wanted to spend time sweating, and pulled into the Best Western Motel hoping they wouldn't turn this funny looking person away. My next destination would be Douglas more than 100 miles to the south. I had the time to get there but did I want to ride for two more hours in this hot sun?

I might be crazy but not that crazy. When I saw the aquamarine water of the only pool in town at the motel I prayed they wouldn't turn me away.

It wasn't long for me to throw my belongings in the room and change to a swim suit. I looked at myself in the long mirror and wondered who that was looking back at me. It wasn't the Marion who left Michigan 14 days ago.

My hair was flat from sweating in the helmet, my legs were still winter-white. I had worn a tank-top shirt for days and had a perfect sculpture of it on my bare shoulders. In the room light my arms looked like well tanned leather. It was the face that looked back at me in the mirror I didn't recognise. This person had white rings around her eyes like she was wearing a white Halloween mask. Her nose was the color of red-brown with flakes peeling in strips. Even her chin and upper lip were of this color. A definite line of brown and white descended along the far cheek area near the ears. I hated to admit this was me, but there was no one else in the room. It must be me. My back had blisters on the burned skin. On my shoulders hung strips of dead skin with bright red under them.

Oh, God! I'm going to pay for this, I thought out loud to myself. I thought of the folks back home. If they could only see me now.

I ran for the pool and its cooling waters. Wow, was it ever nice! Two other women were in the water talking. We exchanged pleasantries. All I wanted was to float along, to hydrate my skin. They wanted to talk. I didn't have the opportunity to talk to many people today. Their banter was welcome after I cooled down.

"We saw you come in. You're on that motorcycle, aren't you?" one asked.

"Yea, that's me." I answered.

"Where you from?"

"Michigan."

"Michigan," they gasped, "that's a long ways away."

"Sure is. I've been on the road for a couple weeks. I usually camp but I had to find something with a pool."

"I don't blame you. It was hot just driving in the car!" They went on with where they were from, where their husbands were but mostly asking about riding the bike. I fed them as much information as I could. This was one way to give biking a better name. Most people had thought of the sport in terms of the *Hell's Angels*. I gave them a different outlook on it.

I stayed in the pool till my fingers and toes turned to prunes. Later I wandered across the busy highway to a drugstore for some lip balm. I smeared it on my chin, nose and lips. Making a purchase of Zinc oxide probably saved my nose from any further destruction. I should have bought it long ago. The dry air was definitly helping to dry and burn my skin. I had lathered my exposed skin with sun tan lotions since I left home. I had a hard time reaching my back.

I had a good night sleep in an air conditioned room. It even seemed cold as I pulled up the blankets toward morning. I was up by 5:30 a.m. to get an early start to beat the heat.

I had about 100 miles to go on 59, a long two way ribbon stretched out dividing the grassy slopes to Douglas. After passing

81

through Bill the wind became a problem. It was pleasantly warm this morning. I still wore the flannel shirt with the sleeves rolled down and buttons unbuttoned, a tank shirt underneath. At Ft. Federman I felt rather lonely. A feeling most any soldier must have felt arriving at this small, bleak outpost in the plains. It was situated on a ridge, giving a view from all around. It must have afforded a good view for the sentries. A notice on the museum's boards told of the wind being like this continuously, year round. It made unusual mournful sounds as it rounded the few buildings still left. It cried passing through trees. The whole place gave the feeling of extreme lonliness or death. Only one person, the caretaker, was here. The fort was well maintained. The realism was absolute.

As I wandered the grounds reading the plaques a United Parcel truck pulled into the dusty drive.

"You deliver way out here?" I asked incredulously.

"Sure, why not. This isn't that far from town, you know."

"Oh." I hated the thought of my competition delivering anything anywhere. Another couple with kids arrived. Too bad the buildings could not be preserved better here. What a shame to have history deteriorate before your very eyes.

It didn't look like the relentless wind would ever die down or ever did. The few trees here were all stunted, bending to the east, misshapened. I left.

The archeologists told me to go down another road out of Douglas to a place where the pioneers crossed the North Platte River. I followed the road as far as Shawnee and Lost Springs but found nothing. A river was there with cottonwood trees shedding their cotton. It looked like snow falling. I returned and crossed the Platte just south of Douglas thinking they had the wrong road in mind. Highway 25 crossed the Platte, perhaps this was where they meant.

Following 25 to 26 led me to Guernsey. Fort Laramie was located here. I thought Fort Laramie would be in the City of Laramie. The park service set up a regular visitor center here with bakers in the bakery and men dressed in cavalry uniforms, and horses. Another self-guided tour showed a museum on the rebuild. So far they had refurnished and fixed up three old Victorian houses complete to the fine dining silver and china. Diggings showed where a prison was built over a pre-existing prison. Old stone walls were discovered under the latest prison with concrete cell dividers still in place. They were only large enough to call small closets.

They had set up a temporary tent area complete with cotton duck bivouac tents, occupants belongings piled inside and out.

The parade grounds were still being worked on. Many more building foundations were preserved. The barracks had deteriorated with just foundations left. The service was hoping to rebuild the structures in the manner of the times.

The relentless wind remained. Black clouds rolled overhead dropping a few drizzlies now and then. I thought I'd better go find a place to camp. My map indicated nothing between here and Laramie or even Cheyenne. I wasn't yet sure I wanted to go to Cheyenne.

Another monument was set up a short distance from here showing the ruts made by the wagon wheels through rocks on the Oregon Trail. I walked the half mile or so to see these. The rocks were soft. A path was worn through a long string of them. Scrapes were seen from the axles. Looking about, I wondered how much of this area might have changed from the days of the wagon trains. So much of the ground was without rock I questioned why they would have hauled a wagon through the rock instead of going the short distance around. This was my first question on the reliability of the monuments.

A long rock called Inscription Rock was fenced off from modern day predators. On it could still be read the names and dates of the pioneers that passed through here leaving messages to loved ones yet to come and for us to still see. Some you could reach through the chain link fence to touch. Touching it gave me a spiritual feel of kinship. I knew I could never really feel the hardships of their day but I felt a binding in spite of it.

I passed a National Guard camp in Guernsey with some stores and a nice city park. With the wind, I was going to have a hard time putting that tent in position for the night. I chose one spot and then chose another with a little better view and shelter from the wind. Perhaps the wind will die down a little later, I thought to myself, so I sat and pondered over the maps for tomorrow's journey, wrote in my journal, investigated the sparse bathroom facilities and read my book. A large tree branch cracked behind me and fell. Looking around quickly, I thanked myself for changing places. It fell in the first site selection.

Finally, not wanting to wait in case it really did rain, I struggled with the little brown dome tent. Bad choice for wind but this was all I had. I tied part of it to a tree and to the picnic table. It finally looked a little more secure.

Charles, Louise Hansen and son, Jim pulled in next to my site in a truck camper. Good, I thought, they will help make a windbreak. I found they were here with the National Guard on maneuvers. The family came along for the vacation. I was invited to come for supper. Several other guardsmen were coming and they would be bringing hot dogs, hamburgers and beer. This was to be last night on duty. It was a celebration of sorts.

"Sure, why not," I responded. I would have a hard time cooking in this wind unless I cooked inside. I was a little afraid of doing that.

I had a great time. Five others showed up and we all exchanged stories. A fire was built in the fire ring and kept small. It wasn't what I would call a cold evening to have a fire. They all thought they needed one if they were camping. Besides it was hard to roast marshmallows without one. They were all from Nebraska. I was invited to come to Lincoln on my travels anytime. Another address was entered in my journal. If I kept this up, I was going to have new friends in every state.

Darn,! I wish I had the archeologists addresses. Later, I sent a card to them in care of the park but it was returned "unknown".

In the morning, the Hansens were packed and ready to go before me. They offered me the last of their coffee and I exchanged my aging cheddar cheese. Several 90 degree days did nothing better than to turn the edges green and melt out a little whey. Carrying English Muffins with cheese, peanut butter and jelly was a good back-up for breakfast and lunch but I've had to devise a better system for carrying the jelly so it didn't leak over everything. It took a while to clean up the slop this time.

I said good-bye to Guernsey, wishing I could spend more time sitting, just trying to absorb the memories of the pioneers near the wagon ruts or in the miles of grasslands. If it weren't for them and the National Guard post Guernsey itself would be one of those ghost towns someone faintly remembered.

My Honda again faithfully hummed. It was ready to roll on. It started with exuberance. Laramie was not quite 100 miles south. I thought I could be in town before noon. Perhaps the sun would not be as hot today. I had one mountain to cross. The wind still blew but not nearly the gale force of yesterday.

I dubbed Highway 34 with all the superlatives I could think of for such a short distance. The windiest mountain pass of only 7300 feet, the lushest farming area before the pass, the longest straight road after the pass and the coolest wind. Crossing U.S. 30 I made a right turn to Bosler for gas and found it an abandoned town. Just a railroad and empty buildings. Back at the railroad crossing I met the train that undoubtedly in my mind was the only time of day it must go through this crossing. I turned off the engine while I waited for longest train I ever saw pulled. I should have counted the cars. I could not see the beginning nor the end. It was the slowest, I presumed because of the weight it was pulling.

I still made it to Laramie without having to push.

Jubilee Days were a big event here. A parade was forming along the main street. Traffic was not allowed. I followed the side streets and found the house of the daughter of a friend back home. No response to my knock. I left a note in the door that I was in town and would be back later. This would be a good diversion, this parade. Perhaps they, too, were sitting alongside the road observing the festivities.

When it was over, I drove around on the now free streets to find a breakfast place, but encountered only one family restrauant. I consumed a large cinnamon roll and coffee, filling in more words in my journal.

I tried again at Bev and Carls' house to no avail. I gassed up and left.

I continued south over the Snowy Range wondering if it meant anything in summer. I never rode in snow and hoped I wouldn't ever have the chance. I did have to put on some warmer clothes as the height of 10,000 feet brought me above tree line again. Gosh, it was pretty up here! The mountains around me most generally had pine trees standing so erect, pointing to the sky. Just beyond in the distance, the Rocky Mountains loomed higher with their rock faces still facing the morning sun. Clouds were forming over those mountains making today a relief from the burning sun of the last few days.

I made another stop along the Poudre Falls of the Laramie River. What a spendid place to eat lunch, I thought. There were few trees along the rocky hillsides but the river cut deeply into one side of the roadway tumbling noisily over rocks. It produced frothy white water. It splashed spray high along the sides but made soft rushing sounds as I opened my bag of sandwich makings. All too soon I had to leave.

Chapter 7   Colorado

The road markers changed as I crossed the border to highway 127. It meandered for many miles through the mountains in a slow descent. Campgrounds were many in this Rocky Mountain National Park area but all had signs printed indicating they were "full". It was such a roller coaster ride through here I didn't care if I had to stop. It would have been nice to have found an empty camp just so I could stay put, perhaps finding a nearby trail head to hike. This was Sunday. If I were here on a week-day I probably could find a spot.

I was more determined now to just go on to Denver. The black clouds behind me didn't look any too friendly.

Once out of the mountains the terrain became flat again. Open grasslands extended east but I turned south on U.S. 85. I had an aunt I hadn't seen in years living somewhere in Denver and several cousins. One, Dennis Champine, was the mayor of Aurora. I shouldn't have had too much difficulty finding one of them. I was here once before and only remembered many one way streets. The main street was Broadway. Since I had not planned to be here this day my Colorado map was still folded under the Wyoming map.

The black clouds were not going to dissipate. I found my way to Broadway by way of the poorest part of town. There being no place to safely pull off to change my maps I kept right on riding. Stopping at a light made me uncomfortable. I spotted a restaurant ahead. I pulled in the parking area. Hurriedly I found my address book, ran inside to find a phone.

Aunt Margaret was home but she knew nothing of the roads to give me directions to find her. I took my map with me so I could locate where she was. She suggested calling one of her sons and return my call. I waited what seemed like an eternity as the storm kept building outside. Finally after downing a cup of coffee the phone rang with directions. I followed it on the map, said good-bye and jumped on Honda.

It wasn't long before I was parked in her apartment parking area. The black clouds were still with me.

It never rained. The sun appeared shortly after.

I saw her last, years ago. I was a little girl. She had a hard time visualizing I had grown up and I was there on a motorcycle. Just like the rest. But this was different. This was family. Family wasn't supposed to think you funny.

She accommodated me as best she could in her one bedroom apartment. We talked and talked about family affairs. She cooked us a huge steak and we had a few beers. She finally tired of that and we retired for the day.

She was off to church. Before she left she produced a big egg and bacon breakfast.

"Here are the eggs and the bacon. You cook, while I get dressed for church. We stayed up so late I just didn't want to get up this morning," she hollered from the bathroom.

"I haven't had such good meals in a long time, about three weeks."

"Well," she said," you just help yourself. Make yourself comfortable. When I get back we'll start getting ready for the boys. They are all coming over today for a cook-out on the patio."

We had a fun time as I met Danny with girlfriend Tina, Tim and wife and their two girls. They brought the food, charcoal, even a bar-b-que cooker, and a cooler full of Coors beer and pop. The girls all wanted rides on the Honda so I took them around the block. Aunt Margaret wanted a ride but kept telling the rest of them to go. We finally convinced her it was safe. She got on the back, holding on to me for dear life. I finally had to get her to relax a bit so I could back out of the drive. She loved it. I didn't go too fast. She was no young chick. We had to take pictures of her. She'll remember that for a long time.

We walked out around the apartment, watching the girls play in the little pool and some black kids break dancing. Danny and Tina made ice cream for dessert. We had a nice time.

I seemed to need this brush with family. I was on the road only a short time alone but there was still a sort of lonliness that strikes from behind. I had the feeling I needed to touch base with family before I trekked on home. I would be gone from there for another week yet.

It was long after dark and the girls were getting sleepy before they all left. I had one disappointment. I did not get to meet Mayor Dennis. He excused himself with a cold.

Saying my final good-bye in the morning with hugs and promises to write and return I was on my way again. I didn't want to leave the mountain area yet.

I aimed the Honda to the west again through the mountains. Taking U.S. 10, I retraced the route I had taken with the friend in the sports car. By 11 am I had just gone through the long Eisenhower Tunnel. The air was crisp and cool but sunny. I wore my flannel shirt more for the little warmth it provided than a cover from the sun. Snow was still abundant among the trees. I stopped as often as I dared till I was in Leadville, a town I missed before. I parked the bike and explored. Sitting on the curb writing out my postcards for home I noticed my watch band was on the verge of breaking. Fine thing. Without the band on my arm I looked like I was wearing something anyway. My tan line was very distinctive.

I scrounged around in my belongings till I found a strip of Velcro. This has always come in handy on one occasion or other and now it became a watch band. I wore this out about every year and made more until the watch itself gave out. I began preferring it to metal or leather bands.

I mailed my cards and walked around the cosmopolitan old town. It used to be a gold and silver mining town in the days gone by. I toured a mine out in the back country by taking an excursion bus. It was very interesting. Many stories were told by the guide of miners and the people out to get the most of them. It used to be the roudiest town in the area.

In town again, a tour of the opera house was about to begin. Why not. Since I found myself "forted out" I might just as well see my share of other things now. I put the Indians and Army conflicts in perspective. Now may be the time for mines and operas.

My friend and I thought years ago, we should come back one day to do some gold panning. We bought maps of prospective gold areas and even gold pans and mercury. Books bought at the time told us how to go about it. We never did it. The gold pans became rusting reminders and then planters.

South on U.S. 24, I was running out of tall mountains. Gone were the tall lodgepole and Ponderosa pine trees. Now short scrubby pinon were scattered about in clusters. Bueno Vista boasted a KOA ccampground nestled in the small rounded rocks that reminded me more of Arizona or New Mexico. I stopped for the night. It proved to be my last night near any mountains for this trip. Just to the south could be seen three peaks at over of 14,000 feet. This would remain another "some day" return visit. No paved roads led to them.

The camp sites were nice here. I felt I was all alone in mine. Huge boulders and short pinon trees hid the rest of the camp from my view and me from them. If I didn't know better I would have thought I was the only one here. I set up camp, sitting on the picnic table doing my usual chore of writing and reading the maps. I was stalling as much as possible. I wasn't ready to go back to reality. The longer I could stay here the better I liked it. I didn't know I could have hiked in those distant mountains. I could have but found out too late. I watched a couple little chipmunks scurry around my tent, thinking I better zip up the door to keep out their unwanted company later.

Climbing over the boulders nearby I could see a field leading to a river. I grabbed a small day pack with my camera and snack and headed out. I thought it to be the Arkansas River that I read about in *Centennial* . I walked through the sage brush imagining I was on my way west. This was ugly stuff to have to walk on. I could have taken a road but wanted to learn the feel of this. I came to the edge of the field but found the only way to the river ahead was to get over the barbed wire fence. I walked along parallel to the road searching for a safer place to do this. We never had barbed wire like this at home. These little buggers were like razors and probably just as sharp. I examined the tension. I felt every car passing was watching me when I saw a sign attached to the fence with "No Trespassing" written in plain sight. I had to get out of there. I would have been just fine but there were wires running vertical to keep whatever they kept in here from separating the wires and squeezing through like I was trying to do.

Very carefully I put my pack on the other side of the fence and pulled myself in to make me as small as I could. I made it.

There was no path here. I didn't think how difficult it would be to get up once I got down, I just wanted to get down there and put my feet in the water. It became a ritual of sorts to say that I had done so. I took pictures of the river with the three mountains in the distance, sitting for awhile eating an apple and soaking my feet, watching the water flow by. This was a good time for thought. Climbing up was more difficult. I dug my feet into the bank and held onto roots of trees and weeds. Some would not hold my weight. I had fleeting thoughts of myself falling back down to this river that I only read about, never to be seen again when a root held and I pulled myself up and out of the steep revine.

I had so much fun walking across the prairie, a walk along the highway into the camp was well warranted.

I was back at camp resting, watching the billowy clouds above when a neighbor poked his head between my trees and reverie.

"You here alone?" he asked

I looked up from my reclining position on the table.

"Yea, is that O.K.?" I returned.

He looked around like he was expecting someone else to show. "Where's your other half?" he inquired still.

I sat up and turned around to face him. "What do you mean?"

"Don't you have another half?"

I stood up and looked at myself. Patting my right side and then my left, I returned, "I have my right side and my left side. How many more sides am I suppose to have?" I knew what he was after but I just played him along.

He stepped out into the open then.

"You're shitting me! You're here by yourself? Nobody else? No husband? No boyfriend?" He looked incredulous.

"That's me. Here alone. No husband. No boyfriend."

"Hey, Gay," he yelled behind him, "come here. My wife will never believe this. Tell what you told me. I want her to do this with me."

Just then Gay came around the trees with a dark, curly headed boy on one hip and a set of twin girls about six years old trailing behind.

"Go ahead. Tell her what you told me. She'll never believe this."

I told her the same thing. I've told it so often now.

He walked over to my Honda pulling her with him. "See here. Michigan."

"You came all the way from Michigan?" she asked.

I gave the long litany of places I'd been on this trip. Invited to have dinner with them, I couldn't refuse. Bob was cooking some chicken and dumplings. I wouldn't want to pass that up. While he prepared the dinner, I volunteered to take the twins off their hands. The little one seemed to occupy her time and the twins kept getting into things. A dog with them also barked a lot.

"I hope that dog doesn't bark all night."

"No he'll get used to you and shut up. Don't worry."

Where did I hear that before.

Rags continued to bark at any stranger while I learned more about them. They were from Texas on vacation. Bob had white curly hair and beard. Gay long straight dark hair. Both reminded me of the hippies of the 60's.

At sunset those billowing clouds made the most spectacular scene. There were pinks, blues, yellows and even an array of green. I quickly photographed them as the sky changed color before my camera lens. Yellow didn't seem right. I kept thinking of tornado weather back home. The sky usually signaled some sort of disturbance when it turned such an unusual color. That night the stars filled the sky. If any more wanted to get in, they would have to wait till tomorrow. I didn't want to sleep.

Chapter 8   Kansas

As it was I didn't sleep much. A van door down the way kept getting slammed and opened. Ka-whomp, shoom. Shoom, ka-whomp. Over and over again. Some other kids didn't settle down with their whining till late. The wind picked up in little bursts lifting the tent up. I could not anchor it as the ground was as hard as Casper's surface. Sounded like little varmints scampering about around my domain outside. It could have been debris the wind picked up but in the darkness it sounded like varmints. I had thought of ring-tailed cats for some reason. I remembered the guides telling us they were around our tents on the Colorado. They left footprints. I opted finally to think it just the chipmunks eating the pine nuts that laid all over the ground. But all at once it became very still. No kids. No wind. No varmints. No van doors. I slept.

Reluctantly, I packed, leaving what I perceived as the west. I wanted to find a leather shirt. Perhaps I could find it in Colorado Springs. I stopped along the road once to photograph an old abandoned cabin and mine shaft, thinking it was surely in a region my friend and I planned to pan gold. In Colorado Springs I only lingered long enough to send off my post cards at a drop box. It was too busy a town for me. I had been so used to the slow laid-back town of the last few I hated to have to get back into the fast lane. But such is life. I didn't need that leather shirt anyway.

Before jumping on I-70 I stopped on U.S. 24 at a truck stop for an ice cream cone. I knew I-70 would bring back the boredom of the ride home. Nothing much to stop for but rest areas, food and sleep. Today was Tuesday. I had to be back to work the next Monday. I should make it home by Friday or Saturday and still have time to wind down.

The bumps on the road were the only things to keep me awake. Even the banter of the truck drivers on the radio held no interest as I relived my last three weeks' experiences and thought of the future. Where would I go next? Would there be a next time? Sure, I'd tell myself, there would have to be. Would I return to see the things I missed? Of course, there were still so many things.

I put up for the night at Goodland, Kansas just inside the border. The campground had the trees as advertised by the KOA book I used for a guide. Thank God! Could hardly wait to get into the shower. I didn't feel dirty just dry. No pool here. In the shower room two women from Twin Falls got into a conversation with me. They invited me along to the Kentucky Fried Chicken place just down the street. I didn't feel like greasy food that night but again I wasn't going to look a gift horse in the mouth. They had a vehicle that had more than two wheels and didn't require a helmet every time you sat on it. "Sure, I'll go."

One of them was a farmer's wife, the other a librarian and teacher. We had a nice dinner.We again exchanged stories of travels and home life. They were sleeping in their covered pick-up truck and invited me to sleep there if I wanted to get off the ground. "No, I'm getting used to it now," I lied.

I sat at my table reading and watching a bird about the size larger than a common sparrow with a longer tail and wings. I thought it might be a magpie but had no book to look it up.

Then two more birds flew in looking like sparrows but with yellow bellies.

By 7:30 p.m. the sky turned black, the wind gusted dust violently and then the clouds opened up with all their vengenance. I ran for the tent as I didn't get all the pegs in the hard ground. Just then, the wind tried to pick it and me up off the ground. Before I zipped the door completely shut, I saw the fly unfix itself from the point it was attached. I grabbed hold of what I could reach and dragged it into the tent sopping wet. The wind blew so hard, my tent billowed and shook. By this time there was so much water on the parched ground, I found myself sitting in a river under the tent and in the tent. I grabbed for my space blanket to lay on while putting my sleeping pad and sleeping bag on top. Some of it was wet. The wind still blew hard enough to put a real scare in me. I lay prone holding the floor down. I thought if I held it down so the wind couldn't get under it I would have a better chance of staying in the campground.

I heard my pots and pans and whatever else I left on the table rattling outside. I laid this way for about an hour or so when the wind finally subsided. The rain stopped, leaving only the dripping trees plopping on the tent top. As soon as I was able I unzipped the door to peer out to see the sun shining and people about collecting their lost belongings.

"Weren't you scared?" asked one of the girls in the truck as she rolled down her window.

"Boy, you're not kidding. I thought I was going to Missouri tonight."

"You should have gotten into our truck. We yelled for you but you must not have heard us."

"Good thing, I wouldn't have had a house for the rest of the trip. It wasn't staked down very well. I'll bet I can get those stakes in the ground now."

"You won't need them now. It probably won't blow again till next month."

"You're probably right, but no sense taking the chance."

I put the fly back on the tent thinking it could dry just as well there as anywhere and collected my pans across the fence in the next field. I lost one cover and a pen. Walked over to the office building.

"You always get storms like this? I asked.

"Most of the time. They come up unexpectedly about this time of year."

We got talking about harvest times and she explained the large machinery that sat across the roadway. This was wheat land and the farmers here hired men to just come and harvest the wheat in groups. That way they could harvest it all for one farmer at a time and go on a regular circuit as the season wound down. The fields were sometimes planted that way, too. Several campers were these men.

I must have slept late. The rest of the transient camp was leaving while I sat there eating breakfast. After the rain last night I wiped down the Honda till it shone. It was as good as taking it to a car wash. I checked the oil at the same time finding everything in good shape. I tipped the tent over so the sun would dry the still wet bottom, laid out the fly that never dried and the space blanket. It at least kept me dry.

Half way through boring Kansas the wind picked up immensely causing me to remove my sunglasses again to keep from losing them. The sun was strong and the temperature on my fairing registered 96 degrees. I acquired a cramp in one of my thighs while swimming in the pool in Gillette and it still bothered me.

Because I was bucking so much wind, I ran out of fuel much sooner. Only made 164 miles on this tank. I rode along picking up the local radio stations, humming the familiar tunes. My thoughts would return to other things sometimes far away.

It would be good to get home but I wasn't ready to quit the trip.

I gave thought to the Indian nations I just studied. I had such a feel for them. I thought I was born in the wrong era. They professed all the things I professed but because society dictated a way of living I could never punch through that barrier. How could I?

They never abused the land as we, whites, did. Never took more than they needed. Why did we have to be so spoiled? Why

93

couldn't we live their way of life? They say it's survival of the fittest. Is that why we are so abundant and they are not? They seemed so much more fit than we. Was I disillusioned?

As a young mother, I became a Den Mother to a band of Cub Scouts. I learned many things about their way of living through that. Their culture was so rich and pure, I wanted to be an Indian. They weren't always dirty and drunk. They bathed. They didn't have liquor till we arrived. They had values. Not the same as ours but that is what made them so distinguished. They treated the land with respect, took only what they needed and replaced what they took.

Stopping at a rest area for lunch I was attacked by a couple of swallows. Seems I picked their house and wasn't invited. I moved to another shelter.

Eastward to Topeka meant the end of my day. Such a boring day at that. At the exit I turned off to find the campground, I spied a Motel 6 sign. It had a pool. After this long boring day in the 96 degrees I owed myself a cool pool. It didn't take long for me to get to the pool though the room I was given was on the second floor. I hauled all my stealable stuff up the stairs and in no time I was wet. I carried a heavy lock for the front wheel of my bike but never felt the need as I did here. My Honda was ordinarily near me every night. It was an intregral part of me. Honda had a built in locking system but I felt better doing this. I even disconnected the radio and brought in my helmet.

I ate out in an A & W fast food restaurant, then walked it off in a nearby shopping mall before retiring to bed and rare television. The wind was reported to be 10-20 mph from the south. Whenever I was in a depression in the road or behind even a small vehicle I felt the turbulence.

I didn't sleep very well on the soft mattress. I must have been getting used to the hard ground and air mattress. I thought I would like to give highway 24 a try for awhile to get me off the expressway. Perhaps I could observe the state better. Kansas City wasn't far away and it became useful to return to I-70 for a short distance through the north of town.

Chapter 9

Missouri,Illinois, Indiana and Home

Independence was celebrating Harry Trumans' birthday. Not much fanfare that I could see but then I must have missed something. Passing by the Missouri River or across the state border signaled another change in terrain. I was back into hilly country but not mountainous. It was like night and day. Farms were abundant and everything seemed greener. In town every street corner had a traffic light so it seemed, or was I used to the wide openness of the plains and mountains. I was stopping and hardly getting out of second.

At Hannibal I crossed the Mississippi River, first stopping at a little park-like area to photograph. Another biker was sitting here resting on a Kawasaki. I asked where he might to going. He had California license tags.

"New York," he said in a German accent. He had a bundle tied to the back so I knew he was going a distance.

"That's quite a way. Are you following I-70?"

Just then two other riders came riding in. They, were on BMW's. I felt in good company again. They explained they are returning to New Hampshire from Missoula. They had just attended the rally in Missoula, Montana.

"Where you going?"

"I'm on my way to New York," Germany said.

"I'm on my way home to Michigan."

"Great. Maybe we can ride together," they suggested. It was a good thought. I could ride with three guys I didn't know, all on nice bikes. Not the horrible bikers most people warned me about before I left.

"Sounds like a good idea but I'm getting on 24 to take the slow way home. It kinda goes north in a gradual way. What are you doing going across the country if you are from Germany?" I asked the German.

"I'm a student. My visa is only good for so long. I was supposed to fly to New York but I spent most of my money and could not afford the plane money. A friend suggested I buy this motorcycle, see the country at the same time and then sell it for flight tickets in New York," he explained.

"What if you can't sell it," asked BMW One.

"I guess I will have to do the best I can."

"How long before you have to return?" asked BMW Two.

"I've got a month. I'm sure I can sell it there. I might not get what I want for it but as long as I get by, that's all I care."

We all encouraged him to go for it. The BMW's said they'd ride with him awhile. They were all going the same way. I departed.

I took a long time in Springfield finding the KOA. It was ten miles off the beaten path. That path kept getting more narrow the further I went. First pavement and then gravel and finally sand. I had my misgivings but followed the signs down the treed road in the cool shade. I expected nothing more than a cow pasture if I ever found the camp.

It proved to be an interesting camp on my last boring states' travel. It was an old corn field but had fine facilities. Pool and clean showers and the usual store for forgotten items.

My tail bone was beginning to be sore from sitting in one position for so long. The sheepskin was fairly well matted now on this last leg of my adventure allowing less fluff to sit on.

After setting up camp for the night and cleaning up, I tried finishing all my leftover food. I was getting close to home and didn't want to get there with a saddlebag full. Pouring over the maps and measuring the distance I thought I could do it all in one day. I estimated it to be about 500 miles. If I took the expressways I should make it by dark. It wouldn't matter if it was. I wouldn't have to set up camp. Just pull in and die. I rode more than 500 miles in a day before but now my fanny felt it. This could likely be my last camp for this trip.

Before the sun was behind the trees a truck and bus load of people came into the open area of the field. The name on the bus said it was the Springfield Clown Band. Interesting, I thought to myself. We were going to be entertained by a clown band. Sure enough, they proceeded to unload the instruments. There were no clown faces or clothing, just people in people clothes. They arranged themselves in a formation and played till dark.

Another person, who did not play but rode with them, invited me to her table where she was writing some statistics or something. I was told that this was a very popular clown band and they came here to practise for the parade coming up in Springfield. Thela England was the mother of a member. Another mother was with her who was pregnant. Lynn Nusbaum had long straight hair and

9 6

kept throwing it back out of her face as we visited. Thela was writing a letter for some genealogy she was working on for her family. I told her I was doing the same at a much slower pace than she. I was given some information on contacts and she took my name and address to send me some materials she had at home for the same.

Lynn shared my love for the Indians; she was part Indian herself. Perhaps this was where she got her long black hair. She suggested I read *Plenty Coups,* an Indian history story. I bought the book and read it as soon as I found time at home and it is in my library.

The band put away their toys and the two women left with them as I returned to my home away from home. I marveled at the many people I met on this trip. No two alike, so diverse. The people made my days much more fulfilling. The campgrounds were always conversation places. The worse part was staying in the motels when it came to people. Once I was in my room I was behind four walls with a television for company. Out here, I found an interplay. Everywhere I went on the outside I always had someone to talk to. The motels were good when I wanted a bed or to be alone or when there really wasn't any place to stay or the weather was bad. Transient camps were best. But they didn't hold a candle to camping along the foot trail or river trail. Wilderness camping was best for me, but not when I was alone.

It sprinkled through the night enough to make everything wet. I packed up by 7 a.m. to be out on the road. I had to start the engine in the quiet of the campground. At 4:30 a.m., a rooster from the next farm awakened me and probably everyone else. He kept crowing all the rest of the morning till I thought I might just as well get up and get out.

Across the wet grass I steered Honda. Looked like the sprinkles were going to be the item for the day. I didn't want them for my last day. Take them back, I insisted in my thoughts. You're ruining my whole adventure.

I could have stayed on the expressway to go around Indianapolis but thought I'd like 34 better. The road traveled fairly well and I had not been this way before.

It continued to rain. I wore my little used heavy yellow rubber rain suit but without rubber protection on my boots they gathered water. I wore wool socks that day thinking if my feet got wet they would at least stay warm. I coated them well with bear grease before I left. The grease was left in many states in the last month as I felt the water enter the wool knit.

By 12:30 in the afternoon I was again at McDonald's in a different area. I had sat on that seat for the past six hours and my tail bone let me know so I ate quickly. I wanted to get home today.

9 7

4 Adventure

California, Here We Come

Chapter 1   Rules of the Road

For 1985, I made plans to ride the Honda one more time. I motorcycled through twelve states and now I had another insane desire to see the rest. I had three weeks to do them this year, and chose the west again. I have traveled much of the east by car and some by motorcycle. Now was the time to explore my world again. I wasn't done with the west yet.

Upon my return last year, Shirley thought I had too much fun without her. She was determined to get a motorcycle herself. She kept looking around for the perfect used bike. The availability of the model I bought was at a minimum since they discontinued this popular style. It made no difference; she wasn't going to buy a new one.

I did my research over the winter again and poured over the 1985 road atlas to find routes leading to places I wanted to visit. The year I went to Colorado with my friend in the sports' car, he wanted to go to Durango to ride the narrow gauge steam train to Silverton in the mountains. We missed the departure by only a few minutes. We literally raced the 50 miles to Silverton to try for a ride back. No dice. No room. I made that train my trip's objective.

I would aim Honda in that direction, then continue through to northern California to Washington to return by the second tier of northern states. When I mentioned going to California, Shirley must have pricked her ears up a little higher. Her mother and sister lived there and I planned on visiting them.

CALIFORNIA, HERE WE COME

I was psyched up to go. Honda was loaded. I would leave after work on a Thursday. I expected her not to go. She didn't have a bike. Her parents were visiting. Her husband was home for a longer period.

"Marion, I'm going with you," she told me over the phone.

"How can you? Did you find a bike?" I asked.

"I'll ride it over, I got it last night. It's just like yours only gray and I think more CC's. That denotes the engine size, we thought. Mine was 500 cc's. Her's, 650. We really didn't know much about the bikes. Just rode them. Not a good idea but we just weren't mechanics. It was the reason I chose Honda. Dealers were in most every town and I never heard of mechanical difficulties with the bikes anyway.

"Come on, we'll check it out." My mind went over the details of planning a trip alone to planning for two. Some things would have to change. My two man dome tent would be too small. Her daughter had a four man.

I made reservations for the train in advance as was required. She just wouldn't ride it. She would only have two days to be ready. How would she do that? She didn't work. Her parents were visiting. Her husband was home. She couldn't try this used bike out before starting. Unanswered questions filtered through my mind.

She pulled up and we examined her new Honda. It looked brand new. It sounded good.

"Walt checked out the battery before I rode it here. He had a charger on it all last night."

"You mean, you had a dead battery all ready?"

"No, you know how he is with batteries. He just thought he would like to make sure it had the proper charge." Walter worked for the Energy Department in Washington, D.C. They were in the midst of developing an electric car. I thought he should know the business of batteries and this bike would be safe in his hands.

"How does it feel to ride it?"

"I like it. It's really nice. So much better than my little 350. Why don't you take it for a ride and maybe I can ride yours?"

I didn't feel I wanted my baby in anybody else's hands, even if she was my friend. I wouldn't even let my twenty year old son ride it. "No, I'll ride mine. You need to practice up on your own. I'm going Thursday. That doesn't leave you much time, you know."

"I'll be O.K. Mom and dad have gone to Perry for the day so I've been fooling around with it all day." Her husband disliked bikes since he fell off his brother's when he was a kid.

We went for a ride for fifty or more miles. Not enough in my book, but she was determined. It seemed in working condition and that was what mattered now.

"Take it out tomorrow again but load it up with weight like you're going to carry. It's different with a load on."

"Oh, yea, guess I'd better."

"You're darn right, you better. I don't want any accidents happening just because you didn't take the time."

We looked over my itinerary when we returned. "How does that suit you? Anyplace you want to see that I don't have marked?"

"No, it's your vacation. You plan it, I'll follow." That became the theory every time we went on a vacation. She was free to go anytime and sometimes traveled with her husband's frequent flier tickets.

"How about your folks, when are they leaving?"

"They'll be home when we get there. They are leaving tomorrow morning."

"O.K. Can you put a CB radio on this thing, like I have? We will need to communicate somehow."

"I don't think so. You can just wave or something. I'll be following you anyway."

"Which reminds me. You know the way you followed me today? You are too far away. You will never see my wave. You should really try to ride close enough to take up just one car length on the expressway. When we are in the right lane I want you to ride behind and to the right of me. Use your signals to switch lanes, and then I will ride on the right in front and you on the left in the same car length."

"Why is that? I don't like to ride that close?"

"When we get in any traffic you might get far behind many cars. I don't want to have to wonder where you are. I want you right there where I can count on you. I want to be where you know I'll be, too. If you take up too much road space, cars will try to nudge you off the road or get between us when you are on the right of the lane. That whole lane is yours but its best to ride tight enough together to keep angry drivers off our tails."

"I still don't like to ride that close. What if you or I have to make a sudden move for something?"

"That is why you jog to the right of me. It gives us both time to respond. It's not that easy, riding in pairs. But if we practice it always, we'll know what the other guy is doing at all times.

Chapter 2

Indiana, Illinois and Missouri

I didn't see her again till the day of the ride. We left in early afternoon, she meeting me at my house, Mom taking pictures of us again as we pulled out of the parking area loaded for bear. I still had to promise to send home the post card every day. One small consequence. At least she felt a little easier, and with Shirley riding with me, a lot better.

Sometime before we passed the Indiana border, she noticed the left fiberglass saddlebag on my bike hanging awkwardly. A check found it was only hooked on one hook. It could have come off easily on a good bump. Safe, for this time.

We stopped several times on I-69 to rest at rest areas and she was getting worried about when we would eat and what. I wanted to just ride. We took a room at a Motel 6. We had quite a bit of food tucked away in our bags and ate in the room. Next door we settled for a hot fudge sundae, enjoying the coldness of it.

The sun had not set when we returned. A swim was in order. Shirley loved to swim so we made every effort to find a place with a pool when the weather was suitable. Donning our suits we found we were already getting a burn on our arms. Walt told her she had to wear her face shield. It got too hot today so she tucked her jacket into a bungee on top of her bag. She left her shield on.

Trying to read the maps in the room with my sunglasses was not going to work. I rummaged throughout my belongings for my regular lenses but found none. This was not going to do. I could try just reading in daylight. The lights in the room helped but not well. I would have to wait until morning to see in the light.

It being cool in the early hours, we tried to beat some strongest rays of sun by leaving by 7 a.m. We would take I-70 across to St. Louis today. I could read the map much better in this light. I knew I couldn't do this for the next three weeks. We may have some cloudy days or even rain, when sunglasses would be redundant. God forbid!

I couldn't get Shirley to ride close enough to me. She always hung so far back several cars would sweep between us. I just knew we would find it difficult in large towns when she couldn't keep up. It was as if she were still afraid she would not see me make a turn soon enough or something. I would slow down to make her ride alongside and motion to her but she didn't get the message or refused to do what I instructed. I asked her at a rest stop but she still ignored me. I didn't know how to get her to do it. Even when we stopped at traffic lights she hung back like I had the plague. It would be the only time we could talk to each other while riding.

"It's getting hot," she said at a rest stop. "What does your thermometer read?"

"Only 98 degrees."

We hurried through Illinois. I still had my radio to listen and talk to the truckers along the way. I met "Ramblin' Man" David who talked me all the way to St. Louis. We stopped at a truck stop for a cold drink of iced tea.

When we got off the bikes I told Shirley what we were going to do and she agreed to go have the cold drink with him. Since she hadn't any contact with us she didn't know what I planned. I wished she had a radio. We changed our conversation from Channel 19 that everyone uses, to Channel 15. One can't get to know anyone on the radio but he sounded like a nice enough fellow for us to stop for a drink. Not bad looking either. On the bike we were out there in the open for all to see what we looked like, except the hair. We couldn't see much of the truckers.

"I'd like to get to Springfield, Missouri tonight. I want to use the phone to call home. I need my regular glasses. I can't read this map with these," I said as I laid them on the table. Dave stayed and talked to Shirley while I made the call.

"I had her send them by "Express Mail" to the post office in care of General Delivery at Durango, Colorado. I should get them when I arrive in two days if she sends them out tomorrow."

"I hope she does. I can't see much better than you. I didn't even bring mine. What are two old ladies doing out here anyway? We can't even see," she laughed. Dave laughed, too.

"You guys are far from being old. I don't think I ever seen such young looking women like you riding on bikes before."

"We are kinda unique, aren't we? David has a bike, too, Shirley."

"Yea, he told me. I told him he ought to go park his truck and he could go with us if he was gonna be good."

"But I wouldn't promise that," he said smiling. "How about an address and phone number. Maybe I'll call you if I get up your way sometime."

"Not going to give you mine, I have a happily married man living in my house and I'd like to keep it that way. How many men would let their wife go off like this, anyway?"

"I guess you're right."

"I'll give you mine. I don't have one of those, remember?"

The thermometer on the bike hit an all time high. It never was that hot last year. One hundred hot degrees! Even the sheepskin seat was hot as I threw my leg over the seat and sat on it. "

"We will have to watch the engine heat. Signal me sometime if yours get past this area," I said to her pointing to the temperature gauge. "That's way too much for these little engines."

"If you stay on the freeway, you shouldn't have any trouble, Marion. Those bikes are built to handle it," commented Dave.

"I never had any trouble last year in this heat. But let's go, it's hot standing here in the sun, at least we get a breeze out there."

David caught up with us on the road. We went slow for awhile so he could. He was going into St. Louis and we were going around the northern side. It looked better. We could avoid the inner city and jump on I-44 to Oklahoma.

I spotted a cooler, shady spot off the expressway on the other side of town. Shirley followed wherever I went and I pulled into a quiet cemetery. "Did you ever eat in a cemetery before, Shirley?"

"We can't eat here," she replied.

"Why not? Do you see any signs forbidding it?"

"No, but do you think we ought to?"

"It's nice and quiet and shady," I tempted her. I must have convinced her as she opened her saddlebags. Using the open doors for tables we ate our fill of sandwiches, juices and cookies. We could hear the traffic below as they whizzed about their appointed routes. The residents of the cemetery never uttered a word.

At Springfield, our first KOA campground was in order. The ground was open and flat with little shade. I paid for the night with a credit card and discount card I received from American Motorcycle Association. I kept all the receipts and she would reimburse me on our return. She paid for the other expenses like food for herself. Since we both had different ideas on food and what and when we should eat it, I carried what I wanted and she, what she wanted. We would have disagreed too much if we didn't. We also made the same decision I made last year. If we ate dinner in camp, we would eat breakfast in camp. If we ate out at night, we ate out in the morning. Most mornings we might still haul hot water from bathrooms to our table to continue heating with an electric coil plugged into an outlet we didn't pay for, to make a cup of coffee. Shirley brought that innovation. I never saw one before. Many a morning we heated water for oatmeal the same way.

The park was having a hay ride for it's campers that night. We joined in the fun with a dozen or so other families after we showered and swam in the pool. Didn't take long to make supper on instant food. We hopped on the wagon as it passed by our camp site. We had a good time as the driver of the wagon told stories, sang songs and described the territory we were jostling through.

The temperature dropped some by sundown. The humidity didn't budge. We snuck into our tent trying to keep out the myriad of mosquitos. We listened to cicadas whistling in the trees, bomber planes, trains and dogs barking as we slept.

Chapter 3   Oklahoma,
                                         Texas Panhandle
                                         and New Mexico

Not giving thought to the night prowlers running rampant in the close-to-the-city camp, I lost most of my breakfast and lunch for the next few days. My zip lock bags of cooked bacon, and two more of lunch meat and cheese were found on the ground. The only visible animal we saw last night was a cat or two. I found putting jelly in a tight plastic sandwich box didn't keep the jelly from leaking out either. The 100 degree heat didn't help any, so I wasn't alarmed, just disgusted in my ineptitude. I should have known better.

I still had pancakes to make and pulled out my sterno to make them. Sterno is not the best for such an effort but worth the show off to a new fellow traveler. I carried several eggs in an olive jar minus the shells, a trick I learned while back-packing in Isle Royal National Park in Michigan. Kept in an inside pocket, they will be kept fresh for several days. The bacon, cooked, only needed heating and it also would keep several days. I proceeded to make the pancakes on my well-used mess kit fry pan using only a small portion of oil to keep them from sticking. Marvelous! Much better than instant oatmeal Shirley ate. Even without the bacon.

We were out of the camp before 8 a.m. and jumped back on the expressway pushing our way to Durango. We had to be there by Monday. We drove slower today. My speedometer read five mph faster than hers. We didn't know it at the time. When I was traveling at what I thought was the speed limit, I was really going five miles over. This might have been one of the reasons she held back. I never knew this till the next year when we timed it with a police officer.

"I got a speeding ticket here in Oklahoma awhile back, I'm not going to rip through this state again. I wasn't even traveling that fast," she admitted.

Oklahoma has not a good name in either of our books now. She might have received a ticket but the rest of the time other things happened to us. We chose route 44 out of St. Louis. We took the old route 66 to Tulsa and Oklahoma City. We avoided all

105

the biggest towns if we could. The temperature shot up to 101 degrees by mid-afternoon. Elk City touted a KOA campground and that became our destination. It would get us closer to Durango and we had no plan to visit anything in this state.

Uneventful day today. We did see a man get out of his car to shoot a dog that was hit by another car. We didn't see him get hit but he was lying on the side of the road when this fellow came along and pulled a pistol and shot him, putting him out of his misery.

It was somewhat windy but nothing we couldn't handle. The camp was quiet and we both slept well in spite of the humidity. A swim in the pool was refreshing. Not a heated pool so the water didn't feel like bath water, just cool enough to refresh.

The air was a-flutter with little black flies making us scamper off to the tent earlier than usual.

Shirley's bike would not start in the morning. This was the beginning of a disabled friendship, little did we know. At first we thought it was nothing important, maybe the heat. We checked it out as best we could, finding the battery acid far too low to start anything.

"Put some water in the thing," I told her.

"No, Walt said not to do that. Only distilled water if I had to at all."

"O.K. How are we going to get going today?" I asked a little exasperatedly.

"Let's ask that guy over there in the Gold Wing. Is he up yet?" We ran over a hill to see if he was. He was.

"I wonder if you could help me with my bike, I can't get it started this morning," she asked.

"Sure, what's the matter with it?" he asked.

"I don't know. The battery looks too low. It's a used bike. I remember the fellow reminding me not to turn it off in only the "accessories" position but in the "lock" position. I think I have been but I don't know." He helped us push it fully loaded to the top of a little gravel hill and told her how to jump start it. She got on and we gave her a little shove. It bucked a couple of times and then just rolled the rest of the way down. We tried it again and it finally took, leaving it to idle while we got the rest of our stuff together. I tried to get her to put regular water in it but she refused. We continued down 66 in search of a store that carried distilled water or a station that did. She would leave it running while I waited outside, but found none.

Many tries later as the sun was rising in the sky, she took everyones' advise. They all said the same thing, "All we use is tap water."

One of my bungee cords was on the verge of breaking from the dry air and sun and I took some time finding a new one the right size. This held the tent, sleeping bag and pad and even my leather jacket. I couldn't go too much farther with only one.

The scenery had changed from the time we left Oklahoma City from green trees and lush farming district to brown, dry treeless plains. The ground was red. We hardly noticed the change with all the other things occupying our time and the day was not waiting for us. We must have been going through the ravaged areas where unemployment was a way of life. We passed by some homeless people sleeping alongside the road with nothing but the clothes on their back's in the hot sun. At least we thought they were sleeping, they weren't swollen the way the animals were.

Shortly after this, something was going wrong with my CB. In Amarillo, Texas, I found a radio repair store at a truck stop who fixed the ailing radio for $10. Our next KOA was planned at Las Vegas, New Mexico.

New Mexico was an endearing place. The plains were red dirt and blue mesas. Here and there we could spot an Indian hogan from the road with a scraggly wooden fence to keep something in and denote private territory. We needed gas and stopped at a small store with one pump out front in the dirt. We bought a few snack items with our gasoline. One or two patrons inside were Indian or Mexican. We could not tell the difference. Some small children played outside. The heat would have been unbearable if it were humid. This drier climate was good in my book.

We rode through Tucumcari and Santa Rosa without any trouble, admiring the views. Nothing too unusual in rock formations but the red of the earth and deep blue of the sky fascinated me. The few homes we saw were made of the same earth in adobe. Las Vegas seemed a good place to stay for the night. It was not a gambling town like it's sister city. Just a quiet little town with the usual city things like a McDonald's. Before we went for dinner, we set up camp and explored our area to see what was available. Shirley parked her bike on an incline just in case.

We both felt we needed to stretch our legs from the sitting position we had been in for the last five days and put on shorts to go for a run. We only did a mile, I found it quite difficult, at that. Shirley handled it pretty good for someone who never did much running. There was a shortage of water and the showers were turned off. We were allowed to put our smelly bodies in the blue pool. I wondered how many others were as dirty and smelly as we must be after traveling in the open all day. I hoped we were the only ones. The water felt cold on the dry parched skin of my arms, but

Shirley loved it. She's the fish. Our camp site was snuggled into a quiet part of the camp among short pine trees. It gave us our own privacy and would block out any wind that blew up.

Cleaned up and ready to do the town at McDonald's, Shirley had no trouble starting up her Honda. I hoped it would stay that way. Weren't many hills to push her down here in this flatter country. It was dark by the time we finished with dinner and wrote out our post cards.

"Do you remember how to get back to camp?" she sked.

"I think it is down that street over there and then a left turn and then a right at the next light. What do you think?"

"I don't remember. I was just following you."

"Don't you ever watch where you're going?" I asked discustedly.

"Yea, but I didn't this time. Let's try your way, you're usually right."

"Well, if I'm not, we'll say we were just misplaced. Too bad we don't have all our stuff with us so we can camp along the road the way of the other homeless folk."

"No, thanks, I'd rather stay here in town if we can't find our way back." Just six long miles later we were parked in front of our tent, thankful our directions were right. I never did like riding around in unfamiliar territory after dark. It wasn't long before we sat on our bags and dug through our personal bags for sleeping things. I jammed my sheepskin seat into the sleeping bags' bag to use as a pillow and always liked to read before I went to sleep. It made me relax and unravel the days' events in my mind. Shirley brought a small transistor tape recorder/radio with ear phones. She lay on her side of the tent, listening to tapes. I put my book away after I found I couldn't read with sun glasses and wore my ear phones to listen to music, too. We were both lulled away to sleepyland.

We slept very well snuggled in our little groto of trees. Shirley made a call home for the day assuring her daughter everything was going smoothly except for the battery problem. She would relay the information to her father if he called. He was in D.C. now and it was free to call her daughter.

We ate a leisurely breakfast even though we ate out the night before, breaking the rules. I had a peanut butter and jelly sandwich and a McDonalds' cinnamon roll.

I hoped her bike will start.

It did. Off to Santa Fe on 84 north. We would be off the freeways for a long time if the plans were followed. We spent more time in Santa Fe than we thought we would. I pulled off my hot jeans to expose my running shorts and donned a pair of running shoes.

"I would have put mine on but I don't own running shorts and the others would be too bulky for sitting in the hot sun."

"That's O.K. I remember how I hated walking around in the jeans from last year. You know how small my comfort range is."

"Yea, I know, but it won't bother me," she said. We walked around admiring the capital building with its floral gardens, went through the oldest church, shopped in all the tourists' shops. We sat in an outside cafe eating another dreadfully good sweet roll. We knew we shouldn't but we didn't care. The atmosphere was well worth it.

I put my hot jeans back on and my boots and we set our sights for Durango, north on highway 84. The clouds were poking their noses into the blue sky, looking like it might rain as we passed by Chimney Rock formation. It made a wonderfully dramatic photo. The shadows on the rock were toward me and the sun directly behind peeking around the rock. Durango sat at the base of the Rocky Mountain range. Mountains were high enough to have tree lines.

This was what I liked to call an "Oooh" "Ahhhhh" day. The scenery changed so often, it was as if we were watching a slide show. On some of the passes I expected an ambush and some of the outcropings close to the road I wanted to see an Indian scout perched on his horse watching our progress.

Chapter 4   Colorado

We stopped in Pagoda Springs for lunch. I didn't want to linger too long. I had been to Durango before and was eager to check it out. The KOA was south of town.

"Let's set up our camp and then ride into town to spend the rest of the day," I suggested.

"How far do we have to go?"

"Just 30-40 miles, I think," I answered. We found the camp about five miles from town. We could not see it from here but could see the town was nestled in a huge crack in the mountainside. The elevation was a little less than Pagoda Springs at 6,700 feet.

We ordinarily had a ritual of setting the tent up, turning it on its side and facing it into the sun or the breeze. It usually was wet from the morning dew. But for the last couple nights there hadn't been any dew and we were lucky to have a dry tent. She'd pull on one side and I the other to get the material to stretch on the center cross piece. Then we'd stake it all down and we had our home. Throw in the bags and personal stuff.

We fought for the right side of the tent on the first night. It was her tent. She could only sleep on one side and it wasn't going to be facing the tent wall. I had the same idea and I didn't want to sleep facing the tent wall either. But because it was her tent I let her have her way. When we used my smaller tent she had to let me have my way. Simple, petty things to fight over but it must be what happens when you put two females together. I wondered if men fought over such trivial things.

I wanted to get to the post office before they closed but we were out of luck. The doors closed as we rode into town. It was a nice drive and we didn't have the foggiest notion where anything was. I had the reservation for tomorrow morning and wouldn't have time to get the glasses. I wouldn't have time to get them tomorrow because the train trip lasted nine hours.

We parked the bikes along the sidewalk parking area on the main drag. The train station was just down the street a few blocks and we needed the exercise. We went window shopping. We heard a piano playing from one of the old time hotel saloons across

110

the street and hurried to finish shopping on our side so we could take care of business and get to the saloon.

The train station was decorated in old time fashion right down to the ticket window. Employees wore visor hats, white shirts with black arm bands, ties and vests. I confirmed my ticket after standing in a long line. Shirley stood in another line for new tickets and was able to get on the same train and same car with the seat next to mine. We were happy. I was mildly disappointed she could get one so easily after I made reservations months ago by wasting a long distance phone call.

We walked down the street happily anyway together, still window shopping. The honky-tonk piano player still tickled the piano keys. The saloon could have been back around the turn of the century. The bar was of old massive wood with the proverbial brass rail. Naked lady pictures decorated the wallpapered walls with oil lamps made electric. Beer mugs and whiskey bottles lined the back bar. Tables were round with bentwood chairs. We climbed the stairway to the second floor. This was an authentic hotel. The hallways were narrow, we expected cowboys and ladies of the night to come out of the rooms at any time.

"We should have reserved a room here, this would have been fun," I whispered.

"I wonder what it would cost to stay?" she asked.

"Don't ask. I remember it was more than I thought I wanted to pay when I got all that stuff for reservations. Especially if I were by myself. It would be fun to be here on a honeymoon."

"I'm not honeymooning with you."

"I don't blame you. I wouldn't honeymoon with me either." We went back downstairs and watched the piano player play and drank a beer. Plenty of atmosphere. The doors were left open to the late afternoon air.

We continued down the street to Francesco's, a Mexican restaurant. We ordered two different meals. Number 3 and number 5. It was delicious. I always liked Mexican food from the one time I stayed in Albequerque, New Mexico for a week of convention.

We stayed late and it was dark as we tried maneuvering the sharp uphill turn to the camp road. Shirley must have hesitated coming in the turn. I couldn't see her from around the curve. I waited for her to come up the hill and when she didn't come, all I could think of was that she missed the turn. I thought she was right behind me. She stopped the bike and as she put her foot down to balance she placed it in a much deeper hole than she thought was there. The bike rolled over. She wasn't hurt. I parked the bike and went back down the hill to find her struggling to upright the bike in the dark. I helped as best I could but we found neither of us could set it on its two wheels. It was too cumbersome.

111

Another camper came to our rescue. He must have seen what happened. Between the three of us, we were back in business. I never rolled mine over since I had it but this became the first of several roll-overs we encountered on this tour.

We took our showers late tonight. I wasn't feeling very well since our return. I hoped the shower would make me sleep. After the rain, the ground around the camp was slick, grey mud. Carefully we picked our way to and from the bathhouse on patches of grass.

I didn't sleep well, after all. The shower did not put me into never-never land. Nothing seemed to help. I became nauseous and rolled around in my sleeping bag trying to get comfortable all night. I purchased a new mattress that blew itself up. I blamed it. I thought I might have just eaten too much.

By morning I was a basket case. I knew I had these train reservations, had to get to the post office for my glasses and I wouldn't let a little nauseousness stop me now. Not quite 8 a.m., I tried to talk a postal employee into retrieving them for me before opening hours, to no avail. I had to wait in line like the rest of the ordinary people. What an insult I felt.

It was good to wear my clear glasses again. I wouldn't have to ask what the menus had on them anymore, or read the maps only in the daylight.

Shirley jumped on the train. I took easy steps. I was excited as the steam engine pulled itself up to the loading platform pulling its dozen or more wooden, yellow and red cars. I remembered the model train my brother received from Santa Claus when we were kids. Now I was going to ride it around the Christmas tree. The engine smelled of coal burning and cinders flew around us like light black snow. We found our seats and waited what seemed hours. I didn't feel very good. I needed to find a bathroom but found none on the train. I ran back to the station as others were loading and tried unloading myself. I wanted to stay in the rest room longer but was afraid I would miss my train. Luckily, I made it back just before the conductor yelled, "All Aboard!"

Settling in my seat made of wood I tried getting my camera set up for some pictures as we started. My stomach would not let me enjoy the surroundings. Shirley was up with other passengers looking out windows on both sides. The train struggled up the steep tracks into the mountains heading for Silverton. We swayed and lurched as we moved out of the city into the mountains. I saw some beautiful scenes pass by without enjoying it as much as I wanted. I sat doubled over in the seat most of the trip unless she said I had to see something. We crossed over a river, rounded curves and could see the cars behind us. We wore our leather jackets to ward off the cold mountain air. We had a closed car, I was thankful for that. The open cars were probably catching much of the cinder dust from the engine. I learned which car to ride in a long time ago on other steam engine rides.

We had a two hour lay-over in Silverton. I wanted to die. The train jerked and bumped its way here and I felt I had a fever. A headache didn't help and the nausea woudn't go away. The trip took nine hours up and back. We walked around the dusty dirt road of old time Silverton, doing the tourists trap shops, finding a lunchplace where my partner consumed a sandwich and I, a cup of tea and a small slice of cheese cake. It was the only thing I thought I could eat without vomiting.

We boarded the train for the return trip. Shirley used my camera a few times to capture some pictures for me while I cowered in the hard seat. Once in awhile I would get up to see something when everyone would jump to one side of the car to look. I didn't know how to capture the feel and sounds of this adventure in time. I wanted to get the smell of hot cinders in the crisp mountain air. The feel of the train swaying and lurching across the cracks in the tracks. Clickety-clack; clickety-clack. The creaking of the cars as they bent into the curves and over the uneven tracks. Again the crisp, mountain air, the creek waters, the trees as they slowly passed by our rolled down windows.

"What do you think is making you so sick?" Shirley kept asking me.

"I don't know. We've been together for a week. Why aren't you sick? All I want to do is to lay down and sleep. I can hardly wait till we get back to the house."

"Do you think you can ride back? We could find a doctor or something."

"I don't want a doctor. He'll just tell me to go home and take two aspirin. You know that. Do you have any aspirin, by the way?"

"No. They are at the house."

"So are mine. I'll be O.K. Let's just get back to the house." I couldn't get my helmet off soon enough. I didn't even remove my jeans, just fell on my bed and stayed there for most of the afternoon.

"I paid for another night while you were sleeping, Marion, I didn't think you'd better ride today," she told me when I awoke around dinner time. "That's all right. I couldn't have gone anywhere anyway. I feel a lot better but I'm still terribly tired. What have you been up to since I was sleeping?"

"I went for a swim and talked to some of the other campers. I ate your left-over dinner from last night. I didn't think it would keep very well in this heat. It's almost 90 again."

"I thought it had warmed up. I think I broke into a sweat in the tent. But I didn't care if it was hot or cold. I really slept hard, didn't I? Did you try to wake me up or anything?"

"No. I rummaged around in here changing my clothes to go swimming and you never even moved. You must have needed it bad."

"What's for dinner? I'm not real hungry. Maybe a trip to the john will help. I'll be right back."

She was just having something like a can of beans or something with some junk food. Didn't sound very good to me. I ate an apple and fell back to sleep, undressed this time for the rest of the night. She sat up and listened to her radio and tapes to while away the time

In the morning, she didn't want to get out of bed. "Come on, I feel great. I slept good. We've got a long way to go and I've wasted too much time being sick here."

"Ughhh! I think I have what you had yesterday. I felt nauseous last night and have the headache, too."

"Do you want to really stay in bed? If you feel like I did, I can't blame you. I don't want you to ride if you aren't feeling good."

"I think I'll be O.K. Let me get up and take care of things, then I'll see."

"O.K. but I don't want to have to worry about you on the bike. It's hard enough for me to watch the map, the road and you, too." She came back from the bathroom slowly and sat. I had a bowl of oatmeal for myself and asked if she'd like to have some.

"No, I'll make it myself. I think I can ride."

"It must have been the Number 3 at Francesco's making us sick. What do you think? "I asked.

"Could be. I ate your left-overs."

"Yea, I'll bet that's it."

I checked our bikes for oil levels. We had driven far enough to require an oil change.

"You know, the Honda dealer is not far from the laundromat. Why don't we see if we can get them both done at the same time? I could use some fresh smelling clothes, can't you?"

"Do you think they will just do that without an appointment?"

"I never had an appointment in Montana. We can ask."

I was right. As long as we were traveling through they were happy to do the change for us. We asked them to look over her bike for any electrical problem, too, and washed our clothes. In the laundry there were ads on the wall. While waiting for the machines to finish we entertained ourselves with them. One read: 'Love to cook but hate to do laundry.' Bill Goodwin left the note with address and phone number. "Why don't you call him?"

"I don't want to do that. Why should I?"

"It just sounds intriguing to me. You're not married, don't you want to know what he's really looking for? You might find something interesting?"

"All right, it might be fun but I'm not going to call. I'll write later to the post office box he wrote here." We finished our business here in Durango and I asked one more time if she could ride. She said she was going to but didn't want to push hard at going anywhere.

We were going to Utah to the west. We drove through miles of sage brush with hogans and sheep, cattle and horses on and off the road.

We discussed the route to take at breakfast and again in the laundramat. Neither of us wanted to go north to Salt Lake City but in a western direction to go through several National parks in the south. We opted to take 160 to Cortez and turn north on 666 to Utah. South from Montecello on highway 191 and continuing south west to Medicine Hat on 163 brought us to Monument Valley. The earth was a brilliant red. The monuments were so large. I saw them in books before but did not realize they were so towering. Forms could be perceived in most of them. Every once in awhile a sign would name one. The road stretched like a black ribbon laid on the red ground wandering from mesa to monument and back. It would take a long time at regualar speed to bring us near a monument. One would be in view for a very long time before we passed it.

What a wonderous sight. I was awestruck. In Monument Valley we stopped at a rest area near the "mitten" speaking to a couple with two dogs in tow. They were natives of Germany enjoying our United States. What a great sight to stop to see.

I stretch out in Harbor Springs, Michigan.

Son, Don, and I ride his victory ride across the Big Mac.

Shirley and I relax in the Grand Canyon splendor.

Riding a rapids.

We were so scared of these falls when we saw them.
Such joy when we made it over without spilling.

Sheri rope climbing to a trail.

Relaxing after an exhilarating day on the Colorado River.

Havasu Falls fairyland.

My wonderful Honda in Yellowstone Park.

Archaeologists in Casper, Wyoming.

Aunt Margaret hangs tight for a spin.

As we start our adventure to California.

Lunch in a cemetery at St. Louis, Missouri.

Ed Tompkins and crew in Cedar City, Utah.

The steam train makes it up to Silverton around many curves.

Monument Valley had the clearest sky and we could see for miles.

*The highest we were allowed to go on Mt. Rainier
without climbing experience.*

Giant Redwoods in California dwarfed the two of us.

*Almost a week of cold rain in the northern states
and we were still smiling!*

Walt and I check the sights in Emerson, Iowa.

Sheri making sure we find the best food in Iowa.

17,000 bikers take over "flat" Iowa.

*Steve and Deanne smile at the end of PALM.
She rode her first 100-mile day.*

Rosemary and Mary Kay in Southport, Conn.

Finally made it to the top of Mt. Hale.

Our hiking friends at the White Mountains in Vermont.

Nova Scotia's rugged coastline made many unique photos.

Near Quebec City.

Sandy at Moosehead Lake in Maine.

Our destination was the Alamo.
It was so much smaller than we thought it should be.

Florida beaches in October were cold and empty.

Lake Louise, Alberta, Canada.

David Buchanen and friend who instigated
my change in travel mode at Devil's Tower, Wyoming.

Myself, Sheri, Walt and Shirley enjoying
one of our many tours together.

*Packed and ready to start out on our first
tour by bicycle in Upper Peninsula, Michigan.*

A long, flat road that didn't need to tell us of bumps.

*We wished all the hills were down
and we weren't even near the big ones yet.*

Bob Axely of Ontonagon, Michigan comes to our rescue.

Waiting for the mine tour in the cold, damp underground.

Even with this mess to sort, we decided to remain friends.

Chapter 5   Arizona and Utah

We pulled into the red sand KOA park having a choice of sites. A great wall to one side was unclimbable and straight up like a cliff. It wasn't long before we were all set and started to explore the area. Walking into the small town we saw no one but Indians or Mexicans in the whole area. Water was scarce enough that trucks brought it in in tanks. Hours were posted for their arrival and the Indians were standing in line with all sorts of containers to get their share.

We walked back to camp and Shirley stayed home while I explored the rocks on the other side of the camp. I walked a long way through climbable soft, rounded, red rocks with odd formation and ledges. From a bridge formation, I could barely see our camp site. Behind our site, a hogan. It was my first close-up of one but I didn't go too close. After all, someone lived here. I could have stayed much longer but the sun was going down.

We wanted to catch a picture of the sun setting out on the mesa and just knew if we waited long enough it would be a spectacular sight. There was a giant outcropping of rock sitting on the flat red land. I just knew the sun would bring colors to it in its descent. We waited and waited on the high rock. The sun never made its' silent coloring of that mesa. It just died in the dusk. We wanted to take a shower but this was the night the Indians came to the camp to buy theirs. We let them have it and went to bed.

The next morning, Shirley had a hard time getting the bike started again. She'd try everything, even choking it. I was beginning to want to choke it literally.

We stopped in some little town in Arizona to buy gas at a market. The place didn't look like it could sell anything; it looked too poor. Perhaps run by Indians trying to make a living, we felt compelled to buy something from inside for snacking. I bought a post card and sent it off to the cook in Durango, telling him about our trip and when we would be home.

Just past Marsh Pass, we made a right turn on 98, a newer road leading to Page on Lake Powell. Since the new dam was built, roads were added to get to it. Page was one of those towns created by the dam. The people who built it needed goods. It reminded me of a boom town. But this town was more city. It just popped up out of nowhere. Nothing gave us the idea we were heading into a town this size, no houses strung out on the edges or anything. Just town. A Honda dealer included.

We made a stop to see if they could help her starting problem. The mechanic thought at first it was the cellanoid. We both gave up on that as the problem long ago. He made a call to someone he knew in Salt Lake City to help diagnose the problem. We sat around while he played around with books and phone calls and waiting on customers, getting restless. He, then, wanted to tear the whole thing down. He thought it was a bad wire connection between the battery and ignition with resulting fix-it meaning all the fairing had to come off. Sounded like money to us. Shirley took another look and found the wire was disconnected, maybe by the mechanic, maybe not. She connected it and tried to start it. Vrooohm! It started up fine. "What do you think? You want him to tear it down?"

"No, I think we should get out of here. I don't think there is anything that wrong with it," she said as she put her helmet back on. I hurried to my bike parked in the lot and started up with the same Vrooohm! and away we went to try another fifty miles or so.

Neither of us had been to the north rim of the Grand Canyon. We headed there. Perhaps we could stay there for the night. It was a fifty mile trek off the beaten path into the rim area but we didn't care. We wanted to see it.

Made a left on 67 bringing us through the desert. Then we rode past rock and canyon and on to the Kiabab Plateau straight into the forest of the National Park. We passed a private camping park, a gas station-food store and a park camp. Both places were full.

We stopped and got out to look around. It wasn't as pretty from this point across the canyon but we tried to pin-point where we were on the other side two years ago. Without binoculars it was hard. We would have liked to hike the trail but we didn't have a place to stay or the means to carry camping gear down the trail.

Her bike didn't want to start again. We both thought it should be kept running the way things were going. I was getting angry but what could I say? It started and we silently went out the way we came in. Stopping at the store to ask about camping facilities, we were told we could camp anywhere in the park area as long as we were off the road.

We bought some pre-made salads and other food and packed them in our full saddlebags and tried to leave. Her bike refused to go. No matter how she tempted it, the engine would not turn over. She checked the cells in the battery. They were low again.

"Fill them up a little, Shirley, and wait awhile. There might be enough juice to charge it up again." She didn't want to, but relented after we sat there for a half an hour in silence. I began to regret ever enticing her to come along. What was I doing here? I asked myself. Short on water, there was a tanker on a truck for drinking. She filled up her water bottle and I helped hold the battery on the tilt for her to pour.

"Look, the cable is loose again. I wonder why it keeps loosening?"

I grumbled something. She waited some and tried again after she hooked everything back together. I wondered if we were not suppose to be on this trip. After several tries it caught. She quickly put on her helmet and I did the same and we were off. We needed a camp for the night.

"I think I remember a place along the road that looked like it was used once before."

"Then lets go look at it." We found a dirt road leading to something and a little wooden sign on a tree with just initials. All around were old campfire rings. "Looks like a Boy Scout troop stayed here. What do you think?" Looks safe to me."

She got off her bike without turning it off and we poked around to see if it looked good enough for the likes of us.

"Com' on, it looks good. We'll have to go all the way to Utah to get a camp if we don't. It's getting later and later. In the morning we can go back to really look at the north rim, maybe take some time to walk around some more."

She parked the bike on a downward angle so we could push it in the morning if we had to. She put up the tent and I scrounged around for some kindling and wood to make a fire in our wooded campsite. I had a nice little fire going by that time and even made a rock stand to heat our water with the fire instead of the sterno. The salad was good. We hadn't had a salad for some time. Sweets seemed to be our downfall.

Across from our camp, a small pond sparkled in the fading light. It was rimmed with tall lodgepole pines and short pinon. We heard sounds coming from the woods where the dirt road led. We weren't sure we knew what they were. They sounded human. A pick-up truck went down the road carrying some dark haired young people. Then another. They looked at us and we looked back. It was as if we were doing something we shouldn't be doing.

Sitting on a log as the sun set watching for wildlife, one of the trucks stopped.

"What are you doing here?"

"Nothing. What does it look like we are doing here?" I answered.

"Is that your camp?"

118

"What if it is?"

"I wouldn't camp here if I were you two."

"Why not?" asked Shirley. The guy wouldn't tell her.

"Leave him be, Shirley, he can't make us get out or anything. This is public property," I whispered.

"What's wrong with camping here?" I asked then.

"Didn't you see all the people coming in here tonight?" he asked.

"Yea."

"This is a work camp. You know, like a reformatory? We truck them in and out. They live here and do park clean-up work during the day. Didn't you see the sign?

"No."

"It's right up there on the tree."

"A few initials on a sign doesn't exactly tell one anything. Are you saying we aren't safe here?"

"Suit yourself. We can't be responsible for anything happening. They probably all saw you as they came in." He left. Shirley got worried and wanted to move.

"I'm not going to move this late. It's going to be too dark to find something by the time we take everything down and hope your bike starts. Com' on and sit down. Let's watch for deer. I'd like to see a deer come out of those trees to drink the lake water, wouldn't you?"

"This is a pretty spot. I'd rather see a moose." I don't think talking to her was any consolation. She still looked worried. She sat down. Not long after waiting she said she saw an elk or deer come to the pond. I walked around the other side and saw a fawn but mother was near. She must have seen us and shooed her baby back into the dense forest. We went to bed after that. It was too dark to see anything more and we did want to be snug in our beds. Shirley refused to undress and slept the whole night with her fillet knife by her side and her eyes open. That was nice, because I slept like a baby with my jack knife hiding on my side. She didn't know that.

In the morning I got up to use our own latrine and came back to the tent to get dressed. She was still in her bed.

"Come on, get up, it's a beautiful day! The sun is up and it's only 44 degrees."

"Go away," she groaned.

"Go away?" I started up the still hot fire to get it going for breakfast. Water was boiling and ready for coffee and oatmeal.

"Smell this," I said as I opened the screen of the door and plied the cup next to her nose. She rolled over and took the cup. I sat down and tried to finish dressing for the day.

119

"I didn't sleep a wink all night."

"I slept really good."

"I kept thinking I could hear them coming at me through the woods."

"I knew you were scared but I didn't think it was that bad. I figured someone should get some sleep and as long as you were going to stay up, I would sleep."

"Good for you," she said unhappily.

I went out and started taking the stakes out of the ground for the tent. The fly was off and the poles were coming down when I heard her shuffling around inside. She came out with everything packed.

Her bike started after many crankings. We both breathed a sigh of relief. Maybe that was all that was wrong with it, a dry cell and loose wires. She checked both before even starting to turn the engine over.

On to the north rim again. The frost was in the shadows yet and the sun flickered through some clouds. Parking the bikes we walked around the park services headquarters.

"Looks like they build all their headquarters the same way. The south rim is just a little larger scale." We talked to some people as we parked, taking only our cameras and wallets. They were interested in the two of us coming all the way from Michigan together. We told them all the good things about traveling this way and left out the bad.

"The next time someone asks about the riding let's see if they know anything about bikes. We may find someone who knows why you are having so much trouble with yours."

"The only ones who might know will be cyclists."

"Well, that's better than none." We walked in silence for awhile to the path leading to the rim. We could see across the canyon perhaps 20-30 miles. The colors were different in the morning light. So many purples and blues in the shadows on the other side. Some of the canyon was in sunshine bringing out the beiges and browns of the sediment rock exposures. We walked for a mile or so along the trail among short pine trees. Heat radiated up the lower we walked. Jeans were beginning to make us suffer from the heat. We both longed for time to roam in this area. To walk to the other side was impossible in our boots. We didn't have the time this trip. We vowed to return another time to just hike in. Another one of our "Other things to do another day".

We turned north on 89 to Utah and Bryce Canyon. It wasn't far. It was afternoon when we located a KOA park. We rode along in some showers and some sun. The weatherman must have called this a scattered shower day. After our usual ritual of setting up camp, Shirley laid down in the tent for a nap as I went to clean up. I took my time and languished in the water. I knew there was a water shortage so I didn't stay as long as I wanted.

Off to see the Wizard, the wonder Wizard of Bryce. What a fairytale place. The rock formations were so unlike the ones we have seen before. They looked more like stalagmites in a cave. I remembered growing rock in colored crystal forms in a fish bowl. The bases of the formations were larger at the bottom and built up, leaving pointy tops. In reality, these bases were the eroded stone and grit from what was once flat land like a huge mesa. Reading the placards along the walkways we learned the ground here was that same height millions of years ago. Weather eroded layers of different hardnesses to form the shapes we were looking at.

Some formations reminded us of castles with turrets, some, lace in large scale. Hummingbirds flitted around the flowers by the walkway. We ran from one formation to another as the sun played tricks on us in the clouds. Sometimes we would get to one place and the sun would hide making our cameras react to dark. We'd wait till it reappeared to get our shot. The sun was receding quickly behind the horizon and we wouldn't get many more chances.

On the way to the park, the road went through an arch. While the sun was shining we took turns driving through while taking pictures of each other.

Zion National Park wasn't far away. We planned to see it this next day. It warmed up again to a pleasant 100 degrees. Our green forest and red rocks changed to beiges and browns of high rock canyons in a multitude of shapes. Parking our bikes, we took off our jeans to expose shorts under and changed into running shoes. Shirley conceded to shorts.

We walked two trails carrying just our cameras and personal bags. One trail led through some cool green area almost too narrow for a body to get through. On the other side, the sun shone brightly on the beige canyon wall, beckoning. We squeezed through and walked a mile or two along the river that carved the trail. The water had an aquamarine color to it. I wanted to put my hot feet in it. It looked so cool and was so shallow. Mistake. It looked like small pebbles lined the bottom but it was a clay mud. I had to literally scrape the mud off my feet with a stick when I got out. On the other side of the canyon in the shade we could see holes in the wall. Large holes with something flickering every once in awhile.

Shirley looked awfully tired as she walked. I worried about her for awhile wondering if she was doing more than she should. She didn't show any other signs for illness, just tired. I could have walked farther into one of the trails but changed my mind.

"Look. What's that over there?"

She looked where I was pointing and for a long time we both stared, wondering what it was when we realized the things that flickered were car lights. "There must be a car tunnel in there. See over there, there are more holes. Maybe those are vents or something. Sure did look that way. We'll find out later."

We returned to find it was a tunnel leading to the most crooked road we ever saw. We saw it from the trail above first but didn't know the road through here was where we were headed, until we were on it. It wound around in switchbacks from the higher elevation of 6,000 feet to an unknown depth. We were driving into a canyon with steep pinnacles on each side, the foothills dotted with green scrubby growth. It was fun. This was Shirleys' first time with swichbacks. I think it perked her up a little.

Above, the colors of white to pink and vermillion would be a painter's paradise. Below, off the plateaus many shades of green penetrated the pinks.

We stopped at the visitors' center and had lunch. That also perked her up since our usual breakfast did nothing for the mind but only for the body in satisfaction. A slide presentation inside the air conditioned building cooled us off. We didn't want to face the heat but knew we had to don our jeans again and head off to the heat of Nevada.

We strayed north on 91 to Cedar City first. A KOA sported a heated swimming pool. Just what we needed in the heat! Before settling in for the night I needed to find a battery for my watch. As long as we were running around town we bought some food supplies for dinner later and a bunch of donuts and pop. We ate the donuts and were too full to eat dinner later.

We set up camp in a very full camp ground on a flat surface. No place for Shirley to park on a hill for pushing. We would keep our fingers crossed again. We tried playing a game of cards when all of a sudden the sky darkened, the wind picked up furiously, blowing anything in its' path in a flurry. We ducked into the tent to hold it down. The ground was too hard to stake the whole thing down. In a short time the storm was over.

We went for a walk to see the pool but neither of us felt like swimming. A lady sitting near the pool was playing a small organ, playing all the old tunes of the 40's and 50's. We listened to her for awhile and sat in her chairs singing some of the songs together.

"You two come back over here later. We always have a bunch of us singing after dark. I keep the fire burning and everyone brings their chairs and we have a good time."

"I'm afraid we will be too tired to come back tonight." We explained what we did today, how tired Shirley really was. "I need her to be in top physical condition tomorrow. We have to head into the Nevada desert."

122

Later, we went back to playing cards, when a fellow from another campsite came over to talk us into eating dinner with he and his friends. We were still too full to eat but accepted the invitation. It was the first one we had on the whole trip. I had received so many invitations when alone, we perceived that two were too many to ask.

Ed Tompkins, a retired postmaster, and his wife were from Tehachapi, California. We had a lot of things in common to talk about. Corky and Marlene Roberts were from the same city. Two single men traveling with them were Roy Warner from the same city and Jim Mathews from Ridgecrest. Shirley lived in one of the towns or nearby and was familiar with their area so they had something to talk about.

They almost forced us into having a drink with them. We had commented on them earlier as we walked by their motorhome. They were still enjoying happy hour. But we took one drink and then another. After that, we didn't think anything about it. We were treated to a fine dinner served on something better than aluminum mess kit pans. They even had dessert for us. We stayed till after dark enjoying their company, taking pictures of each other and generally having a good time.

Chapter 6   Nevada and California

The drinks must have relaxed both of us. We slept like babies. But we were up early without benefit of breakfast so we could beat the heat of the desert. Shirleys' bike would not start. One cell was dry again. We found that cell to be void of a gasket. Perhaps that was why it kept drying out! I made her a new one from a rubber band. I suppose if we were men, the only thing that would do would be a regular gasket. We have been so used to making do with unorthodox fix-its for years, it was just the natural thing to do. We put in some more of our drinking water and it started.

We continued up 91 to Beaver without stopping to eat. We wanted to get as far as we could. Out of Beaver, 21 would take us to Ely, Nevada. At the border the numbers changed to 73 and then to 50 through the entire state.

This route took us through very long valleys. Some 10 to 20 miles in length. We could see another ridge like the one we were on and it took us forever to reach the next one. Each ridge held a large cluster of rock. It was as though we were back in the mountains for a short mile or two.

We stopped at Eureka, an old silver mining town, in a rest area devoid of anything but a shelter, outhouse and water faucet. We couldn't go any farther. Nothing in town. I made us breakfast of sausage and eggs. It was the second time I did so mostly to get rid of the perishable food. Shirley never offered to reciprocate so I thought I wouldn't do that any more. I even washed the dishes each time.

Looking toward the west the sky was black. They were so low I felt I could touch them. I would like to grab hold and push them on to the east. Looking to where we just came, the sky was royal blue with big, fluffy, white clouds. On the fringe of the black clouds, grey water dropped like a sheer curtain. The white, fluffy clouds were beyond it.

We continued anyhow, trying to get as close to Reno as possible before any storm might hit. No campgrounds here anywhere. We approached Austin, slid down into another valley where the wind was working against us. I leaned over my gas tank behind the windshield to buck it. It would sneak up on us out of nowhere around a bend and hit like running into a door. Watching Shirley in my rear view mirror, I could see her sitting straight up, catching it all with full force. In the ridges, we played a game with the wind. It came from all different directions and we never knew which way it would be. It would buffett us almost clear of the bike, or push from the back, or the side. I saw a tavern in Frenchman and got off the road. Pulling into the lee side of the building to get out of the ensuing storm, I said to her over the noise of the wind, "Let's wait out the storm here. It's too crazy to be out there on those ridges."

"I didn't think they were that bad."

"I did. I've seen people blown off the road in those kinds of winds. I don't want to face that." We waited awhile watching to see if it would blow over. It didn't. I covered my seat with a plastic bag brought for just that purpose. She refused to admit it was going to rain even though the sky was black and lightning struck in a few places.

"We could make it to Reno if we left," she pleaded looking at my map.

"Go right ahead. I'm not going one foot from here. In fact I'm going inside to sit it out. You go if you want to." She kept looking at the sky and then covered her seat, following me.

We never said any more.I wasn't going over those ridges and that was all there was to it. The wind was too strong for that.

"I noticed a sign outside that called this road we are on the "Pony Express" route. I think I'll have to get a picture of the sign. After all, I am a Pony Express rider." We drank a pop while being stared at by the local drinkers. Pop was not the drink of the tavern and you could tell by the look on the barmaid's eyes. We didn't need liquor. We didn't care what she or the patrons thought.

Shirley was getting so tired back when we were at Eureka, I didn't think she would last the day. That could be the reason she wanted to just go so she could lie down. Now she seemed to feel better. I didn't know how to judge her. She didn't talk about herself. It was difficult. We pressed on.

By the time we entered Fallon we had traveled 491 miles. Shirley suggested we get a motel for the night. I agreed we'd never put up a tent in this hurricane wind. Did they have hurricanes in the desert?

We couldn't find the less expensive Motel 6 that we liked but there were plenty of others. This would be our first night in a real bed since our first night on the road. Television was a luxury.

We checked over her battery and found that cell dry again. Another thickness of rubber band and more water and we hoped it would start in the morning.

After a good rest, she made a call home and then to her sister living in California. We stopped at Silver Springs and Virginia City. Early in the morning, Virginia City still held the looks of a frontier town. Stores still maintained the frontier looks, streets still narrow. We walked the several blocks admiring the momentos and buying an item or two. Still uncrowded, I was able to take some photos of the Bank of Tombstone, Territorial Enterprise and Prison. By the time we left it was hard to spot our Hondas between all the parked tourists' cars. The streets were loaded with them.

We elected to not go to Reno but to the south around Lake Tahoe. We were not gamblers as we found out when we went to Las Vegas two years earlier.

It was a pretty ride to Carson City. Very busy. Shirley was looking at everything but in front of her when she almost hit a large dog that I dodged. Up the hillside in the mountains we could just spot the lake through the trees. This must be the place they took pictures for post cards. We found no place to stop on the busy thoroughfare ourselves. We were high on the road. A break in the pine trees revealed the lake with treeless mountains beyond. Around the lake a bicycle trail was built. Many cyclists utilized the road. Most of them looked like retirees' getting their exercise. Once in awhile a skateboarder or roller skaters went by. The Truckee river had so many rafts it resembled rush hour traffic on the freeway. Road traffic was just as heavy. We couldn't keep the speed limit.

At the south end of the lake we turned north on 89 to head around the west side of the lake and then to California's Feather River road. California! I have arrived. Such a beautiful drive. We sailed along this mountainous area with switchbacks for about 100 miles. It just kept going and going and going. Very few places to stop. When there was one, it came up so suddenly it was hard to stop. Logger trucks came from behind traveling much faster than we wanted. I could see Shirley in my mirror watching to make sure she wasn't run over. A two lane road twisting so badly it was difficult to pass. She stayed so far behind me I wanted to get behind her to push her forward. It would be harder for the truck to gamble on passing if we took up the whole lane, but she continued to stay back. I wanted to pick up my radio microphone to tell her but she had no radio. I couldn't raise anyone on the truck. I figured after awhile they must operate on another channel.

Must take a break. This can't go on. She was making me nervous. A truck passed her on a sharp curve, then tried to pass me. I moved over to the right. If he was going to pass, then, pass. I slowed. He didn't. I sped up, he did. This was not going to do. I got off at Quincy at a restaurant. Turned my signal on for a long time so he would get off my tail. He didn't. He just went on. Thank God!

Now, where was Shirley? There she came around the bend. I hoped she saw me on the side of the road and didn't continue. She saw me.

"That was fun," She said removing her helmet.

"But I sure wish you wouldn't follow so far back. You scare me when I see those trucks bearing down on you so close. Doesn't it bother you?"

"No, they won't hit me."

"You sure are positive about that."

"Why would they run me off the road? I have as much right to it as they."

"I still think our chances are better if we are together." She ignored my pleas.

We needed a break. I yanked off my helmet and asked, "I'd like to take some pictures of this area. Are there any places where we can pull off? You know it better than I." She used to live here somewhere.

"I think there might be some. If you would go slower you can turn off. I'll follow you."

"If I can find out what channel the truckers are using maybe I can communicate with them, like tell them the road is clear ahead so they can pass me."

"Lets go inside. There ought to be an owner to one of these trucks parked outside. We did and found they ran on Channel 10. It might help, it might not. Back on the road I did find a pull-out without a truck too close to me and pulled over. She followed. I only had one picture left in my camera and when I was taking it, it wasn't the prettiest. A railraod bridge crossed the river on a slant and a highway trestle high above it crossed both. In the background were treed mountains.

In Oreville, we stopped at a Taco Bell for lunch. Her sister worked and wouldn't be home for awhile. I got all the lowdown on their home situation.

We had a nice visit with her sister, Charlotte, husband and two children. It was time for a rest and we spent two days doing it. We visited the local sightseeing spots. In a parking lot, we messed around with a miniature Budweiser truck parked on a little trailer. If we worked it just right I would have a picture of Charlotte's head in the drivers' seat and the top half of Shirley sitting in the rear.

The only earthen dam and Baskin and Robbins' 21 flavor ice cream parlor compared in size. We indulged in more ice cream than I ever ate at one sitting. We washed the bikes. I bought a new head phone set for my helmet. We never gave the battery a thought.

Charlotte's house sat on a site of old tailings from gold mines. They planted an olive orchard in back and she was sure there was more gold mingling among the roots of her trees than olives on the branches. The trees weren't always doing well and she wanted to pull them up and survey the ground under them. There were fig trees and apples trees. They would like to put in Christmas trees thinking the market could use more of them than olives that didn't do well.

The morning we were ready to leave, Charlotte and husband left for work. Shirley couldn't find her key. We looked everywhere. She remembered she always did such-and-such with it. It was remembered she left it in the trunk. The trunk was locked. I was the one who did dumb things like that.

I emptied the stuff off the back seat of my bike to carry her in tandem to town to see about a key. It just so happened our luck was not all running out. A locksmith was just leaving. He demonstrated to the owner a new item to purchase for people like Shirley. She, for some unkown reason to both of us, could remember the number of the key, a prime ingredient to making a copy. Back to the bike.

It was in the trunk. Now she had a spare. I put my stuff back on the seat and tied it down. She tried to start it. It wouldn't start. Oh! great, I thought. This is not going to be my day. She opened the side panel again to look at the battery. All the cells were dry. No way was she ever going to get that battery to run.

"Why don't you drive me back to get a new one?"

This was the best news I ever heard coming out of her mouth. All along I had pleaded with her to do this and she just said it was still good. I took the stuff off the seat and we returned to the store. It would take an hour or so to charge one. We had to remember what side the drainage hose was on but the fellow found one and charged it.

Back to the bike. I put the stuff back on my bike as she installed the battery.

"I hate to say this but this is the wrong battery."

"What?"

"It's the wrong battery. The drainage tube is on the wrong side."

I removed the stuff again from my side and turned the bike around one more time as she jumped on the back. Another hour or so went by. It was 3:30 in the afternoon before we ever left Oreville. Her bike started with the normal starting sound. Thank God!

We couldn't go too far to spend the night. We rode the same type roads as we did along the Feather River. Awesome! We found a private camp ground on the river. Walking over to it through a tangle of wood and weeds and dead trees was more work than it was worth. Shirley liked to fish but found very little time and place to do it on this trip. We kept each other too busy trying to keep her

128

bike running and seeing things. She brought along her roll of string and a plug and bobber in hopes of catching something. We sat in the tangled mess with her line in the water with no results.

"I'm tired and am going to bed. You can fish for nothing if you want to," and left. She followed me.

We left the next day in a foggy drizzle snaking through the mountains on route 299 heading west to Crescent City on the California-Oregon border. How nice it was to see Shirley's bike start up without push starting it. We stopped in Helena for a sweet roll and coffee. Along the Trinity River there was supposed to be some good gold mining. Prospective miners staked out claims and worked the river nearly in the same manner as the earlier prospectors. We stopped at one point to have a look at the river a little more closely. Prospectors were on the river too far for us to see them clearly.

"You see that black sand bar over there?" Shirley asked, pointing down the river.

"Yea."

"Right around that point on the far end is where gold can be found. Wherever you see that in a yellow sand bottom you most generally will find gold deposits. I'll bet there is gold in there. You see those guys down there in the boat? They must have a stake and are running a sort of sluice to pan. I'd like to do that someday. Charlotte and I were always going to but never did."

"Just the way she was going to pull up all the olive trees?"

"Yes, well, you know how it is. You always say you're going to do something and never get around to it."

The temperatures never warmed up since we packed up that morning. The fog wanted to hang around too much for both of us. The farther we got over the mountains and closer to the Pacific, the foggier it was. We began to smell the sea. The surf was smashing into the beach at a low tide. This was my first glimpse of the Pacific Ocean. The sky above the water was a light blue with fluffy white clouds forming over the land heading to the mountains.

Going up the coast on famous highway 101 was a delight. We drove through tall redwood forests and followed, and were followed by the loggers. There was a clear cutting operation through the area. It looked terrible. Such a sad way to cut the timber. Why couldn't they be more selective? I was a conservationist at heart and didn't like this type of operation.

We stopped at a roadside restaurant and talked with a couple on a Honda Aspencade with Alaskan plates. Inquiring, found they were going to San Diego on their honeymoon.

We arrived at George and Mahala Arrisons' to find a house full of relatives. We settled in to a three day rest we didn't really need. We had plenty of time but I would rather have spent it in the woods

129

or in a national park or something. But sometimes you have please the person you're with and I didn't want any repercussions on the way home.

Mahala made a wonderful fresh salmon dinner and then we went for a walk down to the beach a few blocks away in the fog. We walked along barefooted picking up treasures to add to Shirley's pile. I wasn't much of a beachcomber. We also discussed the layover. She pleaded her case that wasn't a very strong one at that. But I relented to see how the days would go by. If there was any unforseen problem I would be wanting to go when I wanted to go. It was my vacation, I reminded her.

Since the house was full of sleepers I elected to sleep on the floor in the living room in my bag and sleeping pad. That was a mistake. I couldn't stay on my pad for some reason. Kept sliding off. A night light burning all night also kept me awake. Having George getting up at an ungodly early hour banging pots and pans around didn't help my situation either. He reminded me of my father-in-law. No consideration for a sleeping person at all. Large and rather cumbersome he'd plunk down in his chair and rattled the newspaper. I burrowed deeper into my bag to try to muffle the sounds. He'd cough or growl something and even talk to himself all the while. I thought him funny.

George and Mahala wanted to take us to town later in the afternoon. We rode along in the back of their van snapping pictures of the sights along 101. Much time was spent walking around in the redwood forests admiring the ancient trees. We had a big lunch and topped it off with a huge ice cream cone till I felt like a stuffed pig. We both felt this way when we got back and Shirley suggested we go back to the beach to run it off in the sand.

I spotted a redwood table I wanted at a tourist trap while there and paid the man for it and for shipping it home. I didn't see fit to strap it down to the back of my bike for 2000 miles.

We walked and ran part of a four to five mile stretch and were gone for three hours. Our hosts were probably getting worried. The fog lifted some while we were gone only to resume it's former position over the land and sea. When we returned we were greeted to a big pizza. I couldn't stay too long here or I will be as big as a pig. It was nice to be treated, just the same. Grandma and Aunt Lorraine had left earlier in the day leaving me a bed to sleep on for the night.

We played Dominos and cards till wee into the night and then started up again in the morning after a homemade cinnamon roll the size of a whole cake crossed our lips. George was the kind who like to show off the area. He was like my dad in that respect. A tour guide. We jumped back into the van and went to some secret fishing hole on the Smith River in his "back yard" and then up the coast again to see the redwood forests.

We stopped at a couple beach openings for pictures and beachcombing and seal spying. We never saw the seal, the fog was still hanging around, the wind was stiff. It lifted shortly and out came the cameras. Just a slight haze. The water turned a deep blue hue. White surf slammed against the many giant rocks along the shore and in the bay. Low tide revealed shallow ponds in the sandy beaches to explore. We watched some kiters fly the tandem kites far below. They looked so colorful against the dull grey and blue of the water.

We scrounged around in the piles of rocks and debris. One inlet looked like a huge bone yard. It was filled with weathered redwood trunks. I got my shoes wet on the incoming tide and lost a new ring on a rock outcropping where I was picking up agates. I slipped them off quickly and waded into the surf to retrieve it. I was lucky that time.

George decided he wanted his favorite food. Chinese. He drove to Brookings where they go quite often to search for the stuff and we had a nice dinner in a Chinese restaurant.

Stuffed again we went for a run around a couple blocks upon returning to the house. We were feeling better about the food since we repaid our debt by running, when Mahala brought out big tubs of ice cream and fixings for sundaes.

Chapter 7   Oregon, Washington and Idaho

I had to get away from the temptations of this house. I lost some twenty five pounds before taking this trip and felt good at my old age at my weight. I wanted to still zip my pant zippers without laying flat on the bed in the mornings. We left early but not without a farewell breakfast and extra food to pack along with us. It was still cool and foggy and Shirley's troublesome bike started at first try.

Along the coast the fog lifted in an hour of our leaving. We could see the waters' edge for most of the time, the surf banging up against the huge boulders fallen off from cliffs. Some could be made to look like animals or other things. The water changed colors from emerald green to royal blue with different sunlight. We stopped to take some more pictures when the sun came out. A small four footed friend welcomed us. I think the little critter was looking for a handout. He found one. We had an over abundance of food.

Our intention was to head up the coast to north of Portland and then go inland across the state of Washington.

The sea lions were not in their caves at the moment. We saved our four dollars.

We stopped on the left of the road at a rest stop, just going around a sharp corner when the wind picked the map off my gas tank and yanked it out from under its elastic bands. In reflex, as I tried to catch it and keep the bike upright I panicked and brought the bike to a stop but also let it lie down very gentle on its side. I jumped off and grabbed the map. Three people standing at the stop ran over to help pick up the monster. I knew the two of us couldn't do it alone from the episode in Durango. So this was my turn to dump. No damage done except to my pride.

We lounged around a few beaches. One had the look of the east coast with an added attraction. A guitar player was playing to the wind. I couldn't understand why we stopped at a donut shop, but we did. We consumed a large apple fritter that would boggle anyones' sane mind. You'd think we had not eaten in a week.

We took our time along this coast and then Shirley dumped her bike again. What could possibly be wrong with us? She thought she turned it too sharply into a drive. I hated to admit it, but my turn was next. I was going to try to watch that I didn't.

A KOA at Tillamook would be our home for tonight. I found my turn to dump while gunning the engine to drive over a driveway filled with rocks the size of golf balls. Right in front of all the other campers while they watched the display. How embarassing! That was my last time.

In the morning we planned to try the inland roads leading to Mt. Rainier. We haden't climbed anything yet!

Crawling out of the bags the next morning and into the foggy air, we looked at our tent and bikes. They were saturated with water. Clinging water. We brought back many paper towels from the bathroom to wipe them down. The windshields needed several wipes before we could set out. The fly stuck to the tent looking baggy in the windless air. Perhaps if we didn't get up so early we would awake to drier gear. We'll try it next time.

Highway 6 was fun to ride with many 10 m.p.h. switchbacks. The road was narrow. We were in tree-filled mountains so that we had more shade than we wanted this morning. The dew would not stay off the windshield until we were in sunlight that didn't come along as often as we liked. We were so far into the hills I thought they had to pipe in the sunshine. We flushed out three deer. The shadows made it extremely dark and when the sun did pop out of the trees it was so brilliant in our eyes it made for watchful driving. Sunglasses were absolutely no help. We couldn't see in the shade. I kept Shirley in my rear view mirror all the time.

In Veronia, gas was not cheap. We only bought enough to get us to a cheaper place. A donut shop drew our attention as we indulged in our test pastime. Shirley worked in a donut shop part time. We thought there could be no other donuts like hers. We tested as many as we could along the way and we were right. They were not any better.

On 47, we followed the Nehalem River to the Columbia River and crossed into Washington State at Rainier.

We steered clear of Seattle, not wanting to drive in big cities.I never liked them and Shirley would just as soon not drive in them. Her road experience was far better than when she started but her confidence level never seemed to hit a high point. I never thought you should get too cocky on the bikes in the first place and always have a respect for the machine. It was supposed to be "boss" at all times. It dictated the terms and you followed them.

In the fog we couldn't see Mount St. Helens that erupted just a couple years before. We really wanted to go to the National Park at Mount Rainier anyway. Hosts and hostesses gave out information about the park and where to find things. They were senior citizens spending their summer in the park helping and receiving free camping fees. We decided we needed to look into that for our later years which weren't too far away.

We found a really nice site snuggled into the scenery of rocks and trees in the park confines. It was hard to see any neighbor. I liked this type of camp. The roads were winding and twisting every which way. We sat for a long time trying to get our soaked tent to dry enough to set it down. In the background we could see the huge mountain at 14,400 feet. Snow covered its upper quarter with glaciers apparent on one side.

Once camp was dry we took a short one mile hike to the 3,500 foot level admiring the vegetation along the way. One plant on the whole trail caught my eye. "Wonder why those Canterbury Bells are here all by themselves?"

"Don't know but aren't they pretty? I've never seen any so big before, especially in the wild. It's a wonder someone hasn't picked them by now."

"Let's see if we can find the water I hear over here. It's getting louder all the time." We wandered off the beaten path into a bramble of shrubs, coming to a river running so fast down the hillside it was more a falls.

Crossing over a dry riverbed of stones, the view of the mountain greeted us again. Tall spruce and pines bordered the river giving the mountain a picture perfectness. Wispy clouds floated by in the sun.

"This is truly a beautiful place. I think I'd like to go to the visitor center and see what there is to do, like hike the mountains' trails or something. Do you want to go?"

I knew she was tired but I wasn't wanting to miss the adventure. "Sure, if we're going to be here long we might as well walk around to investigate. I'm not that tired. Maybe I'll sleep better tonight in the mountain air."

We walked another four miles to the inn for cookies and ice cream cones and maps of trails. George gave us some information about the mountain and where he thought we would enjoy it, so we could decide from a variety of places. When we returned to camp, a ranger was getting set up to show slides of the first women mountain climbers on the outdoor screen. We grabbed our jackets to shield us from the night air but forgot about mosquitos.

After watching that, we both knew we wanted to become mountain climbers. But since we didn't have the expertise, we would just climb as far as we dared the next day. We didn't have the

134

gear required, nor the time. Since the weather turned to winter in the upper reaches, our summer clothes would definitely not do. We crawled into our warm, bug free tent thinking about our trek in the morning.

We both slept very well and were up at the thought of an early start. It was only 48 degrees. Frost on the windshields prompted us to wear warmer clothes while we prepared breakfast.

Since it was going to be warm on the mountain we didn't want to be burdened with long pants. Shirley wore hers to the trailhead but I left mine in camp. I thought my legs were going to fall off in the short two mile jaunt to it.

"Should have worn my pants. Goosebumps and red skin are not very complimentary."

"Ha, I knew it was going to be cold. I'm glad I wore mine."

"But where are you going to put them? All your bags are full."

"I'll just lay them on the seat. I'm sure they will be here when we get back. I have to leave my leather jacket here, too. If anyone wanted anything I guess they'll just have to take it."

"I have room in one of my bags for the jacket but that's about all."

We toured this visitor center and waited for the female ranger who would lead the trek. She was also the park naturalist and could name every piece of vegetation along the trail. I still wished I had gone to school to learn these things. I would love a job like this. To be out in the wilds, even if this is a tame wild. Just knowing what she knew would be enough for me. We were instructed not to veer off the designated trail. The ecosystem was very fragile and took many years to rehabilitate itself to its growth standard of today. We walked with her and the others for some time. They were taking the shorter route. We wanted to continue to the farthest point up the mountain. She explained the trail the climbers took, pointing to base camps and to several climbers that we could see almost to the peak, dressed in bright reds. They were specs in the snow.

We left the group, finding our own way up the narrow path. Water trickled in little streams from the melting snows and glacier. We saw a marmot rummaging around in a hole he must have made and marveled at the meadows all around us abloom with spring flowers in blues, yellows and reds. The pine trees sprinkled here and there in groups among the meadows and rock reminded us of the movie *Heidi* with Shirley Temple. It was supposed to have been filmed in the Swiss Alps. We knew it had to be here. Her grandfather's log house had to around one of these bends. We just knew it.

We branched off to the Skyline trail to a height of 6,900 feet. The sun was warm and the view was vast. We passed the glacier noting the debris in the ice accumulated over many thousands of years. Up close it looked liked like dirty snow. We were told it moved but to us it was stationary.

At the summit of our trek, we sat among the low rocks to count seven or eight mountains that had names, Mount St. Helens, Hood and Adams with a variety of smaller peaks. Most had snow on them. Here we could see many Engleman spruce guarding the tips of the mountains with their branches pointing to the sky just like the sharp pinnacles of some of the mountains surrounding us.

Behind us was still the highest: Mt. Rainier. We sat for a long time munching snacks and writing post cards telling everyone what we were doing and resting before we had to hike down again.

We could still see Camp Muir, the camp for the climbers at the 10,000 foot level. We didn't know now if we could stand that sort of climb. We could see the climbers tied together as they made their approach to the summit some distance away yet.

Returning, the trail led across several snow fields. We were wearing running shoes. Nice for the ecosystem but not so nice on a snowy trail six inches wide on a steep slope. Ahead on one of these treacherous trails, a climbing school taught future climbers how to fall down the very same slope. They would begin a fall and the instructor would yell out to them when to stop their fall with an ice ax placed deftly in the snow. Every other student or so would not get the call till they almost ran out of snow. That wasn't for me. Right now, I had to figure out how to get past them. They were all standing in my trail. They had lug soles on their shoes, they had warm pants to fall on. Some were bare armed. They moved over about an inch. They were all having a good time laughing at their antics. A couple moved over, digging their boots in the old snow. Some laid back on the snow bank as we stepped ever so carefully over their legs. This was the longest of our snow fields. I was never so glad to get on dry land as I was then. I had a bad time with balance. An inner ear problem kept me from ever doing well at these things. Shirley just walked along like she was on bare, flat ground.

The rest of the walk down the mountain was very pleasant. More meadows of flowers and trickles of sun-sparkled river dashing through emerald green mosses. We noted many Japanese tourists on the trail. Once in awhile climbers came down in their heavier clothes. They would strip down as they neared the warmer climb.

We were famished by the time we reached the center. The inn was closed already and the snack bar had nothing we cared to eat. We had some better stuff still in our saddle bags so we sat out in the parking area on a curb to indulge. Our day was not to an end as yet.

Another trail head would take us just two miles into Reflection Lake. We could handle that, we thought. We embarked on another adventure that was botched but in a good way. We walked through flatter terrain in the woods not too far from the road, in fact, probably more parallel. It was much cooler in here than on the mountain trail. Pine needles softened it. It felt good as we trucked along. Nothing here to take pictures of but we insisted on carrying our heavy cameras. After more than an hour of walking, Shirley asked, "What did that sign say back there? How many miles?"

"I'm almost positive it said only 2.1 miles."

"This is a long 2.1 mile."

"My feet are beginning to hurt and I'm still hungry."

"Look at all the weight we are going to lose on this hike. Keep walking. We've got to come to something pretty soon. Listen, I hear cars. There must be a road up there." Sure enough we came to a road, but didn't recognize it. Two backpacking women were on the other side crossing to our side.

"Do you girls have a map?"

"Yea, are you lost?

""No, we think we are just misplaced."

We all laughed looking at the map as they told us it was some distance to Reflection Lake. Looking at the map showed someone was being funny about the marker. No way was it only 2.1 mile. We had already walked that and more. We turned back the way we came. We weren't equipped for an all day hike. We were really getting out of shape. We must have only walked ten miles. We stopped at the center to resupply our sugar reserves and then on to camp and a rest. What a wonderful day it had been. This place was on our list of places to return.

It rained during the night. We woke to a wet and foggy park. No need to sleep late like we said we were going to do to avoid the dew. We packed up another wet tent and left for Yakima on highway 5. At the top of one switchback we paused to look at the fog below us. It sat in the round canyon looking more like a cloud than fog. A camper came out of the cloud with its lights on. We were headed in his direction.

At White Pass we settled for hot coffee and sweet rolls in a ski lodge. The dampness of the fog chilled us to the bone. The warmth of the building helped but we knew we would have to brave the cold again.

Reaching Yakima, the sun was shining and the mountains were behind for awhile. We stopped at a common store we hadn't seen for some time to replenish our sterno and some food.

Wanting to get on with it through not very interesting terrain we jumped on the expressway I-90 and sped off to Spokane. The wind

137

whipped up and a cloud bank showed itself in front of us threateningly.

We found a quiet campsite between Spokane and Coeur D'Alene, Idaho. We put the wet tent up again to dry some before we got it wet again. It dried in the brisk wind in no time.

Our next destination would be Glacier National Park. I did not get that far north when I was in Montana the year before and she hadn't been there in a long time. We set our sights on it.

It was windy and rainy all night and only about 50 degrees. It is important to note that 50 degrees on a motorcycle can be very uncomfortable. There is no way of covering your hands and feet to keep them warm. As far as we knew, we would have to buy a bigger bike or accessories made to fit, making the cost effectiveness of our bikes extended.

We packed up the sopping tent again, laying its heavy burden on a bike and tightening it down with the bungee cords. Pulling on our heavy yellow and red rain suits over hooded sweatshirts and leather jackets and donning our helmets we felt more small children going out to play in the winter snows. A mile into town, we spotted a breakfast place and soon our heavy clothing was reduced in weight while we put away a big food bag.

"They say food is a soother for emotions. Is that why we are eating so much?

"You mean, this will sooth our ruffled feathers or our pruney fingers?"

"Something like that."

"It doesn't look like it's going to be a nice day at all, does it?"

"No, we might have been better off staying in bed waiting for it to blow over." Our former adrenaline was lost this morning as we ate that big breakfast wondering why we were here at all. We did have a good day the day before, we both admitted. We couldn't possibly have good weather all the time.

Highway 95 would take us north to the park. It was wet but the rain and wind had died down to nothing. We gassed up in Sand point and succumbed to another treat of huge cinnamon rolls and another cup of coffee. Drinking so much coffee, wearing so much clothing, gave us another problem men don't need to worry about. We took care of the bathroom problem before leaving, keeping our rain gear on to ward off the now 58 degree temperatures.

We passed through Bonner's Ferry without stopping and into Montana through Idaho. This part of Idaho was the narrowest in the north.

Chapter 8

Montana, the Third Time

It started to rain as we crossed the border. We didn't feel much like stopping to put gear on and off. We were thankful we left it on. The terrain changed from flat to hilly and the temperature changed with it. One minute it was 55 degrees and then 68 degrees and back down again. Surely, the mountains had something to do with it.

We discussed an oil change in Kalispell while eating another sweet revenge. The Honda dealer was easy to find but he had no filters. We took a room at a Motel 6 for the night. Even though we lost an hour it was still only three in the afternoon. We had to stand in line till five o'clock to get a room. We couldn't figure out the reason for the popularity until we saw there were very few motels and most had their "No Vacancy" signs turned on. Perhaps the weather was getting to the other travelers as well as us. We didn't want to put up the wet tent tonight and sleep in it hoping to be happy and cheerful by morning. We knew ourselves well enough to know that close quarters and weather would be the end of a good friendship quickly. Maybe tomorrow would be better.

We passed many small white crosses on the road that day. They must be for auto deaths or accidents.

The room was luxurious after the cold and rainy day. It was just the usual with two beds, television and bathroom with the standard plumbing fixtures.

We procrastinated as long as we could in the morning. The weather didn't look any better as I looked behind the curtains of our room. Our bikes stood out there waiting for us to mount them, their windshields dripping with wet, the seats shiny. A good wash down would be necessary as soon as we had a dry day. The wet magnetized the road dirt.

Black clouds still filled the sky in front of us. In the park, we took the only road through called "Going To The Sun".

"I wonder if that means what it says," my riding partner asked at the gate. "If we find it I want to get all I can. I need to dry up my body of all this dampness I've collected."

"Did the park ranger at the gate tell you about riding a bike here?

"Yes, he said it could be very treacherous up in the mountains. I told him this wasn't my first time."

"You must be feeling better about riding, then," I said.

"No, I just didn't want him to think I was a wimp. We look funny wearing all these clothes. I wasn't sure I showed any confidence or not."

Tucking away the maps we were off to see another glacier. We rode around the parks' large Lake McDonald and then things began to worsen. It was not the most pleasant experience. Our hands gripped the hand grips with wet gloves. Up we went, following the many cars streaming the same way. We could see the switchbacks along the rocky face of the Rocky Mountain trail. The car and camper line crawled along. My thermometer dropped lower and lower. It started to rain and turned foggy. We both held tightly, climbing higher and higher in the fog draped road with rain dropping on the windshield, my glasses, and her face shield, obstructing our view.

We stopped at a pull-out to view a glacier but it was so difficult to get off the bike and unclench my hands I didn't think I'd better. Shirley got off to take a picture but couldn't find the glacier in the fog and rain. She got back on and we continued the climb. The temperature dropped to 42 degrees and the rain turned to snow, leaving a slush on the pavement. It wasn't slippery but some of the edges had no barriers. Just the wrong move would mean curtains for either one of us.

At the summit, the fog and clouds hung around the tops of the tallest snowcapped mountains. We unbent our bodies to walk the flight of stairs leading to the ranger station in hopes of getting warmed. The sun tried to come out but the wind blew it back behind the clouds. The station had a roaring fire in the fireplace. We cozied up to warm our hands and feet. They never reached their normal levels. The ranger said it was too cold for him to go out for a talk on the ecosystem here, but we were free to walk the grounds ourselves. Everyone else was disappointed. I wasn't and I don't think my partner was. We looked around through the big windows and tried to get warm from inside and then headed out. We wondered what we were doing here.

The snow turned to sleet and then to hail on the way down from Logan Pass. Down and down we went, turning into the curves like a giant slolum run. Turn to the right and then to the left and again to the right. The back of the bike felt like I was sitting on the back end of my skis making a tight tellemark turn in the snow. The warmth of the valley below was much better but not skinny dipping weather yet. My clothes were getting saturated through my wonderful rain suit that was guaranteed to keep me dry.

St. Mary's Lake could have been much prettier in drier weather but still held a quality we stopped to admire. In the middle, a small island with several trees reminded us of a battleship on the ocean. The mountains surrounding it had very little foothills but went directly up to towering heights of mostly rock with snow lingering in crevasses. Coming out the eastern end of the park, the dark clouds that were with us all day hung low over the most spectacular mountains across a grassy field. They jutted up with such suddenness I couldn't compare them to anything I had seen in the more southern Rockies. Those same mountains could be seen for miles after leaving the park area off in the distance across the grasslands.

We stopped at Blackfoot for something to eat when we left the cold park and changed our mind. Only one place to eat and it was so dirty we were afraid. We weren't that hungry.

I wanted to go back to Virginia City to show Shirley the area of silver mining and for her to meet my last year's friend, Dorothy. We took highway 89, stopping in Choteau for lunch.

In a KOA park again. The drizzle was still with us but we couldn't spend all our time in a motel. This campground had the new circular shelters. They were made of log, built on a cement foundation, divided into four partitions. The center of each "pie" has a storage place, a cook shelve, table, and hanging pegs built in. Surrounding the whole thing is a grassy patch. The owner of the park was a feisty old women. There wasn't one subject she wouldn't discuss with disgust. Saying she didn't want to talk about it only made her talk about it more. She was cute.

A Honda dealer in this place had filters. He was used to owners of smaller bikes coming in for parts and working on lawn mowers and tractors. He was elated to see some bigger bikes looking for his aid. We helped him do the job and checked over all the other vital signs as well. Shirleys' battery was keeping its cells full. Perhaps she just had a bad battery to start with. Our camp mate in the shelter pulled his bike in to do the same thing.

"There isn't much you can do on a rainy day," he said. We agreed with that. We swapped stories of the weather and trips and we all came to the same conclusion.

Breakfast out again this morning. We didn't feel like eating in the dampness. We dried the tent out some the night before but packed it up wet again today. "Big Sky" was big, but grey.

Wolf Creek Pass was just another warm-up spot on the road. We wished the nasty weather would go away. We still had a lot of mountains to ride through before we hit the Plains states. A bowl of chili warmed our insides but our toes and fingers never wanted to really warm.

We discovered a contest at one of the Honda dealers. A rider had to collect signatures from so many Honda dealers around the state to win a prize. It just happened to be in the states where we were going to be traveling. We needed a signature from Butte. It was on our way and probably the same one I stopped in last year for an oil change.

The rain came down in buckets. That same "Big Sky" emptied all it had on us between Butte and Virginia City. I called Dorothy to see if she wanted company.

"Come on down," was all she said. I explained I had a friend with me and it made no difference. I told her it was raining again and she sympathized with me. It had rained when I first met her.

Took an hour and a half to go the short distance because of the rain and the gusty winds. The rain quit in Virginia City but the wind kept up for a long time. The town was having an art festival or something. We ate dinner in town so as not to barge ourselves on her generosity. I knew we were invited for the night for as long as we wanted to stay but we weren't staying long. She had six to eight students coming in and out while we were there. They were all staying with her. Sleeping bags were piled up along the wall in her family room with a lot of personal things stacked around them. She loved having them with her.

The bikes got stripped down to the bone and everything got dried out, including ourselves. Wiping them down with old rags made them gleam in the subdued light of the ending day.

That night, there was an act we had to see at the "Brewery". Several of the students were planning on going and kept telling us we had to go, too. It was held in an old barn. It started raining again while inside but the act was great. Song and dance. Stray kittens wandered around the barn and water dripped down pipes from the ceiling. It was dark with only oil lanterns for light and dirt floors. It was terrific. Just what we needed to perk us up from our doldrums. Dorothy drove us down in her car but the other students weren't finished with their evening entertainment and were left on the corner to walk home later.

We used Dorothy's bedroom floor for our house tonight. It was dry and the wind wouldn't whistle through it. The heat was on and we just snuggled in for a good night's rest.

We could smell the coffee at first light. Arising, we found her in the kitchen making the biggest pot of oatmeal with raisins and applesauce I ever saw. I didn't say anything about the amount of oatmeal we consumed on this trip already. It was tastier than ours, at any rate. Must be the raisins.

We looked outside and saw the weather had made a turn for the better.

"Why don't we walk to Nevada City this morning. You'd like it there." One of the others were going as well and offered us a ride.

"How about we walk and if it starts raining, we'll ride back with you?"

"That's fine. We'll meet you there," and off we all went. Dorothy stayed home. She had been there many times and had bad legs.

It was only a mile or more to the town that I explored last year so I was sure we would have no problem walking. One of the restaurants were open to sell breakfast items. We met the others there also indulging in a cinnamon roll. We couldn't let them have all the fun so we joined them and we all went our own way through town.

Upon leaving the rain began again and just then Dave, the driver, showed up and drove us in the cramped little car back to Virginia City. Then they took us on the city tour of all the places I had already seen. It was a fun day.

I bought over $100 in gifts and things for myself to keep me warm. A hooded sweatshirt and rubber gloves. Perhaps the hands will stay warm if they stay dry, I thought when I bought them.

Our destination kept us going south from Dorothy's. We didn't want to overstay our welcome. By afternoon we insisted on leaving for Yellowstone Park where we had both been before. Highway 287 would do the trick. It was raining only slightly when we left. Following the Madison River, the sky turned dark again and unloaded on us again. It was so black we got off the bikes to wait it out. This was not fun anymore.

I remembered I wanted to find the tree with the arrows on it along the river but the weather made me forget about it.

The sun tried to peek out some time later and it warmed up a little. Not enough to suit me. The year before was so much different from now. It was hard to explain the good time I had. Crossing over Craigs Pass in Yellowstone at 8,200 feet didn't help our situation. The rain turned to snow and the road turned slushy and slippery. Would it ever warm up?

We stopped on the road for something and then I decided we needed a picture of ourselves wrapped up in our red and yellow outfits. Sweatshirt hoods under out helmets made our helmets sit higher on our heads. Our cameras were self supporting with timers. We came away with many shots of ourselves trying to hurry back into the camera range before it snapped.

We had to go another 57 miles within the park to find a campground with an empty space. We must have had the last one.

143

For awhile we thought we would have to try to beg for one, doubling up or something, or get out of the park itself. We weren't willing to do that yet.

At a camp store, I bought some wool socks. I ran into the kid I met the year before from Owosso.

"Dan?" I asked tentatively.

"Yes?" he returned.

"You don't remember me," I said disappointedly.

"Should I?"

"Yes."

"You do look familiar. I held up my helmet with the "Pony Express" lettering on the back. "Oh, my gosh, I remember you. Yea, I met you last year over at Ole Faithful. You ride a motorcycle." He held out his hand for a shake and I accepted it. Introduced my partner to him and he was all smiles as we told him where we just came from. We renewed old stories.

"This rain suit is the worse buy I ever made," I said as I removed it to try to dry my sweatshirt underneath.

"What kind is it?"

I showed him the label on the front. "Dad sells that stuff. Why don't you give him a call and ask why it isn't repelling the water? He is working out of Grand Haven and sells that to the sailboaters. It's supposed to be good. Just tell him, I'm sure he'll do something for you."

"I wish he could do something for me right now. I paid enough for it."

"I know what you mean. Hey, why don't I come visit you tonight. Where are you staying?" I told him but I didn't think he would come to our camp. He didn't. The coffee shop was about to close. We indulged in some coffee before settling down for the night. We had not had the chance to pay for our site yet but the fellow hawking firewood said if we got out of there by 8 a.m. we won't have to pay. We planned on a quick exit.

We were sitting in a restaurant at 7 a.m. enjoying a warm breakfast in a warm building. The temperature dropped to a low of 38 degrees by that time. We didn't look forward to our days journey. It was getting old, the adventure left long ago. The sky was partly cloudy with dark ominous clouds to the north and east. It looked like we would be following each other all the way home!

Shirley had not seen Old Faithful in a long time so we returned to that part of the park. It was colder than a well drillers butt! It only got as high as 42 degrees this morning. Not good. I already toured the walk and was too cold to do it again. She went alone while I sat by the fire in the inn.

144

We took the long way out and still had to negotiate a pass at the 8,800 foot elevation. It snowed hard here and kept snowing until we got down in the flats again and left the park.

We needed a signature from a Honda dealer in Livingston so we headed north again, and hoped the clouds would go about their merry way. We never won the big prize for all the signatures but we did get a nice enamel pin in the mail.

The KOA in this town had an indoor swimming pool. Heated. The bait was laid and we took it. It was so soothing to the tired and cold body. Only to have to go to a tent to sleep. Our site was so close to the pool we didn't worry about getting cold between the two. We stayed in the water till our fingers looked like prunes.

John came by our tent in the morning with an offering of some blend of French and something or other coffee. He was fishing the night before and tried to find us while we were in the pool, to share his trout he caught. Fine thing! We talked with him when we first came in and he was on his way out to go fishing. We had the coffee but then hit the road. I think he was trying to hit on Shirley. They had something in common. Fishing. She wanted no part of him.

It didn't rain all day and we made it to Hardin to enjoy Custers' Battlefield again. I still admired the Souix Indians and their fight to regain their territory. More articles found in the archeological dig a few years ago were displayed in the museum. So many things! They were not finished digging either.

The hot tub was hot. A long soak relaxed us for the night. I ironed out the damp map with an available hot iron.

Chapter 9   South Dakota, Iowa
Illinois, Indiana and Home

Up early to sun. How wonderful, a dry day. It was cool but not cold. Still on the Cheyenne Indian Reservation, we stopped for our second breakfast. We took our time, enjoying the ride in the sun and ate often.

We were out in the middle of somewhere and nowhere, just riding along thinking our own thoughts about whatever was on our minds. The Rockys' were to our right, off in the distance. They were a hazy blue with a sky full of puffy clouds floating on top of them. Now, we were back into the "Great Plains", the yellow-browns of the grasses waving on both sides on the two lane ribbon of road. A few cattle here and there. No houses, no buildings, only a few trucks on our road. A fence running parallel with the road and a road marker sign now and then. Our rule of stopping every fifty miles for something had been working for the past three weeks or more. There wasn't much to stop for out here. We were past our fifty mile stretch when I spotted a truckstop on the left of the road several miles away in this flat country. Small signs along the road advertised the stop. I turned my signal on to turn left at least a mile before the stop. I saw Shirley in the distance as ususal, too far behind for hand signals or talk.

I slowed to make the turn in the gravel drive, watching to make sure I saw her signal turn on. It didn't come on but she was approaching much too fast to make the turn.

It happended so fast. The next thing I saw was her bike spinning in front of me lying on its side in the gravel. She wasn't seen. I almost hit her bike as I braked around on the gravel coming to a stop and trying to hold my bike in a vertical position. All I could do is yell, "Shirley!"

I turned around to see where she was and she was walking toward me picking up pieces of debris, carrying her helmet in her hand. "Oh, my God! What happened? Are you all right?" I asked as we fell into a hug.

"I'm O.K. Walt will never let me go again. I didn't see you turn. You didn't have your signal on." I wasn't surprised she thought of Walt first thing.

"Yes, I did. Look. It's still flashing," I said as I picked up some of the stuff. We examined her to check the damage. Her helmet struck the gravel tearing the face shield off and skinning off some paint. She had a few cuts on her face that were superficial but bleeding some. Her leather jacket protected her the most and when we were inside we examined the rest of the damage.

The owner of the sparsely filled stop was inside. I ran in to ask if he could help get the bike up and move it off the drive. He came out wanting to know what happened. We explained to him and asked if he had more bandages than what I packed in my first aid kit if we needed any. He gave me what he had and we found the bathroom where she stripped her pants and jacket off.

"Good thing I was wearing all this stuff," she said as she peeled to reveal a pair of long johns. The gravel tore through the jeans but stopped there. The leather of the jacket was skinned up but we were surprised to see her arm bleeding at the elbow where she landed. She had several other layers over her skin and all were torn to some degree. It was the first time she left her gloves off. They were like my gloves. Bicycle riders wear padded palms with mesh on top for air. They were still on the bike.

"I always wear those gloves. I don't know why I forgot them this time. I was trying to reach behind me to get them earlier but thought I would go without for this little while." Her knuckles on both hands were sanded down, bleeding. I helped her put as many bandages as we could use, adding Neo-sporum to the wounds before.

She thought she bruised her hip and rib section and walked out of the restroom-emergency room as if that were so. We went inside the restaurant and ordered a cup of coffee. "Do you feel all right?" the owner asked when I gave him back his empty first aid kit.

"I'm a little shaky."

"We're going to sit here awhile if you don't mind."

"No, that's O.K."

I went back outside while she sat at the table to see if the bike could be ridden. The right side, of course, got all the damage. The saddle bag was scraped, fairing cracked, a couple riding lights were missing, brake foot pedal bent and exhaust pipe scraped up pretty bad. But she was O.K. That was all that mattered. I got angry with her while outside. My mind kept telling me to calm down, maybe it wasn't her fault, maybe mine for being so bossy. But I kept shifting back and forth. If she'd only ride like I tell her she might not be in this fix. Maybe this will change her attitude. Maybe not. She might ride farther back. Or maybe not at all. I wondered if she could or

147

would. It was a long way home. How would she get there if he couldn't?

I sat awhile with her talking over the present situation. She still blamed me for not putting my signal on sooner.

"How much sooner do you want me to do it?" I asked getting upset and concerned.

"Well you just didn't. I never saw it till you were making the turn. I tried to brake because you were in front of me, but I just lost control."

"I think you were just out there looking at something and not paying any attention. Do you think I told you about riding correctly for no reason? If you would pay attention to where you are going you might not be in this fix. Do you think you want to ride?" I felt terrible talking like that to her.

"Yes, I'll be O.K. Just give me a minute." We sat in silence. She got up to go.

"We better see if the bike will ride anywhere. It might not go two feet."

"O.K. if you're game, so am I. You're sure you feel up to it?"

"Yes."

She got on the bike to see what worked. The brake handle was bent some but still usable. The pedal was pretty bad. "I don't think I can use that. I can use the front brake instead." We tried bending it back but couldn't. The garage man gave us a long pipe to put over it to winch it but it wouldn't fit over the pedal itself. She was sure she could handle it.

"How would you like to be the leader for awhile?" I asked.

"Sure, it can't be that bad. Maybe I won't put my signal on till just before I'm gonna turn."

"Whatever rows your boat," I quipped. "Let me strap this map to your gas tank. Remember, you not only have to watch the map, you have to watch where you're going. Read all the signs, the cars, your bike controls, and don't forget to watch for me in the mirror with everybody else in there. We'll be coming to Belle Fourche soon. Remember, we get gas before we run out, so watch the mileage."

We drove off with Shirley in the lead. She never was much of a leader in anything we did so far together. She would have good ideas but seemed to want someone else to take command. She always took the back seat and was content. Now she could see what it was like in this situation. Maybe it would help to activate some leadership and get her off my back. I thought I could be happier going alone.

She took her first unsure steps quite well. Arriving in town she had a hard time reading the map without glasses. I could see her doing a lot of nodding. I presumed it was to read and watch the road. It was.

148

We spent the night at a private camp. Nothing special. Had dinner at Horse Creek Ranch. Nice. It was needed after today's episode. I thought she deserved it.

The tent was wet in the morning as usual. We stayed long enough to try to dry most of it. The sky was clear and it was sunny. We stopped at Leadville and Sturgis. Sturgis is the popular place where hundreds of cyclists ride for a several day rally. We came in after they were gone. There were a few leftover bikers roaming the streets in their black leather and chains. It wasn't our style. At Mt. Rushmore we walked around quickly taking pictures and returning to the bikes. We checked the progress of Crazy Horse monument. I had a vested interest in that. A hole had been blasted through the mountain where a gap would be in the top of the horses' neck and Crazy Horses' outstretched arm. Someday, it will be finished. I wondered if it would be in my lifetime.

"You can have the maps back, if you want."

"Had enough?"

"Yea, I can't see them without glasses anyway. It's too hard."

I chuckled to myself and strapped them back on my tank and led us out of the parking lot with the "I told you so" look on my serious face.

A side road led down a river. The Black Hills is a pretty region. Prospectors came here after someone found some gold and it was quickly confiscated from the Indians as usual. They had a spiritual attachment to the hills and are still fighting to regain ownership. We explored the area, checking out the river along the way where many picnickers were busy splashing in the waters and eating lunch. We joined them and returned to the highway wanting to get on expressway I-90 to rush the rest of the way home. A stop in Rapid City necessitated for more bandages for my injured friend.

That same black cloud returned and wouldn't budge. On went the rain gear and some cussing under our breaths. The rain came down in torrents as we tried to fend off the cold that returned with it.

The temperature dropped to a low degree as we pressed on to Mitchell. We could procure a room in a town that size. My knees squeezed the gas tank, trying to get what little warmth the engine emitted to warm them. I leaned over the tank to keep as much of the rain as possible from hitting and stinging my face. My hands were freezing. The rubber gloves I purchased in Virginia City did nothing to warm them with or without the rain. My feet were frozen, even with the wool socks. Plastic bags in them held out water but not the cold. I could feel an ache working its way into my body. Stopping was a chore. My legs were held in this position and cramped so much it hurt to straighten out.

No room at the inn was the word we received from two motels. A convention in town took all of them. Disgusting! Didn't they keep one or two rooms aside for travelers in peril?

On to Sioux Falls. It was 300 miles of this kind of driving before we found room. A small truck stop with about half a dozen rooms for truckers and a small restaurant must have felt sorry for us and rented us a room.

What a blessing! Another couple on a bike from Minnesota were in the same fix as us and I thought we would share our room with them if they couldn't get one. But they, too, were in luck. Spending time to lay all our wet rags on anything hangable warranted ingenuity. The room was small. I was wet to the skin in my expensive waterproof rainsuit. Shirley was mostly wet on the bottom half, boots, socks, pant legs. Sitting on a bike for a long period drew up the rain pant leg making the jeans get wet from the bottom. We turned the heat on in the room to help warm us and dry the clothes.

Putting on something more presentable and dry for dining, we ran across the parking area to the restaurant for dinner and devoured some fillet mignon as a reward. The clouds behind were no longer angry black but a nice fluffy white against a blue sky. It was the wrong direction of our travel. The eastern sky was still black and menacing.

"Sioux City here we come!" I whooped as I looked out the window in the morning. Sun was shining and only a few clouds in the sky."Let's make hay while the sun shines, Nellie!" I teased.

Instead of riding the expressways we wanted to ride the old roads through Iowa. We didn't know at this time that we would be riding our bicycles through this same area just a year or two away. And we did it for two summers for a week with 17,000 other nuts like ourselves. I might not have ridden the bicycle if I would have known Iowa was not flat!

We zig-zagged our way to Carroll to the freeway, I-80.

"You know, Granny, we could make a project out of this riding around," I called out.

"How so, Pony?"

"If Walt will let you, do you want to try to ride through all 48 states?"

"I don't know. He may want me to get rid of it."

"If he doesn't mind, what do you think? Do you want to give it a try? We already have twenty just on this trip. I have an added five from last year."

"Yea, that sounds like fun. Have any idea where we could go next year?"

"Not right off but I'm sure we could figure out something. Maybe we should go to the east."

"Sounds good."

For the longest time on I-80 I listened to some truckers traveling together. One female and a few male drivers. They joked and laughed and were making a good thing out of a bad situation- working. They kept me in stitches untill we turned off at a KOA camp. I wished Shirley had a radio. It would have made the time go much faster on this boring road. Nothing to see and no one to talk to. She didn't have ear plugs for her FM radio either. The truckers were always trying to get close enough to swat each other with a fly swatter. A dangerous thing to see them do, but they were play acting most of the time and never got close enough to hit each other. I could see the swatter out the open window of one of the trucks.

I slept badly. The exit ramp of I-80 is not my idea of an idyllic sleep promoter. A truck stop was at the next exit just a half a mile away. We heard trucks downshifting throughout the night, trucks parked for the night with their rigs running and those starting out at any given time revved them up. At six a.m. we thought we had a good chance of getting home by nightfall if we scooted right along. Wrong. Three hours ahead in fog was not fun. Radio reports indicated it got worse before it got better.

Rolling along, I heard familiar voices over the radio. My gosh! It was the same truckers I heard last night. I couldn't believe it! I picked up the microphone and wished them a good, gloomy morning.

"Are you the same guys I saw swatting each other yesterday with fly swatters?" I asked innocently.

"You didn't see a thing," responded one.

"Oh, not me. I didn't see anything like that. I only heard someone talking like that was what they were doing."

"Where you at, little lady?" came on another.

"I'm passing by marker, let me see, marker 267 goin' east."

"You can't be. I'm at marker 267 and I don't see no car. Are you in a truck?"

"No. I see you. You are in that green and white striped truck, and there's four of you all heading the same way as I."

"That you on that motorcycle?"

"You got it, that's me, and behind is my riding partner. She's missing out on all my fun. She doesn't know what is going on. She has no radio," I answered.

"Well, I'll be darned. Where ya' all going? asked the lady trucker.

I went into details about where we've been and where we were going and about the accident. All too soon they had to get off at a weigh station and I kept on rolling.

"Maybe I'll see you down the road. Keep up the laughter. It's much better listening to you do that, than all the garbage that usually comes over this thing. They split and we went off to Chicago.

I still had no love for Chicago driving. I didn't want to burden myself with the extra burden of my partner's driving technique. It had not changed to my specifications since the accident, in fact, it may have worsened. She would be much farther behind, letting a multitude of cars come between us, I, still not knowing where she was. I refused to go any slower than the speed I thought was legal. If she didn't want to keep up it was her problem. I expected she thought I would baby her, but I refused. If she was going to ride with me she was going to have to be more forceful. We were both too stubborn to admit the other might be right or wrong.

The nearer we got to Chicago, the more I wished Shirley would ride closer. I was having a terrible time keeping track of her. I got us off at 42A going south for a few miles and east again on 30. Then I heard too late that 30 was under destruction! I always used that term for construction. Made another turn to the north only to learn of an accident tying up traffic. It was too hot to sit in hot traffic with the engines running. Another few miles and we were going south on 141 to find 6. Finally I settled and stayed on 6 till we were out from under the largest portion of city traffic. It might have been better to stay where we were all along.

On one of the side streets I stopped to look at the map to figure a better route. We stopped along the curb in a residential neighborhood staying on the bikes when a gentleman stopped, got out of his car and told us it wasn't a good neighborhood to be sitting in. We never questioned him, but looking around we didn't see anything wrong with it, but moved on.

The rest of trip was just ordinary. Shirley still rode several car lengths behind, sometimes in the right of the lane and sometimes in the left, looking around like someone else was driving. We had lunch on one of our breaks at Big Boy and then closer to home had an ice cream cone. I should have gained at least ten pounds because my jeans were much tighter. Surprised when it was only three and a half.

The next day I received a phone call from a Bill Goodwin in Durango. He left the ad in the laundryroom. Shirley wanted me to answer it but I only sent him a card. He was originally from San Diego and was working there as a surveyor in Farmington, New

152

Mexico not far over the border. We wrote for a month or so, exchanging pictures and then more for religious beliefs, we quit.

We chalked up almost 8,000 miles and rode through 20 states. I now accumulated 25 states on this motorcycle. Now I had the desire to travel to all the states at least once on this machine. Some of them, I went through twice and then there were the ones I'd already gone through before. But I wanted to do all 48 on this same machine and maybe the provinces. Shirley agreed but was still optimistic of Walt letting her. So was I. I liked traveling with someone. Traveling alone meant you had to rely on just yourself. I wasn't afraid to do it any more but company was good, too. Alone, I could go where I wanted, when I wanted and make all my own right or wrong decisions. I would be responsible for whatever happened to myself.

I knew what I was doing here, and so did Shirley. With someone else with me I could blame them for getting misplaced, wet, hungry, tired, cold or maybe even being happy and having a good time!

.......................I continued to ride my bicycle along U.S. 2. The sun was warming me to the extent I had to stop to remove another layer to be comfortable. Thinking of other times and places gave me something to do while alone, making the time fly past. We rode our bicycles just as much as we did the motorcycles in the coming years. We knew we had to keep our middle-aged figures in check. We couldn't do that on a motorcycle. Mostly our bicyling centered in Michigan. Shirley had a couple grandchildren ride with us as well as her daughter Sheri and sometimes even Walt took time to ride. He rode his bike in Washington quite a bit. He knew he needed the exercise and I suppose it was catching when he saw his wife doing so well with it and enjoying the outdoors in a different way.

I was surprised when her 11 year old grandson, Donald, and granddaughter, Sherlyn, a couple years older, rode across the whole state their first year some 375 miles in a week. They both did well with little complaint.

The tour was devoted to those who could not ride long days and it was perfect for kids. They were catered to the whole week. Some parents carried their little ones in buggers behind themselves. Others rode tandem bikes and outfitted the bike so short legs would get a work out as well. Not necessarily were they doing much work unless they were older. One fellow had two children on his tandem. Mother rode along on a single. They switched the bugger from one bike to the other pulling a fourth child. A fifth, rode alone. A nice family project, at best.

We had a lot of fun on these rides with other people. We were catered to ourselves and the camaraderie filled our needs. I continued to pedal alone without that camaraderie but still enjoying the quietude of the moment. I remembered we rode so well and tired so little any more that we groped for bigger and better bicycle rides with groups...........................

Adventure #5

Pedaling our Butts Around

Chapter 1   Traveling Circus

It was the late winter on 1986 when Walt brought us information on a prestigious bicycle ride we only heard about from other riders. RAGBRAI. Just the name ran chills down backs. People from all across the country wanted to be a part of it. It started out as a dare between two fellows on the Des Moines Register in 1973 spreading to more than 7,500 riders in a few years.

RAGBRAI stands for Register's Annual Great Bicycle Ride Across Iowa. Yes, I said Iowa. Out there where nothing is supposed to happen. Out there where it is supposed to be flat. Out there in nowhere.

Wrong.

First, we found that Iowa was where it all was. It was not flat where we were in the middle south. We just knew that if we were a part of this ride, we would be given more respect at other events. Everyone wanted to know more about it and how to get there. It was supposed to be difficult to get a ticket. The mystery made us want to be a part of it more than ever.

Inquiries were sent in. We were chosen from thousands of requests and given a choice of staying with the main group or joining a smaller club. They would look after us in a smaller way but still keep us together with the rest. We signed up for the latter. The Out-of-Stater's Club sounded like it was meant for just people like us.

They would meet us on the east side of Iowa where we parked our vehicles for the week. Our bikes, gear and selves would be carried in a U-Haul truck and bus for the trek to the west side. From there we would ride the bikes and they would transport our gear to the nightly site pre-planned for the whole week. With 7,500 riders that seemed an impossibility to us but they have done this for the past 13 years and we felt they must know what they were doing by now.

We would be camping out every night in some sort of camping area; fairgrounds, city parks, schools or even private residents. Meals would be served at a variety of places. We would be on our own for that. Entertainment was everywhere and anytime. We would travel approximately 500 miles in seven days or 45 miles to 100 miles in a day. The temperatures were usually hot and humid. Non-biker friends could hardly believe we thought it would be fun.

The club would maintain cold pop and beer for us at each night's stop. We would be given full maps. Most needed at end of day to find our campground. The only other things we received for our ticket price was a wrist band for identification, and a daily newspaper just for us. Every other souvenir we would buy during the week.

We had a very good friend Mary Jones, from South Bend, Indiana with us. Us, meaning Shirley, Walt and their daughter, Sheri and I. We were pleased she wanted to tag along with us. She being a gregarious 72 year old senior who regularly rode and cross-country skied.

We were as prepared as possible for this July 17. The temperatures were in the 90's and very humid. I wondered how anybody could ever get used to riding in the humidity when I rode my first ride in 1983, DALMAC. As time passed and you did more and more in it, I guess your body got acclimated to it. I felt good.

We picked up Mary Jones, saying farewell to her husband, Tom, who did not ride and were on our way to Muscatine, Iowa in two vehicles, bikes strapped to the backs. Registration was that evening in a city park on the river near the locks of the Mississippi. Temperatures read 105 degrees in the shade.

We arrived plenty early, set up camp, watched the ships go through the locks, ate at a Mexican restaurant and generally passed the time meeting fellow riders and waiting for night. Perhaps it will cool down. Sheri and I shared her tent that Shirley and I borrowed the year before. She bought another one like hers and shared it with her husband. Mary was used to traveling alone and had a one

156

man tent so short it was meant for midgets. But then, she was only 5 feet and weighed a whopping 100 pounds soaking wet.

"You and Walt will try to sleep slightly away from the rest of us, won't you, Shirley?" I pleaded.

"Why?"

"I know how he snores and I want to sleep."

"Yea, mom, make him turn over when he starts, will you?"

"I don't snore," came back Walt.

"The heck you don't. You could wake up the whole town."

"Sheri, how can you say that? I've never heard myself snore like that."

"Don't worry, you guys, I'll shove him. I can't stand it either."

Walt slept well despite the heat and humidity. We could all hear him and a few others nearby between the toots of the boats and trains. I don't recall sleeping in such noisy environment before.

"I wonder if we will have the same noise in Council Bluffs on the Missouri River when we get there," I asked in the morning when we went to find a bathroom. We did the best we could in the just-better-than-an-out-house facility. We weren't prepared for what was coming for the next week. We were to ride to Council Bluffs with only a hundred or so riders on the bus. The others with the club would be meeting us there and we'd join with the thousands of others.

It took us five hours to get across the state on the air conditioned bus. We all watched the prairie-like hills fly past our windows. The corn fields were high and green and lush. Here and there only fields of grass. We drove up to a college surrounded by corn fields at least as tall as ourselves. The grounds were covered with multi-colored tents of all sizes and shapes, bikes everywhere. Dozens of buses were expelling their contents and semi-trucks were releasing bikes out their tails ends. In several places, rows of port-a-johns were placed. When I say rows, I mean hundreds in long rows.

"Wow, look at all these people. How are we going to find anything?"

"I don't know, but I think we'd better find our own stuff so we can find a place to set our tents before more come."

"We should be looking for a U-Haul truck. Isn't that it over there?"

"Yea, let's go see if it's ours. There are more than one of them." We walked around and inspected it but it didn't look like our driver.

"Maybe it's not here yet."

"There comes another in the drive. I wonder where it's going to park. There isn't much room left."

157

"Come on, let's follow it." We all trudged around with our bags between other excited bikers carrying bags and pushing bikes. We had to stop for the port-a-johns on the way thinking we should get used to this.

We found the right truck and were instructed where it would be in the morning. We would load our gear on the truck and the bus would go on its' way elsewhere. The bikes were packed tight together with cardboard boxes between for protection. Handlebars were turned sideways and pedals removed to make them pack tight together. Everyone grabbed their own and returned them to their original shape.

There was a small clearing under some trees out of the sun, but as soon as we claimed it, someone said it was being saved for the rest of their group. We looked around for another and claimed it for ourselves. It was one of the last ones around. It was in partial sun but as it went down perhaps we will have a little shade to cool us off for the evening.

It didn't take long for us to stake our claim and put our belongings in them. Off we went to a cluster of booths set up nearer the school. If there was anything we forgot or needed it could be found here. Many booths sold t-shirts honoring the ride in different designs and styles. Short and long sleeves, tank tops, sweat shirts, shorts and everything imaginable in accessories for the bike and even bikes. People mingling just like a fairgrounds or carnival. We all bought a shirt. We were used to having one given to us with our ticket purchase, but here, these were all things that enterprising business people sold themselves.

With this many people doing the same thing, we thought we ought to find a place to eat before there wasn't anything left. God forbid, we didn't eat! Next to our tent, a new tent was set up. Ken Nu from Burlington, Wisconsin invited himself to go along with us to eat. He said he knew where to find a good spaghetti place. It was always a good feeling to have someone lead us around. The need for carbohydrates was top priority. We rode our bikes, rounding out our fivesome to six. I liked riding in twos. Ken was in his fifties, a tad older than I. I was the youngest of the six. His wife didn't ride. He came by himself.

He also knew where we could find a place to dip our rear wheels in the river. Taking our picture for the record was also a ritual, our smiling faces masking any fears we might have had about this ride. There was no lock here, we shouldn't be disturbed by boats or trains either.

Instead, the night went on with noises from many of the riders who were out to party. Didn't they ever sleep? Was this the way our week was going to be? Late sleepers? I would have to get some sleep once in awhile if I had to ride in this heat every day. Since I couldn't sleep, Sheri did. She could sleep in anything. Around five a.m., we were both awake. "I'm going to go to the bathroom," she whispered.

"Wait, I'll go with you. Where's the flashlight?"

"I've got mine."

"O.K. Let me get some pants and shoes on." Unzippering a tent is not a quiet idea. Zzzzipppp! Suddenly, we could hear other zipping noises, groans and rustling. Shirley was just getting out of her tent, too. We all walked down to the port-a-johns in the dark. Some bikers were even pushing their bags on their bikes, carrying them to the semi-trucks for the day. Not everyone had the same idea. Amid all the whispers and rustlings could be heard snorings.

"How can they sleep?" Sheri asked.

"Some people can sleep through anything," I laughed.

"I don't know about you, but your dad snored all night and I couldn't sleep," sighed Shirley.

"I never heard him. He must have learned how to do it quiet or I really did sleep and didn't know it." When we walked as far as the johns in the dark, we saw there were lines of people waiting in front of each one. Some carried lights and shone them on the door locks to see which ones were used.

"So this was how our mornings are going to be. Maybe we should get up earlier than five." We all stood in different lines and then headed back to the tents to get packed up for the start. It was a long way to the truck to haul our stuff. Walt was ready to go the same time as the rest. We liked to do the usual thing in the bathroom in the morning but this morning we could only use a port-a-john and hope we had water to wash out our eyes and brush our teeth from our drinking bottles.

At the beginning of the tour, a large banner hung over the starting point with MUSCATINE 479 MILES on it. With a little ceremony we were off. I rode with Ken for the first flat five miles. It was only 6:30. The sun was just barely out of bed. The flatness was good. It got the muscles used to riding in the warm, humid atmosphere.

Ken was a much faster rider than I and he left me to ride my speed. I tried to match him but was finding it too much. I didn't want to exhaust myself this early in the week. We only had 50 miles to ride today but I couldn't keep up his pace. Mary was a slow rider. She rode very effortlessly and surely. I rode with the group for a long time. We kept the same pace. Not wanting to get lost in the crowd we stuck together. The whole road was full of riders. No cars. One of the points the Register made to the public was that we were going to be there. Please stay off these roads today. It worked.

Motorists often wonder why people ride a bike long distances. I've often asked myself the same question. The only answer I can give is: exercise. When I became aware of the need to do more strenuous exercise than daily work and keeping a house and chasing children, biking came to mind. Knowing friends who rode, seeming to enjoy it, was another reason. It was fun. Once I was into the sport I became addicted to it, made new friends and expanded my horizons. Now, here in Iowa, my horizons expanded as far as the corn fields would let it. Riders were stretched out across the two lane pavement riding singly, in twos or more and riding at different speeds. Some were silent, intent on their own thoughts in the hot, humid air and those who were conversing or in a party mood, laughing and fooling around like clowns.

Name tags on the backs of bikes had their name and said where a rider was from. Everyone had something different on their bikes. Stuffed animals, a mialbox, a real stuffed pig and flags. It made for a conversation starter in many cases. About ten miles out, we had breakfast. Along the way ranchers set up tables to sell us home made cookies, junk foods, fruit and vegetables ready to eat and drinks. Water was the most needed and we found it in different places. Hoses, milk bottles, huge urns and jugs.

The sun was our enemy. We could not get away from it. Shade was a commodity to be sold. Signs along the way advertised it for a come-on to buy some other ware.

At Emerson, entertainment was mostly booths of food, the inevitable port-a-john lines and crafts. They must have trucked the johns from point to point. Music came in the form of kitchen bands, dance bands or hay wagons loaded with local country players. A booth for a shower contest invited a cool dunking. It was a clear cylinder with water above. A person sat inside while another threw balls at a target for a price. The prize, of course, was given for dunking your favorite person. In reality, the person inside the booth got the real prize. Cool water. Crowds of riders mingled in places like this for hours eating and watching.

Where a rancher had a booth or a service club sold refreshments bikers could be seen from far away sitting on the grass along the roadside. There was a distance of six miles that was gravel covered. "I hope we don't have much of this," cried Mary. "I don't like it."

"I know what you mean. I'd hate to have a blowout on this stuff," I returned. Flats were commonplace.

We only had ten miles to go to Red Oak, our stop for the night. The sun shone unmercilessly, baking our sweaty bodies along the many long hills. Temperature was 87 degrees.

We would stay at Inman Elementary School, not far from the main campground. We made a wrong turn, and went up a hill we didn't have to go up. How disgusting! A pool made us forget the hill. A beautiful cemetery was behind us. American flags lined the whole thing making a nice patriotic look. The VFW donated the flags. Most of the entombed, were veterans.

We quickly got our stuff together and made our home, circling like we were in a wagon train out west. Ken was here before us and was already in the pool. To cool off we would have to stay in the water and turn to prunes. It did refresh and relax our bodies. Our odometers read 59.5 miles and we still got on them and rode back to town for dinner and watched teens dance to rock music. It wasn't our type of dancing. David hooked up with us that night as we rode out of camp, had dinner with us and walked around the entertainment of the town. With the main square blocked off to traffic it became a festival. We never saw him again. Don't know what group he was with or anything.

During the night it became very quiet. I couldn't even hear flip-flops walking past our tent. Then, in the middle of a sound sleep, came the intruding loud honking of horns. Sheri and I both sat up straight in our bags wondering what was going on. "It must just be some local kids. You know, we are probably the only thing that has come into this town in years," whispered Sheri.

"I suppose we would do the same thing if we were in their shoes."

"Go back to sleep."

"Good night."

We awoke at five a.m. to 67 degree temperature. At this school, we were privileged to have real bathrooms and showers to share with our own group of 300. We've been on rides with this many before and have gotten used to waiting in short lines to use the toilet and sink. One would be brushing their teeth, sharing it with someone putting on make-up, or worse, brushing their hair. We did the best we could.

"How did everybody sleep last night?" I asked when we got back to our spot. Seems we all did a good job of getting rest.

"Didn't you hear our welcoming committee, Walt?"

He just smiled his usual smile. He was from a small Missouri town and I wouldn't doubt, did the same thing when he was forty years younger. "Yep, I heard them."

"He was just getting into a nice snore, too."

"Too bad. You don't suppose this will be our usual wake up call every night, do you?"

"No."

"Well, is everybody ready?" It was only 6 a.m. Walt was the slow one of our group. We were always having to wait for him. He must be very methodical in the bathroom. We wiped down our seats if we hadn't covered them last night. The dew was heavy and all the metal parts were soaked.

161

Ken thought he would not ride straight through today. Riding as fast as yesterday tired him out too much. The three of us stayed together till breakfast and then he and Sheri left me to wait at the next town and then we'd all wait for the other three slower riders. We at least kept tabs on each other and still rode at our own paces and with other people.

"Gather our bags when you get in so we don't have to look for them," I teased him in the morning before we left.

"Let me see what I have to look for and how many," Ken returned. Maybe he would do it, maybe not.

Ken was too much for Sheri, too, and he left her less than half way to Autoban, our destination.

The hills were treacherous today. If anyone was to tell me Iowa was flat, I would debate it with them quite seriously! The hills were very long and very high. It was supposed to be 72 miles that day but ended being just one mile longer.

I had to walk the last few feet of one of the hills. Sheri was on ahead and Walt and Shirley were behind me and Mary in the tail. At the top of the hill just before a town, a woman sat on her porch watching the many riders passing her house. I pulled in and talked to her while I waited for the others. Her little three year old tried to show off her prowess on her tricycle. Stopping to talk to the public was something I really enjoyed. They liked that someone did that without asking for something, too. It made friends for bicycling at the same time as giving me a rest. I always was a gabber anyway. I liked to talk to these friendly people. Michigan people weren't friendly.

Walt and Shirley pedaled up the hill without stopping. I ran to the edge of the road to get a picture of them with the long hill in the background. As far as I could see were riders. I could see at least two miles away up and down three hills. It looked like a long roller coaster. Ahead, the town was crowded as everyone stopped to congregate and eat or rest. "Where's Mary?"

She's back there. She said to go on without her. She has lots of company and is used to going at a much slower pace than we."

"Where's Sheri?"

"I haven't seen her. She must still be with Ken. Do you want to eat lunch here?"

"Let's see what they have first," she said.

"How ya' doing, Walt?"

"I'm doing O.K."

"You don't sound too positive. Is this more than you thought?"

"No, I've been here before. I knew how it would be."

"Bet you never thought you'd be riding with all these people though."

"No, I didn't." We found some more things to do here, watched a clown act and ate some hot dogs and ice cream in the sun. Sheri was found eating a dish of fresh vegetables, talking to some others sitting on a picnic table.

"We thought you'd have the tent up by now."

"Yea, what are you doing here?"

"Hey, Ken rides too fast. I can't keep up with him. It was all right for awhile but I just got too hot for that. My knee doesn't feel all that good to book like that either." She hurt it out on the hike along the Colorado River a couple years ago.

"Is it bothering you?"

"Just a little. I'll just have to be more careful.

We arrived by 3:30 in the heat of the day. There were all our bags in a pile. Kens' tent was up but he was nowhere in sight. We hurried to get set up and get to the pool. Walt and Mary took their time. Ken was found in the pool. We all enjoyed the refreshing water and regrouped to find dinner. At the regular campground, a large bill board directed everyone to different places in town that offered food and pools and showers. Another was half filled with notes from one person or group to another.

We left at 6 a.m. the next day to beat that heat. Ken would wait at each town for us. He would say that every day but didn't much heed his own words. We only had 58 miles to go today.

We were in Perry by noon. It was good to beat the worse heat of the day but now we had to find something to do with the rest of the day. It was hot. We didn't see Mary for much of the day after breakfast. "I wonder if she's mad at us for not waiting for her," stated Shirley.

"Let's at least get her stuff together so she won't have hunt for it." We found her clothes bag but not her tent. We looked everywhere for it in the long line of bags on the lawn, and then headed for the pool, hoping she'd find it.

Our camp ground tonight was at a private house. They had a large field out back and we used it and the front yard. Two port-a-johns were set up and a hose for a sprinkle shower. The pool was in town. Several of us left, loading our bikes with clean clothes. Another Ken and another guy pedaled along with us as we went to dinner in a church.

We didn't stay long in town. There wasn't too much to offer. The pool was away from town and we would have to get all sweaty if we rode there and then back. We went back to the house. Shirley and Walt brought some comedy tapes to listen to. We sat around listening to them and laughing, writing in journals, reading and resting in the only shade from our tents. We could sit in the shade in the two-car garage but there weren't enough chairs. Walt did some maintainance of their three bikes. I didn't want him to touch mine. He was putting some grease on their chains that didn't coincide with mine. Nice thought. Sheri would roll up her eyes at dads' efforts. "I wish he'd leave my bike alone. It doesn't need that kind of stuff on the chain," she'd say.

"He better not get overzealous and do mine," I quipped. Just then, he approached mine. I got up and saved my bike from its' fate. "It's O.K., Walt. I took care of that before I left home. It won't need anything for a couple more days."

"O.K. just thought you might like it to ride smoother."

"It's riding smooth enough, thanks."

Mary came in and was not upset but didn't go to the pool. She washed up in the hose shower even if it was cold. She did go to dinner in town with someone she rode with some of the day.

We packed along some instant coffee and a sterno can with a couple spare cups. "Why don't we play like campers and make some coffee, Shirley? Do you have any junk food left?"

"I've got some regular coffee, not the decaffeinated stuff you have and some cookies."

"I've got the sterno, let's put it to use." Nobody wanted any until we got the odor passed around in the shade of our tent. Then a couple decided it would be a good idea. We had all the cold drinks we wanted in the baggage truck, but somehow relaxing in the shade, coffee and cookies sounded good.

That night, someone found a tape deck with speakers for all to hear and we played the tape to the crowd on the back porch to hear. Giggles and snickers were heard off in the tent area. We sat around in the garage and porch talking with our hosts who were just some very nice Iowans. The Dwight Fazels.

We were all very rested by our 5:45 a.m. leaving time in the morning. We had the option to ride 100 miles today. "I'm not riding any 100 miles," I said. "You guys can if you want. I'm having a hard enough time getting in the 88 we have to do today."

"I'll wait till we get to St. Anthony where the option is," replied Shirley. "You want to, Walt?"

"We'll see. I'm not committing myself this soon." Sheri was all for it and so was Ken. Mary wouldn't and neither was I. But if the ride went well I would think about it in St. Anthony some 70 miles into the day.

We had hardly any breakfast, no fault of anyone. Melon and cookies didn't seem like much to eat. Lunch consisted of two skinny hot dogs. We all rode apart again. Walt and Shirley stayed together. Ken waited for Sheri, they waited for me and we waited for Walt and Shirley. We didn't wait for Mary who told us to go on.

164

It was sometimes hours before we could regroup. I rode along with others, discussing other rides we were on. Everyone usually wore some sort of t-shirt advertising a ride in their home state. There were many who wore as little as they could in the heat, but everyone had such a positive attitude on life it was a pleasure to be one of them. I stopped several times for snow cones sold by service clubs from their trailers. They moved each day to a new place on someone's lawn. Some of the residents would dress up as clowns to get your business. A few miles from town cardboard signs were erected to tell of meals in churches, parks or fire departments. They were feeding a moving army and really knew how to put on a feed bag. I didn't feel like eating all the time but probably should have eaten more than I did for the energy.

At St. Anthony, the others did the extra miles. I had no desire. Instead, I stood on the street corner talking to some local people who came to town to see our parade. I theorized a person could sit themselves out at the beginning of the day's ride to count the riders and would have to sit for 24 hours to count them all. Everyone left on their own and some before dawn while others left late and rode in the early evening. We heard there were many more than just 7,500 riders, closer to 12,000.

I would ride out slow till the others caught up with me. Then I saw an older gentleman sitting on his porch in the sun with his dog, watching the parade. I stopped to sit with him a while and then on another porch with a big group of folks who offered me some cold lemonade. They were such a delight! All inquired about our bikes and the gears and such, watching the antics nearby and the continuous flow streaming by their house. I might not have explained everything to them the way I should, but gave them my views as we explored the sanity of riding in this traveling circus.

The hills bothered me more that day than usual. It could have been the sitting around in the shade, not eating enough or the extra miles. I was sure I could be better by the next day.

Even though they took the extra ride around, we still came in around two or three in the afternoon. Still too hot. My butt hurt and so did theirs. They all said the extra miles weren't bad. The worse part was riding against the strong wind.

I couldn't find my prescription sunglasses when the sun came up in the morning and surmised I left them at Fazel's house where we stayed the night before. I asked the baggage truck driver for a ride back or if I could call them and he produced the glasses. Yes, I left them in their bathroom.

We sat around in the shade of the baggage truck exploring our options for the night. We could get a shower across the street in a house. Residents who would offer showers to us displayed a

"Shower a Biker" sign in their window. "I don't want to do that," sighed Sheri wrinkling up her nose.

"Why not, it's a public service and we are ambassadors of good bicycling to take their offer," I came back. The others didn't want to either so we trudged our tired bodies to the school shower room a half mile away.

We were far enough from town and there were enough of us that the city provided shuttle service. We just jumped aboard and they made a circuit to the several pools, downtown areas where we could eat, party or mingle and to the main groups lodgings at the fairgrounds field.

We waited for the bus while sitting on the coolers after we were all cleaned up. The other Ken always came out of the shower with some unique t-shirt he found in some unknown place. Todays' touted a road kill picture. A black cat spread-eagled with bicycle tracks over his inert body.

In town, we wedged between the crowd to hear singers, and see dancers entertain us. We ate ice cream cones and one of the 2" thick pork chops grilled in the open. The griller usually stationed himself about 25 miles out of each town to sell them. Somehow, some of us could not bike on pork chops at eight in the morning. Having enough of the revelry, we'd find a bus and circle the town to see where other clubs put up their people. Some elected to stay at individuals homes that were prearranged months before the ride. Usually tent space in the backyard but with house privileges.

We all started again early the next day. I would be happy to sleep past 7 a.m. one day. We were all supposed to meet at the pork chop place but today it was set out 32 miles from town. Instead, we had breakfast in the next town for only $1.50.

The wind picked up. I heard it was 30 m.p.h. and we were headed for the Bohemian mountains. We didn't know what they were, but were just told that by the baggage man. It was a tough day. Only 76 miles. We should be used to it but the wind and hot sun did not make it easier. Our butts hurt more each day.

We would stay at the high school in Belle Plaine that night, walking distance from town. A masseuse looked like he was helping some very sore people feel better. We filed into the warm water showers and on the way in, I made an appointment. A long line was waiting for him to ply his trade. OH! What good, strong hands he had. He rubbed out soreness in my legs. I didn't want to have him quit. The other girls declined this wonderful treatment. By the feel of it, I would need this treatment every night.

Wandering in town for our usual jaunt, I told them I had to find a pharmacy for something to put on my genital area. It was torn enough to promote bleeding in fine tears. "Walt said he was having trouble there, too," offered Shirley. The pharmacist recommended Hydrocortesone.

"You people should know better than ride in those pants with the chamois seats," he chided.

"Those are the official bike rider's wear," I corrected. "They're made so we can spend longer periods of time in the saddle without saddle sores."

"But you do have saddle sores," he reminded me. "You use this stuff and give the area plenty of air. The problem is that the chamois doesn't breathe. You sweat and it has no place to go. It becomes an irritant."

"That's true. I'll give it a try. Thanks for the information. Maybe I'll stand tomorrow."

We watched the festivities in town. Some kids were doing tricks on those little bikes for hours. Quite a show. We watched a troop of mimes go through their antics to a loud round of applause. Upon return I offered some Hydrocortezone to Walt who was lying in the tent resting. Shirley and Sheri stayed in town to browse some more. Ken was around somewhere doing his own thing. I went in the tent to apply the cream and treat with air. Hard to do in a camp full of people without zipping up the door. It was so hot and humid I didn't want to do that. I draped my sheet over my backside till it got dark enough not to be seen.

We no sooner got ourselves settled in to a humid night of sleep later, when a bull horn announcement came booming across the open school field. "Take cover in the school building. The National Weather Service has issued a tornado warning. A tornado has been sighted and we could be in its' path. We may only get the severe thunderstorm accompanying it but we don't want to take the chance. You have 10 minutes."

The message was repeated as the speaker roamed the grounds in the dark. "Oh, God, Sheri! Are you going to go?"

"I'm not staying here," she said as she pulled on some clothes.

"Mom, Dad, did you hear that?"

"We're up," they shouted back against the coming winds.

"Maybe it won't be that bad," I said as I tried to find my stuff in the dark. It started to rain as we spoke.

"Hurry, up," she yelled. "Mom, are you getting it on?"

"We're taking the tent down already." It started to thunder with the rain. We gathered up stuff and just rolled it up in a ball and ran for shelter some distance away up a long incline. Everyone was running and yelling at each other carrying as much of their belongings as they could. I dumped my load in a corner of the school building and looked for Mary and Ken in the dark. Mary was already inside, leaving her tent on the grounds. I couldn't find the others as I ran back outside.

The wind picked up furiously and the rain pelted me with needle sharp drops. I found the place where I thought we were camped, only to find everything gone. I searched around to find the bikes. We would leave them there, locked together in a stack but I couldn't find them. Hardly anyone was left. A few tents were there blowing in the stiff winds. I spotted Kens'. "Are you in there?" I called to the tent.

"Yea, I'm staying here. It'll be o.k."

"You're crazy. You won't last out here if the tornado hits."

"It won't. I'm staying." He unzipped the door a little.

"Can I wait it out with you? The school stinks and its early. I'll never get any sleep in there. My tents down."

"Come on," he said as he unzipped the whole door and zipped it quickly shut against the rain.

I didn't want him to get the wrong idea but I was cold from that wind and rain and it would be nice to share the storm with someone other than the 300 in a smelly school hallway where everyone was piled on their wet belongings.

"Here, dry yourself off," he said as he gave me a towel. I was only wearing a tank top and running shorts. My feet hurt from running through the field on stones and gear and tripping on tent guy ropes. We huddled together while it continued to rain and I was dry, then I found a comfortable place to sleep on his bag. He carried a sheet that helped keep both of us warm throughout the night except for my feet. The storm quit after an hour and we slept undisturbed the rest of the night.

By five a.m., I was up to find the others in the school. Walking into the building I was glad I stayed in the tent. The smell was overpowering. People were sleeping anywhere there was a flat space, their belongings piled in wet blobs all around them. Some were snoring, others were up and trying to make some sense out of their mess. The lights were turned off in most of the hallways so in the dimness it was hard to sort out anything.

The girls were not near where I thought they should be. They must have moved to more comfortable quarters in the night. I found them in the bathroom. Then it was a matter of getting our own things together so we could start another long day on the road. Maybe it wouldn't be as hot now that the storm cooled things down.

"Where were you?" they asked when they saw me.

"When I went out to get the other stuff, I couldn't find anyone. Ken was still in the tent and wasn't moving so I stayed with him," I explained.

"I made two trips. When I came back, I didn't see anyone or anything. I thought you were in the school. All I saw were the bikes," said Sheri.

"I couldn't even find the bikes. They weren't where I thought they should be and I kept running around looking for them."

"Yea, sure, you just didn't want to sleep in the school with us," she teased.

"Walt did real good on such short notice," said Shirley. "We even folded the tent up."

"You didn't do that in the storm!"

"Yea, in the storm."

"She didn't do it in the storm, they repacked it in the school when they couldn't sleep. I packed ours, too."

"Well, I got some good sleep snuggled in Ken's tent, and don't worry your little heads off. Nothing happened."

"Oh, darn, I thought you were going to tell us some really good stuff!"

"Come on, let's get loaded," I said as I walked away from her tease.

Even with the cooler night wind, it did not change the day's temperatures or humidity. The wind was in our tails or side most of the day. We had to make Washington that day, 82 miles south. To look at things you would never know it rained unless you used a corn field for a bathroom. Feet came out with mud caked to them. To know where a rancher did not mind you using their field you looked for a roll of toilet paper on a stick. It was not courteous to use one unless invited, they told us. They wanted to be invited back.

We learned a lot about the state and how they ran this prestigious tour. Most of the cities in the state bid on having the group. A lot was at stake. We spent an enormous amount of money and every year the tour grew to an astounding 17,000 riders with the added support team. We bought goods on the road from ranchers as well as the service groups in the towns and cities. They entertained us well. It promoted their lifestyle, too. The tour paid them fees for usage of fields, schools, busses.

But the Iowans themselves were most gracious to have us there. They were the friendliest people I have ever met, always wanting to help in anyway they could. The use of their facilities was a major concern and most gladly gave whatever they had. I, personally found only one household that backed away from letting me use their bathroom in a crisis. I was allowed to use their personal corn field out back instead.

Ken was in first as usual, with Sheri hot on his trail. I lost the trail to the school grounds, delaying me awhile. We couldn't just follow the crowd like we did on the roads. Everyone had their own camp area to find. We would make friends with someone all day and they would go off to wherever they were to camp. We usually looked for our truck when we were closest to the main group which wasn't

169

often. They put a large green flag on the truck proclaiming them the Out-of-Stater's Club making it much easier for us to find them.

Ken was realizing how much better it was to ride and wait. He was more relaxed as he rode and not so tired at the end of the day. The three of us rode together more that day than most. Mary was still doing her own thing and she sometimes accompanied us out at night and sometimes not. I thought she was upset with us but she usually did things the way she wanted to do them and it didn't matter we didn't agree with them she told us.

With the humidity, I found I drank more water than ever before. I didn't seem to ever get sated. I don't know where it went. I hardly ever needed to use the rows of port-a-johns or the corn fields like the others. It was determined by all of us that it just evaporated. We were all getting a nice brown to our bodies and used a tremendous amount of lotions during the day and after showers. It also evaporated or was absorbed in our dry skin.

In town, we did our usual browsing and looked over the general campground wares. We bought more shirts. They were cheaper now the tour was almost over. The best ones went early. I found a gold necklace with a bicycle charm at a jewelry store. That has been coveted by many people since. Shirley found some ear rings to take home as souvenirs.

We rode through the large town of Tallyrand, population 11. They also sold shirts with a pig on them and their town name. Iowa is known for their pork as well as corn. We could tell we were nearing a pig farm from a mile away. It was enough to clear our sinuses of any congestion we might have as we rode past. It was especially awful if we were passing it on an uphill, breathing hard.

We watched the hoard of people dance on into the night, drinking untold amounts of beer. Some of these bikers never slept. They rode and partied. We all slept well this night.

Our last day came. Inwardly, I was glad of it. I had enough of trying to get to the end of the day without dying on the way. I liked the party effort but it was getting to wear on me. I wasn't used to a week-long party. We only had 53 miles that day and it should be easier than the miles we had on other days. The terrain was flat for a change and we all waited for each other at each stopover.

We had breakfast in a bar. The owner was not alerted we were coming through his town and did not prepare for the onslaught. We waited and waited for someone to take our orders. When we could see they were having trouble keeping up, we dove right in to help.

"Sheri, let's help them out. Clean off the tables. Shirley, you're good at taking orders. Why don't you take orders for those folks over there." Walt just kinda slid dishes around the tables for us to gather. Ken and Mary were way ahead or way behind. The waitress looked at us in surprise and we just kept on helping.

"Thank you," she said, so frustrated with so many people. "I've called the owner and he's sending over some more help.

"That's O.K., we don't mind helping. What can we do?"

"Whatever your little hearts desire," she said breathlessly as she ran to try cooking some eggs. We washed dishes and even cooked our own breakfast, making bacon, eggs and toast. We didn't think we should do someone else's. Coffee was distributed so fast Shirley had a hard time keeping the pots full. It was fun and it didn't hurt us a bit. Other bikers couldn't believe we were doing it and began helping us a little. They cleaned off their tables when they were done and went on their way. We didn't take money, we let the girl do that. Help came and we went on our way, paying for our meal but tipping ourselves. It was enough that we waited on ourselves.

Through Lone Tree, a fire station set up a shower for us to run through over the street. A long rod with holes in it sprayed us as we went past. How refreshing! I went through a couple times. The others went around. We met Ken again and he ran through. We dried off in minutes.

In Muscatine, we were greeted with the townspeople all cheering our return. Musicians were set up on sidewalks playing any style music imaginable. Revelers were still partying and we made our trip to the river with the others to dunk our wheels and ourselves in it. What fun we had!

Our mileage ran almost 50 miles farther than the proposed 476 miles. It was added because we rode our bikes into town after getting in for the day. That was minus the extra miles the others put on doing the 100 mile day. We said our farewells to our new friends and hoped we would see them again sometime. Mary was in town before we were that time. She did not stop to make breakfast and bust tables. She was already showered and found our truck and car and waited for us. We said good-bye to our tour director, and the Korean college student who did our bags and supplied our cold drinks every day. We were on the private list for next year and wanted to return. The route was changed every year and they never revealed it to anyone before hand.

................I stopped in a restaurant for a cup of coffee and roll for a rest, talking to a few people who were interested in knowing where I was going. "Do you know where Brighton is?" I asked them.

"No, but isn't it somewhere in the lower?" asked Jenny.

"Do you know where Ann Arbor is?" I prompted.

"Oh, yes. Way down there?"

It seemed like such a long distance to them and to me. From here it would be almost a five hour drive by car to my home. I explained where I intended to go with Shirley and they all approved until we split. Too long to go alone, they said. I recounted the RAGBRAI thoughts I had with myself to them and about the another adventure...................

Chapter 2

One Day Ride
Across Michigan

..................."We didn't think we would go back to Iowa again," I explained to Barbara, Jenny and Ted.

"Why not? Was it that bad?" he asked.

"It was fun and we did get a lot of respect from other riders like we thought we would. But we didn't savor riding that hard every day," I tried to tell them. We probably rode more than 450 miles in Iowa the next year.

"That's a long way. I don't know how you can do it," sighed Barbara.

"It isn't bad. You have to get used to it slowly. You can't just one day say you're going to ride across Iowa, you know. We gradually get used to it in the winter by riding our bikes on training stands in the house. At least I do. My friend, who isn't here, is hardier than I and just waits for spring. So does her daughter. But she has an exercycle in her house that I think she rides occasionally."

"I couldn't ride around the block." Looking at her I would guess she got very little exercise, and eating a very fattening breakfast with her skinny husband who just drank coffee.

"Well, I guess I'd better get going. It's too nice of a day to waste it here inside even if it is nice talking to you. Why don't you sign my journal?"

"Sure," said Ted, "I'd love to. Remember us when you're out there riding around. We'll pray for you and that you get home safely."

"Why, thank you, I appreciate your thought." I left and repacked my journal and wallet in my paniers and attached my helmet to my head. Slipping my feet in the toe clips, I pulled back out onto the road.

RAGBRAI the next year was a lot better. Of course, we had many more miles under our seats every year that passed. I was averaging 2500 miles a year by this time. Much better than that first year of only 400 before we went on DALMAC. Iowas' terrain is much flatter. "Someone must have heard us complain about the hills last year, Shirley," I'd say as we whizzed along.

Mary talked us into doing what is called the "Hilly Hundred" in southern Indiana, her home state. We thought we were in great shape and could handle it after doing RAGBRAI XIV. It was held in the fall when the weather was cooler and it was for two days of fifty miles each.

We never thought there could be this many hills anywhere. We walked up several. Much different than Iowa. These hills were quick and short. Vertical would be a good description. What was I doing there? After those two days, we said we'd never do it again and to date, have not. We get a lot of respect wearing that t-shirt, too.

Another respect ride was the time we decided to ride across the state of Michigan in one day. Now, talk about being a glutton for punishment, this should have been the ultimate punishment! Shirley refused to ride. Sheri, friend Gregg Mallow and I rode. Shirley was SAG driver for us, catering to our needs along the 152 mile route.

Since we were going to be so crazy as to attempt to do this, I suggested we take some kind of bet from people that we could do it. Sheri was not for that. She didn't want to take money or even ask for it until I said, "Why don't we take pledges to finish? We can give the money to a charity."

"That wouldn't be so bad. Which one?"

"How about Special Olympics?

"O.K." We only approached our co-workers. They knew we would attempt to do such a feat and probably finish it. A sure thing for us.

We started in the early morning in October in the dark. Only 100 hardy riders showed up for the event. It was the first time it was done. We were among 25 other women riding along but the rest looked like very young, crazy guys who thought they were more macho than they were.

The state park hosted us overnight on Lake Michigan. We would go to the east hoping for westerly winds if we had any and end in another state park on Lake Huron. No provisions were offered. It was an endurance ride only we few thought we could master. We were encouraged to do it by Denny, the host with whom we participated in other rides over the years.

In the evening before, we watched the gold ball dip into Lake Michigan leaving a red sky. I remembered the old addage "Red sky at night, sailors delight; Red sky in morning, sailors take warning" and hoped it wouldn't be red by morning. The water was calm as it lapped at our toes. Gregg stripped down to trunks and ran into the lake for a late swim. "Too cold for me," I said. The others agreed. We walked along the beach in the twilight, content to just get our feet wet. Morning would soon be upon us, we didn't want cramping in the legs to stop us now.

174

In the dark at 5 a.m., we gathered together for instructions before setting out without lights to guide us. Gregg had something wrong at the last minute and Sheri went off to help. She was riding strong this year and he had no trouble himself. "I'll start out then. You'll catch up shortly, O.K?"

"Yea, go ahead, we'll be right there." I started to get in line in the glow of some flashlights and with the extra aid of car lights. I had no lights on my bike. There wasn't any street lighting. We pulled out onto the empty tree-lined road behind the start car. Some riders had lights strapped to their arms or on fronts of their bikes. Cars were supposed to follow us to give us some semblance of light until dawn. We got the call to start.

It was a cool morning. I wore ear muffs, gloves and flannel shirt over a t-shirt and tank top shirt and bike shorts. I could take layers off, if needed. I had a handlebar bag for such times. We decided it would be best to carry as little as possible. We carried tire repair kits and water and maybe some fruit to sustain us.

We began an odyssey I knew I could finish. I didn't know many of the other riders. I had a hard time seeing in the dark and keeping up with the lead car. We laughed and talked as we scooted down the road in the dark. Then we spread out as faster riders went on ahead. I saw a rider with a tail light. I thought if I could keep him in my sight I would know where to turn. He was going too fast for me so I had to put my body in high gear. It was too early in the morning for that but I didn't want to fail. I didn't hear my riding partners anywhere yet. I wondered what was detaining them. Gregg had a light, I thought. We could at least see the map if we had to. I refrained from turning around to see if anyone was behind me in the quiet for fear of losing my tail light guide. What was I doing here?

"Aren't we supposed to turn pretty soon?" asked someone. There was someone behind me. Good.

"I think so. There's a road just ahead. See that street light? I think it's the corner light."

"That guy up there turned. See him?"

"Maybe he knows the route."

"I don't know, but I think we oughta follow him." We followed him and then he was gone past me and I felt alone again. It finally turned a little lighter with the dawn. I never saw the lead car after the start.

In the first town, the map was wrong. Others were on the corner trying to figure it out. It became foggy, they all headed to the right. I followed after they yelled something about being surprised I was just behind them. I got the idea that they thought women weren't tough enough to do this ride. I wanted to prove them wrong.

The hills were few. The middle of our state is flat, but the hills, if any, only near Lake Michigan and I hoped they would stay there.

175

We had to really push hard to get done before dark. With the time change just weeks before we were no longer saving daylight. I rode as hard as I could and as fast as I could. I wanted to get as many miles as possible under my seat.

Shirley passed me one time after the sun came out at about the thirty five mile mark. I threw my flannel shirt in the truck, ate some food we kept in the cooler in the back, refilled my water bottles and got caught up on Sheri and Greggs' progress.

"I haven't seen them for the last couple hours. I know I've followed the wrong road myself once. They had a flashlight when they started but I haven't seen them."

"Don't worry, too much. At least she isn't alone. What was the matter with Gregg?"

"His back was hurting. I think he was doing some stretch exercises or something before he left. That swim last night might have been the culprit."

"Well, I'm going to keep going. I'll stay on the road. I'll keep my bike in sight if I have to get off of it."

"I'm going back to see where they might have gone now that its light."

"O.K. With this sun out now, the fog has burned off and we can see.

I couldn't believe it. I had put 75 miles on by the time I reached Blanchard. I was feeling good. One half done. I ran into a store and bought a couple peanut butter cups while waiting for the familiar brown truck to show or Sheri and Gregg. Only one or two other riders were here. Another surprised look that I was still here. I called home from a phone booth to tell the good news and how good my progress was going. Mom was happy for me as usual. I could always count on her to be behind me in my crazy stunts.

I rode up and down the streets looking for my two itinerant friends, when I spotted them. Gregg had to lay down a few times to stretch his back. They could ride faster than they were going but his back was holding them up. It made me feel good just to stay in front of them. I went on ahead as long as I knew they weren't far behind. Good incentive for me.

Clouds formed shortly and it began to rain. I was glad I brought all the right stuff to wear but now the rain gear was in the truck with my warm flannel shirt. Turning a corner I saw a log cabin grocery store. I pulled in to get out of the rain and buy some replenishments of food when Shirley pulled in behind me. "Boy, I'm glad you're here. Good timing."

I hopped in the back end and changed my wet shirt into dry one, no longer caring if anyone could see or not. I had nothing to hide that somebody else didn't have. Slapping my rain jacket on, I hollered to her, "See ya' down the road."

176

Another twenty five miles, the rain quit and I had to do something with the rain jacket. Off it came while I devoured another apple and banana. Another ten miles and it was time for lunch. Shirley parked in a town and I put away a sandwich and fruit drink when the other two showed.

"Gregg is really hurting," reported Sheri inside the truck out of ear shot. He was laying on the grass, stretching his back out again.

"Do you want some Doans' Pills, Gregg?" I asked out the door.

"No, I'll be all right. I took some Excedrin. I'll take some again as soon as it's time. I'll just lie here and eat for awhile and rest it."

"Well, I'd be a lot farther on if it wasn't for his back. I thought I'd better stay with him," replied Sheri, digging into the cooler.

"I'm going to keep going. I can't believe I'm feeling so good yet and only forty miles to go. Can you believe this?"

"No, I feel good, too. It's not as bad as I thought. We got caught back there in the rain storm but I had my rain jacket I was using for a wind break and didn't get real soaked. Either did Gregg. It felt kinda cold though, didn't it?"

"Yea, but your mom was right there when I needed her for clothes. I got wet. Sure glad I brought more than I needed. I'm gone. See you at the next stop."

"O.K. Be careful."

Off I went. I was beginning to feel the last forty miles. I was feeling it in my butt and my legs. The other two caught up for awhile. Then they were gone on ahead and I was left to try to finish. We never rode more than 109 miles in one day before. This would be a feat of real endurance. I stopped more often, down to every five miles. At the end of my rope at one rest break, I told Shirley I only said I would do 150 miles. "Meet me at this corner. On the map that looks like it says 150 miles. I'm not going any farther."

She agreed and I saw her several miles away from the 150 mile mark as she approached the corner without stopping.

"Shirley, where are you going?" I called out in agony. I was getting so tired. Did she not believe me? Did she want me to finish the whole thing? Her daughter was on ahead and looked like she would, but now I was tired and my back was hurting. I pedaled on for two more miles. What was I doing here? There she was in the light of the gas station. It was getting dark fast. If I hurried I could be there before she left. I didn't want to be on the road in the dark anyway.

"I thought you were going to make me ride the whole thing," I complained breathlessly.

"It's not that much farther. I thought you were just kidding."

"Come on, Shirley, this is me you're talking to, remember?"

"How many miles did you go?"

"My odometer reads 152 miles. Sheri is going to have a lot more since they got lost in the morning," I said as we drove in to find them. They did do 158 miles in their extra effort. There was no fanfare at the park when we came in. We got a congratulations from the other guys who looked at me and were wondering what I, a female, was doing riding today. I felt good about that. They knew I wasn't any wimp, anyway. I knew I wasn't a wimp. Either was Sheri.

We collected over $350 for the Special Olympics. We felt more special ourselves when we found we were the only females who finished the whole ride. It was advertised to be 150 miles. We knew we could ride just about anywhere with that and proudly wore the t-shirt only few had.

For several years now we rode another group ride that wasn't quite as adventurous as that. It was too tame for me. But it was a good one to do for a week early in the summer season.

Chapter 3   PALM

PALM means Pedal Across Lower Michigan. If we traveled the north-south route and across the middle we might just as well cross at the lower end, we thought. It was advertised as being quite tame and catered to children. We were children at heart. To make it nicer, we took Shirley's two grandchildren with us, aged 10 and 12. Activities were planned for all and to make the riding less painful for the kids.

We planned on tubing down the Muskegon River the next day. Every night the whole group gathered in the school gymnasiums to hear about weather and to be warned about the bad habits of some of the new riders. It was a good learning experience for newcomers and kids.

Here we were again with the early risers. At 4 a.m. we could hear zippers opening tent doors. We only had to ride 39 miles today and there was no need to get up that soon, so we slept in to 5:45 a.m. The tubing would not be done today. It rained. It rained all day. There weren't any fun places to stop and everyone was getting crabby. Sheri had trouble with her brakes but let them go unfixed till later.

The rain lasted so long the officials had to make decisions to let us sleep inside the school or let us take chances of kids catching colds outside. When we arrived the decision was: inside. The schools insurance and liability is in question when they do this. No sooner did we stake out a claim inside when the sun came out. We put three of the four tents up and slept out. Shirley slept inside.

Some of the meals offered were not that great on the ride. We opted to buy them out in towns that had enough restaurants to provide it. Our better friends, Deanne and Steve bought their meal. They also had another couple with them from Seattle, who just came for the ride. How nice! We walked to town to find our meal and promised to wait for them to finish the school meal and have a beer with them. They found us later. They waited so long for dinner, they changed their minds and ate out. It was a slow day. It turned nicer in the afternoon. We only averaged 13 m.p.h. One steep hill gave us a speed of 26 m.p.h. Not as fast as I have ever gone before

179

but the best for the day. Even our odometers on our bikes were better than the ones we used to have.

.....................As I ride along on my own here in the Upper Peninsula, I am riding at a speed of 18 m.p.h. or slower. The odometer sits on the handlebars and tells me not only how fast or slow I'm going, but how many times my feet make a full circle in the pedals, called cadence, what my maximum speed, average speed is and the time it takes to do whatever miles I had gone, and the total miles. It even tells me the time and I can set it like a stop watch and it beeps. So many improvements. Some have a pulse monitor......................

Grandma and kids ate breakfast out of the grocery store while Sheri and I opted for a real breakfast eighteen miles down the road. We waited for them with another fellow who rode with us and then the kids wanted a real breakfast, too. Passing Steve and Deanna on a dam with their friends we continued to a fruit stand where we found Gregg was lounging around. Off and on the rest of the day we rode comfortably and easy trying not to push the kids. Our chains were pretty dry from yesterday's rain and today's gravel. Gregg carried some lubricant with him and we were saved from wearing the chain out.

Since we got in too early, we were sitting around doing nothing. Sheri and I offered to help unload the bags into the gynasium. It is quite a sight for a first timer to see 700 or more duffle bags expelled out the baggage truck on the ground. It can be quite a trick to find your own when everyone uses the same color. Khaki was the color of this tour. At least half of the bags were that color. Imagine what it was like in Iowa!

Breakfast was bad. We packed up our dewey tents and were on our way for another leisurely day. Sheri and I went on ahead again and rode with Arnold and son David till .lunch, eating with them in a restaurant. The others caught up with us and we stayed together the rest of the day finding a cold water creek to play in.

Shoes and socks came off quickly to splash around. It wasn't long before a dozen more riders stopped to enjoy the water and we got out and fled down the road leaving them to have their turn at playing.

Met an older fellow who had just fixed some ladies' flat tire. His hands were greasy black from her chain. I offered some hand cleaner from my tire bag and was thanked for it the rest of the trip. He was a tight hugger and it became our way of greeting each other for the rest of our acquaintance.

Sheri and Gregg took an optional twenty mile ride making their day just 68 miles. Dinner was a huge salad bar, much better than what was offered at school. A magic show was in store for the entertainment.

We all got burned today. Catching up with Steve and Deanna, we found that Steve did another option of 100 miles today while Deanne entertained their guests. Century rides are commonplac on most rides. The DALMAC ride had one for all four days. We talked Deanna into her first century last year and she was so proud of herself. All you get for them is a patch that says you did them. We have so many patches and no place to put them any more that winning a patch doesn't enter our enthusiasm stream.

The next day was 90 degrees and no real places offered things to do to break the day. In camp, the school opened the pool for us. It was cold but nobody cared. Three hours later and many more conversations with new and old friends, we were invited to go dancing in town. Our own group were having dancing in the gymnasium, so we went there first. It was to records and it was mainly for kids. We walked into town to a bar and found there wasn't any music. Another mile away we found the invitor and stayed until late into the night. Grandma took the kids back earlier and the rest of us stayed late.

Back in camp, we tip-toed as best we could in the dark field trying not to trip over bikes and tent guy ropes. We could hear an assortment of snores and giggles and even a few noises from the rear. The dew was already settling on the tents and ground.

Frankenmuth is always a fun place to spend some time. It was on the agenda today and we did just that. We toured the brewery, got a free beer and generally browsed around eating ice cream and looking. Frank Kral, the hugger, was searching for a packable kite. We shopped all over without finding just the right one. I rode with him more today. He was interesting to talk to. He was in his seventies, lost his wife some time ago and decided the only way to stay young was to get out with a younger crowd. He has traveled all over the country now and rides many of our states' rides and helps out any way he can. He said he wasn't helping any more people with flat tires. He didn't carry grease remover. He gave me many tips that I still use. The only one I could give him was the hand cleaner.

Donald and Sherilyn were doing very well on the trip. I clocked Donald against his Grandma's wishes at 22 m.p.h. sprint on his new but clunker of a bike. This was their second time doing this ride. The first year they had worse bikes. Donald was our repairman. Every night he would look over everyones' bike to see if anything needed fixing, grease the chains, adjust brakes and all that stuff.

181

We let him ply his new trade as best we could. Most times it was useful. We taught him how to do things and he taught us a few. He was only 10.

I rode at a good clip for most of the day and then took Donald in tow for the rest. He kept complaining that Grandma and Sherilyn rode too slow. He liked riding my speed which was slower for his benefit but not a lot. I didn't want to discourage him. Ernie rode with us for the last few miles. He was a promoter of foreign rides. He kept instigating me to go to Denmark to ride.

In camp, Frank was there to give me my hug a couple times. He was doing that every time he wasn't on his bike, at rest stops, in stores and at school.

A festival was in town and we all bought white Bicentennial sweat shirts at a museum and had our pictures taken dressed in them. Our last night was always a slide show of all of the riders along the six day event in any given pose. We all watched to see if we were in any and laughed at most of them. With 350 riders, we joined a camaraderie with all. We recognized everyone in the slides and became a tight knit group by the last day, something that happens on long trips with strangers.

The statistics showed the oldest to be 72 and the youngest, 6, who all rode the entire 326 miles. Everyone was praised for doing a fine job and we were off to find the rest of the festival in town, walking several miles.

A tent was set up in a field where dancing and a lot of beer drinking was going on for a long time by the time we got there. Too many rowdy "Hells' Angels". We walked around the carnival, ate elephant ears and walked through the Hall of Mirrors.

In town at an old fashioned saloon, we saw other friends, Chris and Bob. We stopped in and had another beer with them on this last night. I left with Grandma and the kids to go to bed by midnight. Gregg and Sheri stayed till after closing and by 3:15 we were all awakened by a loud siren. It was usually a good way to warn everyone of a tornado and many got up and ran to the school building with their kids. I sat there trying to figure it out in the still night air when I finally gave up wondering why it was still blowing and went to sleep. Later, I found it was an accident victim in a car that needed help, but the siren ran too long even for that.

Our destination was Port Huron on Lake Huron. As a finale, we were to be escorted over the Blue Water bridge into Canada. Since we wouldn't go through customs, negotiations had to be sorted out when we arrived while we waited and gathered. We all wore the same emerald green t-shirts for our last ride. We gathered outside of town and paraded through with escort and then over the bridge. We looked nice together after a week of being rowdy. Parents pulling buggers with kids, tandems, and a lot of young kids riding themselves with the others in the rear. On the other side, we were all penned into a fenced yard to be escorted back and then to dispurse for our trip home.

A final picnic was in order with pizza and McDonald salads and more fruit. As we ate, clouds came over and dumped their load on us. We all ran for cover and then the sun was back again. It was a scramble to find our bags and readjust our bikes for the final ride on the trucks and buses only to do this same procedure another time.

Chapter 4   RAGBRAI Again!

....................I kept the riding cadence of about 75 along U.S. 2, rounding the curves into a park at Cut River. A park on the north side of the road was waiting for me to stop for a rest. Picnic table seats would be a welcome reprieve from the bike seat for awhile.

I thought about our next year in Iowa. Mary didn't want to return this time. Just the four of us. She said she did it once and it was enough. We wanted to have another go at it. I don't know why. Maybe we hoped the roads would be better. We wouldn't know till we were given maps at the start point and then we, the out-of-staters, didn't know the terrain anyway.

We were in luck. It turned out to be the best ride we had in that state. Enough to make us believe it would be very hilly the following year and we should refuse. They couldn't possibly have two good years without a bad year. From people who rode this every year, we were told about the south and its' monster hills. The south was due to come.

We began RAGBRAI XV in Onawa and would travel to Guttenburg. The weather was the only real thing that did not change. Waiting for the morning again to be bused to Onawa, we spent time eating an incredible white fish wrapped around a wild rice dinner in a Bar-n-Grill. A paddle wheeler was having a "Booze-Cruise" later that evening. We bought tickets and had an exceptional time aboard while they plied the paddles over the Mississippi River. A band played "fifties" music for dancing on the top platform. We drank a few beers and danced the night away in the warm air. We could view the river for only a short time and then it was only twinkling lights affording us any kind of idea what was out there.

At the city park, the rest of the bikers were revving up for the week of partying. We could see this was going to be another non-sleep week.

Bussed to Onawa, we started by camping right behind the reception center where a red carpet was layed out for us. It rained in the morning and cleared up by our arrival. The grounds were saturated. A spigot was our companion and it was well used from teeth brushing to cat baths. We expected to swim away in the morning from its overuse. A pool was nearby and we spent the rest of our afternoon lolling in it.

One of the nice things about having the Register sponser this ride is the publicity and daily paper just for us. In it could be found trivial information and important things like: where food was offered, pools and showers, just as before. Some of the trivia interested us: 90,000 people have ridden since its conception15 years ago; all 50 states and some foreign countries are represented; two marriage and four deaths in previous rides; two thirds of the riders are professionals or managers; an over-nighter in a town is worth $100,000, economic impact for week-long is $1.5 million. It costs us $25 for a ticket. The oldest rider ever was 85 with his wife of 70. A birth happened this year.

We inspected the usual line of port-a-johns. The walk was about a half mile long. We now knew how to do the Tour de Shirts, Tour de johns, Tour de tents, and Tour de eats. We bought several new shirts before the best ones were gone and untold number of food stuffs.

Ute opened a fire hydrant for us to splash in because of the heat.

In Charter Oak, a church service was being conducted. I wanted to sit in and we were invited. Church members were selling cookies outside. It was cooler inside. A baptism was going on and we sat with the parishioners with no problem. I felt it would be a blessing in more ways than one to attend.

We rode on to Denison, our host city, one of the most hilly. By mid-afternoon the temperature rose to a hot 92 degrees. Maxwell Park was away from the town and hard to find. As a subdivision park it was quiet and we were surrounded with houses. I finally thought it would be the ideal place for an in-house shower. There was a sign on the window on the next street. To get one otherwise, we would have to take a shuttle bus mixed with hot, sweaty bodies to another school or Y. Jim and Lois Beymer were our hosts. Luckily for us they just added a second new water heater. Bikers were lined up 7-8 deep in the air conditioned house.

We caught the shuttle twice. First to find dinner and then the other girls went back to a pool later. Some of the streets were blocked off for the entertainment and we watched some dancers on a platform from our sidewalk seats. I stayed in camp with Walt while the girls returned to town, but I stayed at my own tent trying to write and read the book I brought for just this occasion. It was too hot to be bussing around and I just wanted to relax. So did Walt. Sheri was getting upset with her dad because he was becoming stubborn and slow to do things. He wanted her to listen to some

185

tapes he thought she should hear in the car on the way to Iowa so she rode in the car with me.

"Watch out, he probably will want you to listen to those tapes he has," she warned before they left.

"I'll do my best. I'll just stay in the shadow of my tent. Maybe he'll think I went with you," I returned.

As it happened, I listened to the tapes. They were O.K. but not something I would have chosen if I had to choose. Then I had to give a report on them. I thought I was back in school.

The next day we had mostly wind all day. When we had hills it was in the tail and blew us up and when on the side we were mostly on flat lands and it felt good with the humidity. We lost Walt sometime after breakfast and didn't see him again until the end of the 66 miles at Storm Lake. At Arthur, a Colonial Manor Kitchen Band welcomed us playing everything they knew for as long as we would listen.

Storm Lake gave me chills. Why would anyone name a town, Storm Lake? On the map it showed a big lake and it was reported to be shallow. It was a long way around it and it was flat all day.

We put up for the night at Buena Vista college on the lake with an indoor pool. Fabulous. We put up our tent in the shadow of the building next to the pool but had to go a long way around to get to any other facility in the school.

It was an air conditioned college and as many people were sleeping on the furniture in the halls of the open area as were sleeping on the lawns.

In the middle of the night we had our usual mid-night storm. This was Storm Lake, wasn't it? Without waiting for a call to abandon ship, Sheri was up and rummaging through her stuff. I looked at my watch with the flashlight. "It's only 2:30. They didn't tell us to get out yet. It's hardly blowing. Where are you going?"

"Let's pack up before it starts to rain so we have a dry tent tonight."

"What? That's what tents are for, to get rained on."

"But if we do it now we can have a jump on tomorrow."

I fell back on my sleeping bag. "O.K. It's your tent." She went out and awakened her mom and dad. They agreed. They weren't sleeping anyway. I thought about not bothering to put the thing up and just sleep out under the stars. Much easier than erecting a tent every night and taking it down in the dark.

After sitting around in the school cafeteria waiting for a breakfast line to open at three in the morning, I noticed my wallet was not with my handlebar bag that became my personal bag. We looked all over in all our stuff. It started to rain in the meantime but we put on our rain gear and walked the quarter mile back to the tent area looking in the puddles where our tent was, finding nothing. I rummaged all through our bags since there were few in the truck and found nothing. All I could think was someone had stolen it and the police were summoned, a report made. I called home to alert my mother to call off the hounds on my credit cards.

Walt loaned me some money to last the rest of the trip and all I did was worry the whole day. We found out from the police while making the report that twelve bikes were stolen from the campus that night and the whole group wasn't awake yet to find more bikes missing.

We heard along the grapevine, an inch and a half of rain fell that night. Some people lost their tents to the wind, finding them some 150 yards away in the lake. Palmer, population 288, rolled out the entertainment carpet with high school students providing three hours of jazz music. A donation jar was on the platform sitting mostly empty till some cyclists got on stage performing with them and made other cyclists fill their jar. A basketball game on an open court was formed with RAGBRAI team losing badly.

West of Palmer a farmer entertained by rolling a large bale of hay around what looked like a bike rider in the middle. These Iowans had a real sense of humor.

A bad accident happened not far in front on us. The road was full of bikers across the two lanes. Sheri was ahead, Walt and Shirley, behind. The ambulance came up the road and I could see the lights flashing. Word filtered back of an accident ahead. We were drafting a long line of bikers for several miles at 22 m.p.h. with the tail winds and getting our 66 miles out of the way for the day. I left the line after about 10 miles or so but Sheri hung on. All I could think of, it was her. We made a right turn in the road ahead.

I went by the accident relieved it was not. One of the line drafters went outside the line making the turn too fast and ran head on into a pick-up truck hawling a pontoon boat. He didn't live. I saw Sheri, who was visibly upset. We didn't ride the draft line any more. We met the other two in town and their fears were abated at our rendevous.

At about 50 miles out, I felt I was losing all my umpffff. I found out that my seat had readjusted itself lower than it should be and I was pedaling my legs in an uncomfortable short length. It didn't take much to fix that.

We stayed this night at the senior high school and had a good hot shower. I wasn't feeling too good about losing my wallet and asked everyone all day if they knew of anyone finding it, with no results. We put up the tent, took showers and sat around before I examined all my belongings one more time. There, in one of the corners of folded over material was my blue wallet. I was so happy, I went around hugging everyone who helped to look for it, even the baggage man I made get out of bed to help look in the morning. I returned what I owed to Walt, thankful he had some extra cash to lend. We took a taxi to a VFW hall for dinner where I called off the credit card negotiations with mom.

Breakfast at a fire hall, Norwegian pastries in Thor, cyclists mooning people from the grain elevator in Hardy, and huge cloth canopy over the main street of Kanawa were highlights of the day. At a park, sprinklers were set up to run through. Some utilized the cooling effect as we sat for lunch provided by a service group.

A little three year old girl was lost in a corn field. She was found by one of the many cyclists who stopped along the fields to look for her, coming out with mud caked shoes but feeling better that she was at last found and returned to her parents.

We were treated to some music on a corner by a church and the cookie monster met us with cookies on a hill going into Forest City. Today was the day for the century. I didn't do it again. What a wimp!

We met Dennis, and his young son, while we busted tables again at breakfast. He couldn't believe we would do it and just watched. Today we not only busted tables but made breakfast, washed dished, took money and tips. We had fun. We made friends with him easily for the rest of the week. He was from Stevensville, Michigan.

A rider, Art Hoffman, from Albequerque, New Mexico, created a big stir against smoking by riding a tandem bike with a skeleton on the back seat strapped into the stirrups with helmet and cigarette.

Even though I didn't do the century, I met Sheri at the camp site for the night. The tent was up and was surrounded by several men on a hill. They were standing around looking at all the other piles of baggage the baggage man had piled together for us. They were with the Winers club not far from us. Winers meaning cry babies. They had a couple beers for us and helped us put Shirley and Walts' tent up for them. It was a long day and it was another scorcher. The beer and help were welcome. Jim Taft was a friend of Dennis Buchalski. Jim was from Battle Creek.

The whole group was together in this area tonight, noisy and crowded. We had to wait in line for the pool. Jim and Dennis stayed with us all evening. We also picked up Gary whom we met before. He was good company, too. We hitch-hiked into town several miles away rather than take the crowded school bus. We didn't get a ride soon enough. "Let's put Sheri out in the road. We'll get a ride better if we do." Even though it was a tease, she was put out there and from then on we used her for hitch-hiking. Our ride was in the back of a pick-up truck but we didn't care. It was a long walk.

Jim stayed with me for most of the rest of the trip. He smoked and I had a hard time understanding how he could ride. He was also

188

overweight but still rode well, he said. He walked me back to my tent after the night on the town, buying my dinner and anything else I wanted.

We were to make sure the guys were up in the morning. Their group never got up until late. I tip-toed through the myriad of tents in the dark listening to the zippers again at 4:30 in the morning. I couldn't ride well this morning and kept falling behind. After breakfast I teamed up with a man by the name of Randy from Illinois. He was having trouble with his energy, too. Once I caught up with the troops, he left.

A country music singer entertainer had his speakers blasting his music from miles away. He was good enough, we stayed a long time to rest and bought tapes he sold. We lost the guys along the way and hit a head wind that was about to zap all our energy. We were only using third and fourth gear till we hit a side wind. It never felt so good.

On one of the hills, we all thought we would run out of water. The heat was unbearable. We were all getting burnt more than we should. Out on the long hilltop, after riding against a head wind, a farm lady rode a mile from her ranch on a fat tired ATV with one of her kids. She brought us all water in milk jugs. So welcome! She must have known we were desperate. She made many trips that day.

In Osage, someone had somehow put a bike up on the overhead wires on main street. After leaving a lot of the towns that were host to our nights or even our days, we rode by "thank you" signs. It was so nice to know they were such warm people.

That night we looked for the Winers club to no avail and went to town without them. But in town we met a lot of others who kept saying Gary, Dennis and Jim were looking for us. How could we possibly be found in this crowd? We met one and then the other and we went different ways as we lost each other in the tight crowds.

Sheri broke a spoke today and we had to go to the main camp to find a new one. We were all over today and tonight, none of us really staying together. It was fun anyway. Music emitted from every street corner. It could be heard all night back at our tents. Dancing everywhere. We were again like locusts devouring the town. Walt and Sheri went back early to fix the bike. Jim walked me back so I could go to bed early.

Jim and Dennis pleaded for us to let them ride with us on the last day. Dennis had another member lined up to ride with his son and about 5:30 we were ready. Jim was a little slow to get started but we got going and sped through the hills to breakfast. Sheri rode with Dennis up front while I chided Jim on his cigarette

189

smoking holding him back. He had to walk a hill while I didn't. The temperature rose to 100 degrees and humidity was again high. The hills were getting worse as we neared Guttenburg.

Because it was the last day, many folks wore costumes. We didn't recall many doing that last year. It was like a traveling circus. We stopped in many towns along the way for rest, eating ice cream and having our pictures taken together. Jim cut his finger on one of his gears he was trying to fix and was bleeding all over the place. I found some shade and played nurse for awhile and then onward to get this hot 73 miles over.

The last downhill into town was scary. Long and fast. Cracks in the pavement meant many accidents. People were stationed at the top of the hill to warn everyone going down. We made it safely, drove carefully and found the river beach to dip our front wheels in the Mississippi again. We all jumped in with our clothes on, cooled off in the muddy water and said good-bye to our new friends. Gee, we had another good time to talk about to others and more shirts to flaunt at our local rides.

.................I continued to eat my lunch of peanut butter and jelly in pita bread at the Cut River park. I missed Shirley. It was fun to be on my own but it was still nice to have a companion to share the fun. We had a good time canoeing the Manistee River that summer with Jeff Speer, the young son of a friend of mine and Shirley's granddaughter, Suzie McDaniel. It was only for a week-end but I had fun teaching all three of them. We had a mishap, when the girls tipped their canoe over in the fast running current on a tight bend. The only thing lost was the two-burned cook stove that wasn't tied down and some pride. Then, we went off to the east on our Hondas for our first Canadian adventure.................

Adventure # 6

Nova Scotia

Chapter 1   Ohio and Pennsylvania

................I rode along the road thinking I'd better find the KOA park near the Big Mac bridge for the night. The sun was beginning to fall farther behind me and shadows were getting longer in front of me.

I wanted to find a pasty before leaving for the Lower Peninsula. After setting up the blue two-man tent that would only sleep one man tonight, I jumped on the bike to head for the tavern I saw with a large sign in the window advertising such a delicacy. Pasties are made like a turnover, made with meat and potatoes and half the size of a dinner plate. Some served with gravy, I elected to have my gravy on the side. I didn't like it swimming in the stuff. It was delicious with a cold beer.

The night was peaceful. It was more lonely not having my riding partner with me. In the middle of the night, I had to shoo away the four-legged bandits myself. I watched them through the screened door as they found I had nothing to offer in my panniers still on the bike. I covered them with garbage bags every night to keep them dry and to rustle if marauders tried to steal my precious food provisions that usually were there.

NOVA SCOTIA BECKONS

In the morning, before the dew was off the tent and ground, I was ready to roll off into another day of adventure alone. I stopped just before the bridge for breakfast, not wanting oatmeal again. I was somewhat anxious to get over the bridge. Since I was not allowed to ride over on the bike I had to find an alternative method. I was told to just ask for a ride at the office.

At breakfast, I was finishing when a couple motorcycles pulled in with four people on them. I longed to be on mine, too. I walked over and introduced myself after they finished ordering, finding they were two couples not riding together. They were each riding to the others' home state of Oregon and Massachusetts. We had a very interesting discussion on places we were all going. Exchanging maps and information. I thought I might never get across the bridge.

The big question everyone wants to know it seems was 'Was I alone?'. I went into some detail about the failed seat but I didn't want them to get the wrong impression of my friend. I told them it was fun to go both ways and I was familiar with this area and wasn't afraid.

Allison wanted to know about my visit to their neck of the woods in Massachusetts.

"I lived near there in 1957," I said. "You know, one of those Navy wives."

"Well, what did you think on your return trip, when was it? 1986?"

"I guess I was younger then when traffic didn't bother me."

I continued with the tale of our trip to Nova Scotia.............

Since Shirley and I had been out to the west so often, we thought we'd better see the east and what better place then to go all the way to Maine. I poured over the maps again trying to get as much into a two-week vacation. Finding we had plenty of time to cover much ground, I said, "How would you like to go to Nova Scotia? I hear they have nice weather in August and the scenery is beautiful."

"It's sounds good to me. Will we have enough time?"

"Sure, look here at the map," I said as we spread them out on the table one winter day. We just came in from cross-country skiing and were looking forward to warmer weather. Walt had already said he didn't mind if she went again if we were more careful. She repaired the Honda from last years' accident and it almost looked the way she bought it. We both needed a new back tire. Mine was getting a little thin. I don't ride these babies till the underwear hangs out like I do the bicycle tires. More at stake here.

Other improvements were a radio on her bike so we could communicate. That was the first consideration. I bought a new pack

192

for the back seat. An internal frame back pack so I could use it for more than motorcycling. A new Whisper-Light stove for cooking and a new mess kit set my kitchen up to first class. Peanut butter and jelly would be carried in their containers this time.

We again started out with a primary destination and a date with an old friend. Rosemary, who rode with me on our first excursions into the world of bicycling at seven years of age, lived in Southport, Connecticut. We hadn't seen each other in years and all our children were grown.

We began in a fog bank. It was good to have the radio contact now. Shirley called herself "Granny" for her handle, fitting both of us to a "T".

It warmed up nicely and instead of making it to Wilks-Barre, Pennsyvania, we only got as far as Bellefonte. There was nothing of note in northern Ohio at this time except many people on the road going to Cedar Pointe amusement park.

"Let's stop and get some fresh fruit," came a call on the radio as we approached our camp. Since I was in the lead, she had to speak up quickly so I would do things before I passed them up. She was getting used to it now. We bought a couple ears of corn from a roadside stand, thinking it was too early for corn but not questioning it.

"How are you going to fix them? I asked her.

"I don't know. We could roast them over a fire," she suggested.

"You and I know that instant gratification does not come with fire building."

"I'll think of something." The woman selling threw in a couple peaches that looked like they were around a little too long but we'd take anything free. We hadn't any place to carry them and tried to loop them over the turn signals. They banged along as we drove the final miles, surely bruising them or grinding them to a pulp.

While our corn was "cooking" we went for a swim in the pool. She put them in a bag of very hot water and surprisingly they were quite tasty. The peaches needed much trimming.

Many people in this camp. A hayride was going by as I sat writing in my book and we jumped on for something to do. An All-You-Can-Eat ice cream social was being held in the barn. Leave it to us to not pass up an opportunity to indulge in Shirley's pastime.

We should have stayed up all night and played cards or something. Between the noises of cars driving through, kids yelling, dogs barking, we had a hard time staying off each other with the slanted floor of her tent.

"Which way are we going to put our head tonight?" became the familiar question when setting up camp. No matter how we put our head this time, we were not going to get a flat surface and just gave up. Our feet would be hanging out the door in the morning, for sure.

Chapter 2   New Jersey, the Big Apple and Connecticut

It was thick fog early in the morning. We could just barely make out the way to the rest room. At 7 a.m., the countryside awakened ever so slowly, the wisps of fog lay in low spots wafting across the valleys, lazily waiting for the sun to burn it off. It mingled with the trees in the hills. We listened to the truckers trying to keep their eyes open for another hour or so, telling off-color jokes or trivial things to each other. We needed a break from the fog and the jokes.

In Williamsport, we met Eddie in a donut shop. An older gentleman, he liked to tell us how rich he was and how he was looking for a wife to spend it on. We let him buy our breakfast and said good-bye even if it was foggy. I didn't want her to get any more ideas as she did last year in the laundryroom of Durango.

The sun burned off the fog and now it was my favorite kind of weather. Sunny and hot. I thought I didn't want to go through New York City. Shirley wasn't ready for it either. I felt about this city the way I felt about Chicago. We would have been better off, as it was Sunday.

We passed over the Delaware River at Easton. Entering New Jersey, all the towns we used skirting the city were having some sort of festival or circus or something. We were in the middle of traffic delays that overheated our engines in the hot and humid air. Stopping to cool them down became a necessity. We turned off the engines when the jam came to a standstill.

We passed over the Hudson River, rolling along at a nice clip when I heard over the radio, "Pony Express?"

"Yes, Granny, what is it?"

"How far do you think you can go on a tank of gas today?"

Thinking she was playing a prank I dismissed it flippantly until I looked down at my trip odometer. "Oh, my gosh," I screeched. "We've gone 200 miles."

"I haven't had to put reserve on yet but don't you think we ought to stop for gas?"

"I haven't either. There doesn't seem to be much around here in the way of gas stations either, does there?" I half said to myself. We kept riding and riding and I heard nothing from the back row. At 210 miles, a station was sighted. "We must be riding on fumes. I never ride this far with a load except maybe once out in Wyoming. I was paying so much attention to getting us to Rosie's before the week was out, I forgot to watch. Good thing you were."

"No loss this time. I just don't think I want to push this thing or sit alongside the road in this heat."

A call to Rosie helped save our day, too. They were looking for us and had invited company to meet us. We had to get there by 6 p.m. for supper. I don't think Rosie knew how difficult it was to travel the way we were. She was more used to flying from point to point, or having more time to drive around in a closed car. It was difficult to maintain a good attitude in the eighty degree heat as well.

But we made it in good time, meeting Ed, her husband, a couple kids and their friends. It was so humid, changing clothes became a chore. I could hardly wait to get the hot, sticky jeans off.

Friends, Tony Roman and Kay Burns came for dinner. We had many remembrances to do. Rosie turned into a good cook. I knew she always was but I never had the opportunity to savor it. After the filling meal, we opted for a walk around town. Shirley went with them while I took Tony for a ride around town on the Honda. He had never ridden before and was excited to do it. Shirley couldn't ride anyone or wouldn't. Didn't have the confidence, she said.

"Turn over there," he hollered into my helmet. "Make a right on the next corner. This is fun." I could see a big smile on his face as the wind cooled both of us.

"Go up to that place right there." I pulled up to his apartment.

Oh, oh, I thought. What do we have here?

"Come on, I'll introduce you to my daughter. She won't believe this." We went in and found no one there. Nice place, I thought.

"Darn it, she's working," he said as he looked at a note on the table. "Do you like it?" he asked, looking around his apartment.

What am I doing here? I thought. "Sure is nice. You live here alone?"

"Just me and Mary, my daughter. She must have been called to work. Let's go there."

Whew! I thought again. I really didn't want some intervention get in the way of a good friendship. We got back on the bike and found his daughter working in a fast food place. We stood in line and he bought us both a yogurt cone to make it look good while he introduced me to her. Pretty girl. He could hardly hold back the fact he was riding a motorcycle. He held up the helmet he was wearing.

"Dad, you didn't!" she said as she looked at him incredulously.

"Yea, it's right out there," he said as he pointed out the window at my bike. He told her the truth laughing and we said good-bye and went back to the house to find the others. They were still out. We groped our way around in the darkness of their neighborhood with just house lights lighting the way. We spotted them coming up a hill. They went to the wharf. We thanked them for a perfect evening as they left and we both hit the beds like dead weights. It was a long day.

Chapter 3   Rhode Island and Massechusetts

This was the third night with no sleep. It was so humid I felt the sheets clinging to my skin. The open window did little to relieve the humidity. A thunderstorm worked itself up and I needed to close the windows. Tomorrow, I'll sleep.

We said our fond farewells later in the day. We spent as much time as possible with Rosie and Mary Kay, her daughter. They showed off the town as we went to get a car repaired. The trip around town was driven by Mary Kay, who must have received her drivers licence at the race track. It was time to put on those hot jeans again to go to Mystic Seaport. I heard a lot about it. We could go aboard the Nautilus submarine.

Traffic built up in a steady stream in the afternoon heat. We couldn't find what we wanted but instead found Patrick from Chicago, who invited us in his cramped house for a very hot cup of coffee. While his wife was at work, he proceeded to tell us where everything was in the area and that the Nautilus was there but it was closed the day we wanted to visit.

The campground wasn't far from the harbor. We set up to the usual chores of drying the tent and heading out to sight-see the town.

Dreaded No-See-Ums were prevalent here but the tent had insectproof screens. We spent the time along the reconstructed harbor taking pictures and strolling along the walkways looking at the picturesque tall ships. The town was once a whaling village. A lot of memorabilia could be seen in the windows of the closed shops. Reluctantly, the rest of the evening was spent inside, cross-legged on the mattresses playing cards away from mosquitos and no-see-ums.

On the way to Newport, we made friends with three older gentlemen who were out to enjoy their daily McDonalds breakfast together. They were sweet. They couldn't believe we were traveling on the iron horses and had tales to tell of their younger, more foolish, days.

198

A sign directing us to Jerusalem attracted us. It looked like a bridge would take us across the village to another road but found out differently. It was a wonderful area for the camera buff. Signs all over forbade parking everywhere on the sand dune beach road. We backtracked and went on to Newport, disappointed.

I lived in the Newport, Rhode Island area for two years. Returning is sometimes a disappointment. It was this time. All the things important to me back then were gone and the build up of commercial places were blown out of proportion.

"They never had a tour bus operation when I was here and now there were several. They never even had buses other than Navy buses. Sure, this was a historic town but did they have to ruin it? How could the town fathers do this?"

"I guess that's how they get their big bucks back."

"As long as we're here, do you want to try for a tour? It would be easier than trying to find the things I'd like to show you from my limited knowledge of the place."

"I think that would be a good idea. Didn't you say this was where the millionaires lived?"

"Yea, but I'm not sure I could remember the streets. It would be faster on the bus." With that we attempted to find a tour bus but all were out and it would be hours before we might get another. Reservations were needed. We would try to find them ourselves. I felt I was in Disneyworld.

We drove down the main thoroughfare, Thames street and Ocean Drive. I could hardly recognize them. A walk along the beach front where the mansions were used to be a nice stroll. I couldn't even find the entrance. A stop at the Kennedy compound took our money instead. We toured the house and grounds.

"Granny? There used to be a house we called the "Haunted House" on Ocean Drive," I said to the microphone as we drove along the ocean road later. "It was abandoned and everyone went there to fool around in it. It probably is gone but I'll try to find it for us." It was gone. "It was fun to explore it. I suppose too many things were happening in and around there." In its place a state park was bustling. We left for Cape Cod.

Staying at a campground in Buzzards' Bay sounded different. Were buzzards here? It was right on the ocean with a lot of sand. The drive in was not the best for two wheels but it was done. The owner wasn't about to take us in to her camp.

"We don't usually take in single people or motorcyclists," she said.

"What? Do we look like ruffians? I can understand if we were," I protested.

"Well, you don't look like there should be any trouble. We just like to give families a family atmosphere without riff-raff."

We paid our money and proceeded through the park that reminded us of the northern Michigan woods with lots of pine trees and woodsy smells. She told us of a great place for a seafood dinner back in town and as soon as the tent dried and we could stash our belongings, we found the best dinner we had in a long time. At least since Rosemarys'.

We slept so well in this secluded spot. All we could hear were the rustling of the wind through the pines needles and far off, just the faint swish of the ocean lapping against the sand.

The rest of the day was full of dodging crowded freeways and roads that the locals thought were freeways.

"I havn't ever been to the tip of the cape. I remember it being nothing but a spit of land." It still was till we got to   Provincetown. Nice resorts. Many bicyclists were on the edge. We made comments on how we should be out there pushing our way around instead of the luxury of pushing the accelerator hand grip. Taking the southern route to Provincetown was our biggest mistake. Once we turned around and headed back, we took the northern route that was a freeway. We could handle the traffic much better on it.

A stop at the Cape Cod lighthouse gave us a break from traffic. We enjoyed lighthouses. In Michigan, we would drive long distances out of our way to take pictures of them and this was no exception. The day was sunny and warm with a stiff breeze. The sea grass bent over the sandy dunes providing a pleasing foreground for the tall structures. It was afternoon before we returned and then we were getting hungry enough to stop in a rest area not intended for resting. Out came the peanut butter and jelly and twinkies. We watched an ant carrying a dead insect for our entertainment. Cars and trucks zoomed past at high speed. We were oblivious to them for a few minutes.

"What are we doing here? I've had enough of this. How about you?" I asked her.

"I really don't like all this traffic. They would just as soon knock us off the road."

"Let's look at the map and try something else inland." We studied and circled a few places and then changed the itinerary for the day.

"I'd like to go to Sturbridge. That's where they make all the Early American furniture and junk. I think it's called the Yankee Peddler or something."

"O.K. Where is Palmer? We have some friends there. I could call Walter for their phone number. They'd be glad to see us."

"O.K. Let's do it. This other stuff is nuts. We can't enjoy this."

Off we went inland and away from the frantic pace of the other world we wanted nothing to do with. We intended to go to Boston and see the historical sites but not at this cost. Perhaps a car would be better. At least there was a little more armor to shield us. We felt so exposed.

Webster had a campground. We were running out of clothes already. KOA campground had a pay laundry. Doing the mundane things like clean-up and eating a microwaved pizza should have settled us down to a nice rest but somehow we became hostile toward each other. It must have been the long day traveling in the conjestion. By morning everything was better.

We visited with her friend at his office in Webster and found his wife Gladys at home in Palmer. The atmosphere was much more pleasant. The furniture shop wasn't open for an hour and we were lucky there was a donut shop across the street so we could indulge in a very large cinnamon roll.

Chapter 4

New Hampshire and Maine

While this east coast is a far cry from the west, it has its own values. I prefer the west. I like the ruggedness and mountains or even the openness of the plains. In the east, inland is no different from territory in Michigan. Rolling hill, conifers and pines fill the landscape. Then we came into the mountains and this euphoric changed.

I located Mt. Hale in the White Mountains. How convenient. Maybe I can talk her into hiking it, I thought. I tempted her with the idea and it wasn't long before we were at the base of it, map in hand. I hoped for a day or two of backpacking but settled for one. She didn't have the equipment. We quit biting at each other since we were out of that traffic. The mountains always made me feel good, perhaps it did her, too. Our whole attitude changed. Perhaps it was the naturalness of it.

Examining the maps for the best route up, we started to the first trailhead. It looked like a cloudy day and we expected nominal rain, if any. We only carried cameras without any drinking water. The day was warm but cloudy. Wearing the jeans almost became unbearable but we would be thankful at the summit. The White mountains are not the tallest mountains but are nice.

We started straight up and continued straight up till we lost our breath. I kept trying to keep up with Shirley. She must be half mountain goat, I thought. But it was even getting to her. We heard the sound of water and followed the trail to a rushing river crashing down the mountainside. I was so thirsty I took a small suck on the water leaning over so far I thought I would fall in. It was a good reprieve from the walk up. Nevertheless, I became sick on this trek, the farther we walked the more I wanted to lie down and die. Diarrhea set the scheduled stops from here to the top of the crest to the consternation of my partner. The sweat was running down my back and I wondered why I put myself into positions that make me sick. I was sick hiking the Colorado River, sick in Durango, even if it was the food, and I was sick here. Was this not my forte? Was it the water?

Rolling up pant legs helped cool down my body. I would have to put on the heaviest ones today!

We passed a couple Boy Scouts coming down who were surprised we were going up. We'd look up the trail and thought we were near the summit only to see more trail continuing on over the next bump in the trail through the trees. What were we doing here? The thoughts crept into our sparse conversation after two hours or more. There had to be an end and as sick as I was the more I was determined to find it.

We stopped long enough to really look at the map.

"Look, here, there are three routes we could have taken. But this one is not the beginner route, Marion, this is the expert route."

"Let me see that," I said astounded. "It was the shortest one, remember?"

"See here. It says, "If you have never walked a mountain trail, this is the one for you."

"You're right. And we aren't on that one. But this doesn't look all that bad on the map. What do you want to do? Quit now and go back or go a little farther. I'm not going to want to quit but I sure wish it would end soon. My stomach is so churned up it isn't sure which way to go."

"Let's try a little farther, if you're game. My calves hurt. We've been sitting too long on that bike."

"I know what you mean. So do mine, along with the stomach," I said as we continued the climb. It wasn't a hike, it was a climb. Many times we had to hang onto roots to pull ourselves up and over rocks in the trail. Several places were narrow enough on the edge of the river to put little scares in me with no balance ability. Shirley went on sure-footed as usual.

At long last, there were no more trees in our view and only a sign stuck in the ground with milages on it. We, indeed, went the wrong route. The wind picked up while we were on this summit and we could see for miles over the tops of these and other mountains. The Whites are mostly in the 5,000 foot range. An old fire tower still erected invited us to climb a little farther. We declined its invitation. It was windy and cold on our now overheated skin and we returned to camp.

Descending was just as hard as the ascent. It went quicker as we more than walked, but slid, jumped, tumbled, and ran down the steep trail through the trees. The sound of the river and the neighboring mountain occasionally caught our attention. Our mountain did not get us and we were happy with that.

I consumed a cup of herbal tea and chicken soup when I returned and then a nap in the tent. I felt much better in a few hours.

I was finding I didn't like my Whisper-Light stove for cooking. It would have to go. It clogged too often and wouldn't light. It ran out of gas too often and it was hard to replace. I only needed a pint. It was hard to buy just a pint. The neighbor fellow in camp gave me some out of his three gallon jug. He was the cook for a 6-boy climbing group.

When the rest of the six returned with their adult leader from hiking Mt. Adams, we were offered some left-over food in the name of reconstituted raspberry cobbler and coffee. It was delicious! We enjoyed the group. All youngsters had to carry their own load up and down the mountains. The youngest was almost smaller than his pack. We felt better about our climb when they told us the route we took was a real "bear", too.

I made a little camp fire and listened to the boys next door sing camp songs around their larger fire while resting my knee that also began to hurt on the downhill plunge. Shirley tried to sleep in the tent. Her shins were aching.

We missed the Old Man Of the Mountain formation and returned in the mist of morning to view it. Another trail led us up a path to the "Flume". A flowing river careened over boulders for a mile and a half. Walking the extra miles in boots wasn't bad. The dampness warranted wearing our leathers. In a few places, the water fell from the rock into emerald green pools below. It made the misty day seem much more enjoyable and lent a better contrast to our finished photos. A covered bridge added to our portfolio.

With a brochure of a cog railroad in the mountains in our hands, we set tracks for it. After looking around, we found the trip we wanted would show nothing and we would have spent some $30 to see nothing. The rail road went up Mt. Washington but the mist turned into fog and then to rain. We reminded ourselves about the narrow gage train trip we took in Ontario one winter. We went in a blizzard and could see only little of the mountainous area.

We went on to find some other misadventure to get into. I mailed my daily post card with a rural New Hampshire mailman after talking shop for a few minutes.

Highway One would take us south along the sea, across many bridges and through Rockport. An artist colony, but today all one could paint would be foggy pictures. This town has been on every calender in the country, I think. I searched for the little red fishing hut on stilts but didn't find it in the fog. Setting our sights on a KOA campground offering lobster dinners, we kept on moving.

The sun appeared just in time to dry out our wet house. It was thirty miles to Bar Harbor where we would take a ferry to Nova Scotia. We made our dinner reservations thinking they would be less expensive in the park. In Bar Harbor, we could have had more elegance even in our casual clothing for the same price.

The sun gave us a treat. We found the ferry dock and made reservations for the morning, spent some tourists' dollars on remembrances of Maine and sped back to our lobster dinner served on paper plates. Over our hot fudge sundaes, we met two older gentlemen that we saw in our last camp ground. We teased them on following us and then took a short walk. A good stretch was needed after the filling dinner.

We found a pond out back with such still water, it looked painted on the ground. We took off our shoes and socks and waded in the warm water. It was warmer than some pools. Mosquitos became a problem again as night fell. I was beginning to have welts from them and the no-see-um's. Those would get under my helmet and lodge there during the day. My scalp became a mass of bumps. Jumping into the tent and into bed was welcome. We had an early date with our first foreign country.

"I'm afraid to get on the ferry in the morning, Marion," Shirley whispered as she snuggled into her sleeping bag.

"What do you mean?"

"I've had dreams about driving on the boat. I don't know if I can do it. Some guy said it was real hard to do. I think you have to drive over planks."

"I heard that, too, but I also heard there is someone who will help if you have a problem. Let's try to be there early enough to scout it out."

"O.K. I just don't feel comfortable. I don't want to drop the bike on the way over." Now, she started me thinking about it and I also became scared.

Chapter 5   Nova Scotia

Some of those mosquitos invaded our tent and kept Shirley awake. Even though it was warm, I covered myself with my sheet. She didn't have one so the bag was too warm. It was nice of her to keep swatting them for me. All I heard were cars pulling along the road near our site during the night.

We packed up as fast as we could, swatting at the hordes of pesty insects. They became so annoying I left without waiting for Shirley. I couldn't stand them. It was only 5:30 a.m. but the early date wouldn't wait for us thirty miles away and these mosquitos weren't getting any more of me.

Our ride in was difficult with the fog. A quick dose of grease at the local McDonalds' got us to the dock in plenty of time. We only needed to hand our ticket to the ticket taker and zip on the ferry on double car width metal grating. It was good we were early as traffic wasn't up to snuff yet. The fog turned to mist as we parked the Hondas in a special place just for them. Ropes and blocks were provided to tie them down to the metal floor rings. Another biker showed us how to do it. A dozen or so were already parked.

Shirley's dream faded slightly. We still had to get off but I made no mention. I was just as scared as she but there was no sense getting both of us more flustered than we were already.

We had a six hour voyage in the fog to Nova Scotia. A lounge provided comfortable space for waiting to get across. "*The Natural*" was being shown in the theater. We noted many French speaking people with us. Many of the people were tourists but many were residents. It was nice to hear them speak. It was my native country but I never learned it. It sounded romantic.

Getting off the ferry, we both were filled with anxiety. We waited in a long line on land to go through customs and then were set free to go wherever we planned. Our first job was to get our American money exchanged for Canadian. Yarborogh looked like a good town to find anything and the first thing I spied was a Honda dealer. I was experiencing a squeak and wanted to make sure it was nothing to worry about. I was told it had a central shock absorber and to get to it would mean taking down the whole bike. I never heard of that and let the squeak stay. The fellows got such a kick out of us two old bags this far from home, they greased everything they could find for nothing. They were friendly enough. We just felt different here. Even though this wasn't a French speaking province, many could speak it and they all seemed to have an accent of a sort. Different from the New Englanders'. Perhaps Scotch. That was another of my ancestral beginnings.

The mist turned into rain. Welcome to our province. At the campground we were given a spot nestled in the pine trees and black mud. The previous owners were here during a drenching. A trench was still evident dug around a square where their tent must have been. It was still partially dry. Mosquitos were wearing saddles and this must have been the last roundup. We thought we would take in a movie in the recreation hall later to get away from them.

The rain quit for a while allowing us to try again to see something without carrying our load. Off we went to see what was here. It didn't last long. Fields reminded me of what I would picture the "moors" should look in Scotland. Slightly rolling but green hills, with rock patches here and there. Off in the distance, the ocean lay in a hazy light blue without the benefit of a horizon in the misty rain.

Sitting in the log house after supper on benches were many kids of varying ages watching what looked to us, an x-rated movie. We watched for awhile until we could make no sense of it and had our fill. A stop at the office to buy another bottle of insect repellant became a must. We hiked back to the tent swatting the ferocious insects and getting wetter. Inside, we tried to make a decision to stay one more day in hopes it would quit raining or to move on to see the countryside. We would have to battle the bugs all day here and we were told it was better inland.

"If we stay here, I'm going to want to move the tent over there on the hill. This place is too muddy and it's a haven for mosquitos."

"You got that right. Should we go into town tomorrow and fool around while we wait for the clearing?"

"What does the weatherman say on the radio?"

"Rain tonight and clearing tomorrow."

"We'll see how much clearing means after a breakfast of mosquito pancakes."

It didn't look very promising. We made the final decision, moved everything to another site and started all over again. The mosquitos followed us to the other site. We would have taken a shower, but in the shower room a woman was slapping them on her now-uncovered body while trying to wash. I wasn't so dirty I had to do that. Shirley agreed. We'd stay dirty together.

In town, we browsed, spent more tourists dollars, took in a visitor center show and had breakfast at our favorite spot,

McDonalds'. We had a nice conversation with several men with their children. One father was from Boston visiting his young son and the other was a missionary father with his daughter from South Africa. It made an interesting conversation for a good hour or two while we listened to them talk about where they lived and they got answers to their questions about our travels.

Another big fellow sauntered in talking to anyone who would listen or not listen. He was an elder gentlemen from Newfoundland. He said he was a marine but I think he meant a mariner. He reminded us of an old sea dog captain who only needed to change into sea captains' clothes to put him in the right perspective. Perhaps a peg leg and a patch over his eye would help. The fathers left.

Other patrons of the restaurant looked at us with sympathy as they listened to him talk to us and complain about one thing or another. It looked like it was going to quit raining and I got up and Shirley followed suit and we walked out on him still talking or complaining to whom ever would listen.

"Boy, I didn't think we'd ever get away from him."

"I didn't know of any other way but to just get up and leave, Shirley."

The wind picked up ferociously whipping our dirty hair into never-never land. Putting on the helmets held it down and we began our own tour of the Yarborough area along the sea edge. Took a road to Cheboque Pointe that started out nice and wide and before we stopped it was a cow path leading into a pasture for sure. We tried to park the bikes in the soft mushy ground. Shirley thought of bringing a small piece of wood to put the kick stand on that always worked in these situations. I had to find something solid.

We walked out to the water over the marshy ground, climbing over moss covered rocks. The tide was in, preventing us from doing any beachcombing. Walking along the rocks found us taking more pictures of the sun shining on the distant water through the openings in the clouds. Storm clouds were still abundant, offering great shots of them and the rocky protuberances with sea spray crashing against them.

This was just the area we were looking for. No tourists, stores or other commercial establishments. Just the land in its native state. Since we felt we were trespassing we didn't stay as long as we wanted.

Back at camp, we found the tent floor hadn't dried very well and since Shirley's side was the wettest, her bag and pad were still wet. She hung them out to dry on the nearby trees while we tried to make sense on post cards and scan the maps for tomorrow. The mosquitos found us again. The camp store had a corner on the

208

"Off" market. Even at the different rate of money we knew we were paying inflated prices. Supper was eaten standing up and dancing around to get away from them.

Needless to say, the tent was our hide-out for the rest of the day and night. Making trips to the rest room was a chore neither of us wanted. Every time the zipper was opened, a million mosquitos flew in to invade us. They knew their next meal was in there and hovered around the screens for us to come out. Their incessant buzzing was enough to drive us half crazy.

The road to Halifax should get us away from the bugs. It was inland and we were ready to go even if it didn't stop raining. Miraculously, it was a sun that peeped over the horizon that morning with a few lingering clouds interspersed in the blue sky.

The scenic route took us to the south of the island past many fishing villages. Lobster cages were stacked up at every building. We found a nice little cove for lunch watching the waves crash on the sand beach. A store provided the necessary extra calories to go with our peanut butter and jelly sandwiches. The rain returned with sprinkles making our stay all too short.

Passing up Halifax may have been our mistake but we didn't want to ride through cities. An inland campground prompted us to head for the north, criss-crossing the island.

Again, a hay wagon rumbled by carrying other campers. I found myself sitting next to a congenial retired fisherman from Halifax. I received the history of the fishing business as he knew it. He fished when they still used dories instead of the big motor powered ships of today. He also said the land in Nova Scotia was what I thought it looked like, Scotland, his homeland. Natives to the island have Scottish accents, he said, because that was their origins. They all have a swarthy, rugged look about them.

We were going to use the showers as we hadn't done so for two days and were becoming somewhat tacky but quarters were not something we were used to taking with our towels and soaps. Tomorrow, if we can stand each other that long, we would shower. Good thing we had the larger tent.

The skies cleared during the night to allow the full moon to establish its place in the dark sky overhead during the night. It was so quiet and cool it was hard to sleep but I gave in when I heard the slight snore coming from my partner's bag.

By the morning hour, the clouds and the misty drizzle returned. The temperature was a damp 55 degrees. Cold for riding when not prepared. We wore snow suits for this trip after the cold weather we encountered in the northwest territory of the states. Warmer gloves were a big help but we just couldn't warm the feet. I was given a pair

209

of knee length rubber boots by my mother. They kept out the wet and also held more warmth in. They fit nice and tight and were not bulky to wear or carry. I thanked her silently as we drove out of the camp in the early morning hours riding to the first restaurant for breakfast.

It was some distance away before it loomed in the mist. Breakfast was with two couples driving cars who were from near our home town. Two were Chinese, both married to Americans. It provided interesting conversation over eggs.

In the scattered showers day, we waved at another motorcyclist as he rode by our break spot on this beautifully smooth roadway. Down the road, we met him again filling up with gas. He was an older gentleman riding his new maroon colored Kawasaki and proud as punch to be doing it. We had lunch with him. He hinted that he would like to ride with us since we were going the same direction. We let him. Joe Gallant hadn't any radio to communicate but he didn't look like he needed one. He smiled and waved and rolled along happy to be a part of our excursion. He was a local person from Amhurst just riding over to his sisters' house not far from our exit.

We planned on a KOA campground today. It was early in the day but we needed some time to dry things out and the distances between campgrounds were too far apart. There wasn't much time to see things and be a part of them if all we did was ride. The one we selected was one of the nicest campsites on the island. It was far from primitive, with many things to do. The area was where Alexander Graham Bell summered along a channel near Beddeck.

Taking time to lounge around felt wonderful. No rain. No mosquitos. Laundry became the chore of this day after a long soak in the shower. It felt so good. Bug spray coated us like a second skin, becoming an irritant. We tried to sign up for a pontoon trip down the channel later in the evening while it was still light but the list was full even at this early stage of the day. We rented a canoe. The channel was as still as could be. It opened onto a wider channel but the narrow channel was still, the other was not. It had small ripples with the wind. Ours was secluded between high banks on either side covered in pines towering to the sky. If we didn't know better we would have thought we were paddling on a mirror. Letting current carry us along at a slow speed we spotted a bald eagle in the distance. We armed our cameras.

"Don't paddle, Shirley, just cruise with the paddle in the water to steer us. I'll try to get a good shot. I'm going to aim the camera. Watch the bird and tell me if he looks like he's going to take off. I'll try to wait till that time so it will be a closer shot."

"Shush!"

210

"Watch him."

"There he goes," she said aloud as he flew from his perch. I snapped the picture but got mostly a tail shot, sorry it was our best effort. A blue heron was taken and that ended our escapade on the water.

Bed felt good tonight. It was dry. All the mosquitos were smashed. I read and Shirley listened to taped music to lull ourselves to sleep. The Cabot Trail called us for the day. With a 52 degree temperature I was not ready to be alive and well by Shirley's wake up call before 6 a.m. It was damp again as we headed out to the north east part of the island. Through the mountains, the fog layered over the low area and rivers. Nearer to the sea the air cleared and the sun showed itself. The temperature warmed to a comfortable 65 degrees. We rolled along the edge of mountains where we could see the road etched in along the sea in the tree cover, water bursting over the edge of the beachless land.

At the top of the high places we stopped to photograph the mountains as they met the water. Neat homes clung to the sides of hills painted in colorful hues. Breathtaking is the only word we could use for this long awaited view of this island.

We stopped at a swimming beach. The tide was on its way in and where there were rocks at one end, the water crashed so noisily we could not hear ourselves speak. We didn't have much to say but always found something to talk about. We met a couple newlyweds, Keith and Liz Webster, from New Hampshire. We met them on the ferry coming across from Bar Harbor. We shared the beach. Off to the left a huge outcropping of rock was host to straight, narrow pine trees growing several hundred feet from the waters' edge. The rocks around the perimeter were so solid, it was hard to believe trees could grow out of them. The grey water roared into the cove making the surf bubbly and white. Much too cold to swim, even though there were bath houses for changing clothes.

Leaving the Websters to go in the opposite direction, we encountered the road construction they warned us about. It was a rocky ride for six miles as we dodged boulders and sand. One thing going for us was the position in the line of cars. We were first, without having to breathe in the dust from the cars behind us. It billowed in huge clouds behind the cars. We had to maneuver our two wheelers through ruts from the cars and trucks made slick from the rain.

We met other people from the ferry again and found we were, indeed, going the opposite direction that most tourists take. We always thought we were different and by golly, we knew it now.

We needed to exchange more money and took a number and stood in line as we do in home waiting lines. Spending so much

211

time looking at the scenery and getting business done we almost forgot the time. It was getting close to being dark when we realized we hadn't a place for the night. Looking over two camps along the road we didn't like, we opted for one on the ocean that we were hoping for.

Chapter 6   New Brunswick, Maine, Quebec, Vermont, New York and Ontario

The north wind was the factor here. The nice warm sunshine we enjoyed most of the day was no longer with us. Tying the tent to a picnic table seemed the only way to make sure we would be here in the morning. It was too windy to try cooking and we left to eat out. The same thing in the morning. Rain came again and the temperature dropped to 51 degrees by morning.

We had another tiff this morning. I couldn't understand why it was Shirley couldn't find room in her packs to store more food. We were eating out more often than I wanted. Everyone has their idea on what is more important and we were no different. We would have to find a grocery somewhere to replenish supplies. I liked packing dried meals that were small, she liked cans, bottles and other bulky items. She would consume them early to save space and therefore run out sooner.

At least the sun was out. The wind was still with us as we packed. The water in the bay was calm in spite of the wind and a much better color of blue than the grey of yesterday when we unpacked.

We found many new things at our campsite in the daylight. The wind blew in a shirt, almost new, that Shirley kept. A hat and bathing suit snuggled together in a sodden mess in a puddle in the sand. We left them to their demise.

New Glascow provided breakfast as we headed into the New Brunswick Province by way of Amhurst. Traveling along an inland road we saw no water for most of the morning. At St. Johns' we were back against the sea on the Bay of Fundy.

Somewhere along the way we spotted a rocky beach and stopped to explore. On the way, we walked through a wild blueberry patch. We picked as many as we could carry in our hands. A refreshing, fresh snack. At the border, the border guard didn't think it was funny when I questioned him about why I might be carrying a gun.

213

Back on our own soil again, we were thankful to arrive without any problems. The scenery we traveled through in New Brunswick was green and mountainous and into Maine as well. Having difficulty with finding a campground again, we stopped into a Chinese restaurant for supper and were told of one on the Penobscot River. Sounded good to us. The name-Cold Stream Campground-meant just that. The water was cold. The day turned cloudy again and uncomfortable. The sites weren't conducive to tenting but were made to work. A shower made us feel better and we were soon snug as bugs in rugs.

In the middle of the night we were awakened by a thunderstorm pelting our tent with hard drops sounding like rocks were being thrown at us. We felt the water coming up in the tent floor as our Therm-o-rest mattresses became saturated again. We tried to edge away as best we could without being on top of each other and otherwise spent a rotten night trying to be cheerful.

Early morning saw us on our way. I donned my rain gear over my snowsuit when the temperature didn't rise. Packing a drenched tent was getting to be an everyday occurance.

Looking over the maps the night before showed we could visit some mutual friends in Maine and head again into Canada to the north. The warmer clothing would be needed this August. I recalled the warm days I spent on my solo trip out west. I don't remember ever being cold. I never carried cold weather clothing. It must have been a quirk. We were wearing snowsuits and rain gear over sweatshirts and long johns at the same time of year.

We were hoping when we rode into Greenville and called Sandy Neely that we would be invited to spend the night in a warmer shelter. We called her but with the hesitancy in her voice I indicated to Shirley that we may not want to push that thought or plan on it. Sandy invited us to tea when I told her we were so close. We met Sandy and her husband, John, on the raft trip in Arizona. John was out with a raft trip today, as that was his business here, so we instead only visited a short time with Sandy. The rain stopped and it wasn't long before we hit the road again to find our way.

Sandy reported to us that they returned to the Colorado River the next year at the same time of year to find their weather had changed drastically to what we were experiencing now. They fell out of the rafts quite often and needed to be rescued. I was again thankful we had a beautiful weather system when we went.

Down the road at lunch time, we stopped and finished off our Chinese left-overs when it started to rain again. We were getting mighty tired of rain by this time and began to get testy. It continued on and off most of the day.

The temperature never rose higher than 65 degrees but still held a dampness to it. Across the border, I made reservations for a tour bus for us at a tourist center while asking directions to a motel. We knew a campground would be out of the question in a city this size and we couldn't speak the French language to find one. The director spoke English.

The valley we drove through to get to Quebec was one of the prettiest I had seen on all my travels so far. It was fun to make myself feel I was somewhere on a different continent for awhile and this was going to be it.

We had a good, dry time here in the city. It is one that will remain on my list of places to return, to spend more than two nights and a day.

Our motel was a welcome reprieve from sleeping on the ground. It would be the first one on this trip. While we did spend a night in a bed in Connecticut, this would be only the second bed in a couple weeks. We laid out her bedding to dry in the room. Mine wasn't wet. Making supper on the bathroom floor wasn't much better than making it in the wind or in the tent as before. We elected to find a dessert out within walking distance. We needed to walk for awhile. Our exercise was becoming nil.

We met, again, the grandpa and grandson we met on the ferry. We were to meet them one more time after this. We seemed to be going the same places but taking different roads to get there.

We tried to make reservations at a KOA campground outside of town for our next accommodations but they only spoke in French on the phone. We asked the owner of the motel to help us and she did well, laughing at the prospect of herself making reservations to a competitor. She agreed it was a little different accommodation and not really competition and was happy to do it for us.

In the morning, we found the tent wasn't completely dry and hung it in the bathroom before we left for our tour of the city. This day started off badly. While cooking breakfast on the Whisper-Light stove on the hard floor next to the closed front door, I accidently set off the fire alarm. It startled Shirley who was in the shower and she came running into the room with just a towel wrapped around her as I opened the door to set the stove outside. We laughed over the incident. Last thing we needed was a fire department.

I finished breakfast outside on the picnic table. We waited for our bus to pick us up. While we were waiting on the swing on the lawn, the bus came and we were off. We picked up others in their hotels, two who were still asleep, and one at a college, when I realized I left my wallet on the swing. We were an hour away from the motel. The young bus driver made a call for me to the motel owner with borrowed change and I explained to her what I did. She went out to find it still there. The rest of the day I was in debt to Shirley for my spending money. She didn't have much Canadian and I did. My wallet was getting the best of me. I "lost" it in Iowa, too. I felt like an idiot.

We had an interesting tour. It was in two parts. It lasted most of the day. We were shown places in the city, saw the changing of the guard in the palace, left in the center of the city to browse and spend money. Then we were taken into the surrounding countryside to see the strip farms and eat maple sugar bread at a sugar shack and then to the cathedral of St. Anne deBeaupre. I loved this city. The narrow streets and stone buildings fascinated me. I would like to expand my horizons and go to Europe. Listening to the French helped.

We returned, I retreived my wallet giving the owner a cute little gift of thanks and packed up to go to our next reserved over-night place. Our other friends who toured with us came running out of their room. Kueber and Maria Oliveira were from Brazil, touring this country.

"I need to have a picture of me on your motorcycle," she explained. I looked at Shirley and smiled.

"Do you want to do it or do you want me to?" I asked her.

"Go ahead. I don't care." Maria was all excited.

"Here, I just want to stand next to you, I don't have to sit on it."

"No, you sit on it and I'll stand behind it." I put my helmet on her short dark hair and Kueber took the picture.

"Thank you, thank you. My son will get a kick out of it. He won't believe it."

Off to find our way. All the signs were in French and we had to try to decipher them along with the map I was given and drive in the horrendous traffic pattern. Home was a welcome sight. We traveled with KOA for a long time and it was just like going to McDonalds' or Motel 6. We most generally knew what we were getting before we got there, especially when we had a tour book and could read their ads before setting sail for them.

We spent a cold night at 47 degrees. I usually throw my sleeping bag over me like a blanket. My sleeping pad is a short version so my feet hang over a foot or two. When its cold I had to remember to zip my feet into the bag or freeze.

It was getting near time for another oil change. We couldn't speak the language when we found a Honda dealer in Victoriaville, Quebec. I pointed to the oil cans in the display case and the fellow behind the counter placed them on the counter and began to ring them up.

"No," I said, as I stopped him, "in the bike." I made a motion of pouring the cans and pointed to the bikes outside. He smiled and said something in French and ran outside and before long we had the oil changed in both bikes. Shirley was having wobble problems. She indicated it as best she could and the fellow suggested in sign language that she was overloaded. He filled up her front tire with more air thinking it might help. We both laughed at the overloaded part. We were eating much more than we should.

I asked about the squeak and he indicated the bushing of a shock absorber under the engine like the fellow in Yarborough. Let it lie.

We were heading in a southern direction now and intended to enter Vermont soon. It took some doing. We didn't take the freeway but old roads. Some were dirt but we did see the countryside. Restocking in Windsor would hold us till we returned home. This was the final stretch and the rest we traveled before.

After a long ride along Lake Champlain, we found the KOA we were looking for. We came in late and now that we had renewed provisions it was imperative we eat in. Our neighbor wanted to talk to us all the while we were preparing our food and eating our meager offering and swatting the returning mosquitos. Royce, Grace and daughter Tess McConnell were from Kansas and the northeast was not new to them. They related points of interest to us making us wish we met them before coming to the east. It was so pleasant here. The water was warmer than sea water, there were no parties going, no freeway sounds, no lights glaring. I sat in the store and talked to the owners for the time it took Shirley to take her shower. They were a nice couple but I failed to get their names for my journal. It was a good day all the way around.

The rain and wind returned with the mosquitos. The wind battered the tent enough to wake us up and put a scare into us. At least we had a high and dry site this time and the floor did not get saturated as it usually did.

Once up, we decided to spend another day here in the rain instead of traveling. Laundry became the project for the morning. The Essex county fair was held not far from where we were. For $5 we spent the day seeing all the horse pulling I ever wanted to see. Shirley owned one herself and she loved fairs. We ate too much and sat around a lot. Mel Tillis was the entertainer for the day but we decided we didn't need to spend another $8 to see him. We rummaged through the craft building and found things for our grandchildren back home and had an altogether good goof-off day. The rain stopped during the day and we were home before dark.

Turned cold again in the night. The thermometer read 48 degrees by morning. Snowsuits were the clothing of the day. The day was cloudy as we started out with no promises of sun and warmth. It didn't rain all day but the sun had a hard time showing itself, too. Driving through the Green Mountains we remarked back and forth about the bicyclists we saw struggling to get up the inclines. We admired the green area, making a three sided run around the mountains and then on to the south.

Camp was in New York state. On our way home now, we had no desire to venture out of our straight route. North of Glenn Falls was the campsite shared with a couple from New York who insisted we stop and visit with them after our walk down a steep hill in the park. We had coffee with a kicker around their fire and enjoyed the company till dark lowered our lids. We knew from weather reports it would be our coldest night yet and we wanted to make sure our beds were ready for it. We laid our space blankets out to hold our body heat better. We found we couldn't roll up in them as moisture could not get out and we became a sauna in our cocoons.

The temperature dipped to only 42 degrees by morning. It was supposed to be 30 but we were happy it wasn't. I slept like a baby. Shirley may have been cold. She was up, had eaten breakfast and was rolling up her bag before I ever heard anything. If I waited much longer I was afraid she would have rolled me up in the tent or left without me.

It wasn't long till we reached Utica that we could feel comfortable enough to strip down to lighter clothing. The turnpike was taken as far as Buffalo and then we headed Niagra Falls. Shirley hadn't been there in a long time and we could take a short cut across Canada to home.

I slipped on some large rocks getting into the camp and dropped the bike. It was our first drop since last year. It wasn't serious but embarrassing. We never stayed in such a camp before. The security was outrageous. If you put your tent over a white line just a hair you would be charged for an extra lot. Security guards ran around on little scooters making sure there was peace in the park. But we slept well.

We took our pictures of the falls and then trucked on across the border and through the familiar Ontario loop to Windsor. It was a 300 mile day but nothing extraordinary happened. We parted ways on the freeway and we were home before dark for another adventure to add to our credits.

We crossed the border six times. This was our thirtieth state and now our fourth province.

..............."So, you see, Allison, I didn't enjoy the trip back where I lived but I did enjoy seeing all the new territory I never saw before."

"It's too bad you didn't get to Boston," one of them prompted.

218

"Well, maybe another time. Hey, I've got to get going. It'll be noon if I don't move on. Maybe I'll see you guys some other time. Stop in at my place if you come through there." I handed them the journal and they all wrote their addresses and phone numbers in them and I gave out a name card.

As I was outside putting on my helmet and getting ready for my ride across the bridge, Allison came out and put a pin on me. "This is for you. I'm promoting my home town and this will remind you of us, dear."

"Why, thank you, I don't get these kinds of gifts. I'll treasure it and maybe I'll be out there sometime soon and I will definitely look you up."

Off to the bridge, I hustled, riding along the freeway where bicycles are not allowed. A half mile down hill to the bridge office and I was inside asking about getting across.

"See that post over there," the officer pointed. "You stand over there and wait and a truck will be there to pick you up. I'll call one over. They are working on the other side. It'll cost you one dollar, please."

I paid the dollar, happy that was all I had to do and sat on the curb waiting for my ride. In a very short time a pick-up truck with two fellows came alongside, hoisted my bike over the top of the bed and I was riding over the bridge to the Lower Peninsula. Shirley should have been here. She would have enjoyed this. But she wasn't. I couldn't even ask if we were still friends.

They left me off on the other side and I was on my way south for another 400 miles or so expecting to arrive in a week. I planned on spending a few days with a friend in Traverse City.

Adventure #7

East by Way of Texas

Chapter 1   Indiana,Kentucky, Tennessee and Arkansas

The Lower Peninsula was like coming home again. I knew this area well enough, I never felt the apprehension I felt when exploring unknown places in other states. I had a plan. I would try to retrace the DALMAC arrows on the opposite side of the road. Or I could try recognizing places I've seen before. I kept the state map and would use it as best I could. So many smaller roads that I could use would not be on the state map. I pedaled as best I could, following C81, hoping it wouldn't be as hilly as a parallel road closer to the center of the state. I was wrong. It was hilly enough for me to get off the bicycle and push the bike up the hill.

I rode along the Lake Michigan coast line after Harbor Springs. It was a gruelling ride. In Petosky, I stopped for air in one tire and pressed on. I stopped in Charlevoix to see the woman with the beauty shop. It felt good to sit awhile in the air conditioning. I hoped to get an invitation for overnight but I must not have made a good enough impression.

At Fishermans' Cove State Park, I found the dreaded sign out front--Sorry, Full. I stopped in anyway in hopes they were wrong. I was given a site better than all the rest. I didn't know that our state must keep sites reserved for those who come in on our own power. How happy I was to find this out! I was in a nicely secluded wooded

EAST BY WAY OF TEXAS

spot between the ranger station and the beach. I could see none of the other campers and I liked that. I made my supper on the white beach sand and watched the sun slip into the lake as a huge orange ball. The breezes were warm and gentle. I slept the best I've slept in a long time. No traffic noises, just the lapping of the water on the sand and no revelers, no four legged bandits.

It felt good to prepare pancakes while the newcomers standing on the hill in line, watched. On Highway 31, I met a headwind, preventing me from making better time. I bought some sweets at a farm market and ate fruit at a rest area. Met Fred here who talked my arm off for a change. He wanted to hear more about my trip to Texas where he was from originally. He was of Mexican descent but lived in several different places on a continuous vacation. He was retired.

"Did you get down along the gulf?" he asked.

"No, but almost. I only had one prime destination in mind in Texas. The Alamo."

"I'm from Corpus Cristie myself. Tell me about riding a motorcycle. I always wanted to ride one." Fred was 85 years old. I told him about the rudimentary things of riding and about my lost bicycle riding partner who was home padding her bottom.................

That was the first time we would leave for a motorcycle trip in October. We planned it this way because it should be hot in Texas in summer. We planned on going directly to the Alamo, turning east to Florida and up the east coast to Washington D.C. and home.

"I think we ought to take the foul weather gear with us. Coming home in three weeks we may run into cold in the north," I suggested to Shirley when we collaborated on packing.

"I'm taking my snow suit again," she reassured me. I got some warmer gloves from Armond, too, and a different pair of boots." Armond was her son-in-law.

We couldn't have started on a better day. The temperatures were hovering around the 55 degree mark. It was raining and riding the freeway with the heavy traffic we continued to ask ourselves the question always on our mind. What are we doing here? Trucks sprayed us as they rumbled past. We needed our snow suits and rain gear to keep warm and dry. Without windshield wipers, our windshields were splattered with dirty road water. Shirley wore a face shield and it was as spattered with muddy water as my face without the shield.

We only traveled 168 miles to Fort Wayne and took a motel room for the night. We'd keep the tent dry another day. Taking I-69 to the south we would stay on it all the way to Nashville,

Tennessee. "It better hurry up and get warm. This 42 degrees is not my idea of comfort, Pony Express," I heard over the radio.

"If we can get to the south in a hurry, I guess it will be warm enough all right," I returned. "Maybe Nashville won't be cold."

It wouldn't take us long to get through the state of Kentucky. We stayed on the I-65 freeway from Louisville south into Tennessee. It was going to be too cold to enjoy much of anything.

We thought we would like to go to Fort Knox to see if they had any left-overs but decided it was out of our way and passed it up. Nearing Mammoth Cave, I heard, "Have you ever been to the big cave?"

"Yea, we were there when the kids were little, Granny, I don't want to go again. Do you? It's cold in there, too." We continued to roll along trying to keep warm. I hit a big pot hole in the road and it jerked my left mirror loose. It hung there just swinging until I could stop and remove it. At a hardware store I couldn't get any screws to put it back together. I needed regular Honda screws. I had a roll of duct tape. It always came in handy for one thing or other. It held the mirror somewhat even though I had to run the tape clear across the windshield for bracing. The KOA was waiting for us again. It was still cold and I threw all my clothes over my sleeping bag to keep warm through the night.

The frost was on the pumpkin when we emerged from our abode. A stop at Loretta Lynn's Kitchen gave us a good breakfast. It was warming up and the sun was out for the remainder of the day. We met a couple from our state, Chuck and Joanne Schive, and two couples from Louisiana at the visitor center. We were back to explaining ourselves, back in the oddball business. We liked it.

In Nashville, we set up camp and took off the foul weather gear. The sun felt good as we walked around and found the place to board the tour bus for town. We spent the rest of the day visiting the Ryman auditorium, Music Row, Waylon Jennings Museum and the drive around to see where the entertainers lived.

With still plenty of time after the five hour tour, we rode our bikes back into town for a dinner of catfish at the Nashville Palace. Entertainment wasn't going to be for a long time so we left before dark. I hadn't any headlight now. My bike seemed to be falling apart as I rode. The sun had set. With the band-aid fix on the turn signal and now without a headlight I was getting into trouble. It is illegal in some states to not have a headlight working, even in daylight. For safety reasons it is best to be seen.

In camp, we found out there was entertainment in a metal barn. We enjoyed the country music, sitting on folding chairs. I lined up a Honda dealer for a fix-it for tomorrow.

222

The temperature fell to 38 degrees but there was no frost this time. I ate left-overs from the day before and we were off to get fixed, and then out to the country veering west. This was a pleasant part of Tennessee to travel. Not much different from Michigan. After the couple of days of rain and cold, the mild weather put us on the alert. We sat on the grass near a shopping center eating lunch when some geese across the road must have smelled our food. They were curious and looked too aggressive for us. We left.

State road 70 was too slow to get anywhere fast. We turned south again at Camden to get back on the interstate 40.

We spent a lot of time visiting Graceland and toured the home of Elvis Presley. "I never really thought that much of him, did you?" I asked Shirley after we toured his home.

"Yea, he was one of my favorites but I never went crazy like the rest of the women did."

"I liked to listen to him but not watch him. He seemed too prissy to me."

I liked him much better after seeing more of his personality here in his home. Watching the Elvis Presley Story later, I could get a better picture.

We spent so much time in Memphis we had to hurry to the next KOA. We set up in the dark. It was warmer and we wouldn't have to huddle in our clothes in bed.

We picked the wrong place to get a good night's sleep. Because we were in a tent, we were given the site farthest from the rest room. It the worst one in the camp. We were parked next to the freeway, near an exit. We could hear the trucks changing gears as they pulled off for the truck stop across the road and when they left it. A bridge crossed a river on the other side and planks rattled when the trucks drove over and there was much traffic. Mosquitos became prevalent again. We were reminded of Nova Scotia. A large 76 gas sign was shining through the tent walls.

We were up early to get out of there and only made coffee. At a restaurant a man talked to us during breakfast. He wanted to be our travel agent, he said. He knew of a good place to go to in Oklahoma. We found out he had a video film he rented and wanted someone to return it for him. He was going the other way. He smelled of liquor. We left to laughter.

The wind picked up from the north and we felt we were riding on the edges of our tires. In Hot Springs, the wind didn't blow as hard. We got off our iron steeds, parked them and walked around the area to see the old bath houses.

"Do you want to get a bath?" she asked.

"Why, do I smell that bad?" I countered.

"No, I just thought it would be fun to have a real mineral steam bath. Isn't that what these are?"

"Yea, I guess so, let's look around and see what's what." One house was not in operation, another not open till later. We were somewhat discouraged with that. We were on a schedule of a sort. We climbed up a hill in back of the town that gave a better view of the city and then down the hill found a mineral spring. Shirley thought the water too hot. Steam was emitting from it and it smelled of sulphur.

"I remember a spa in Colorado that was an open swimming pool. There were funny white things floating in the water but it was warm all winter."

"Let's walk through one of the elite hotels to see how the other half live." It was elegant inside. We sat in one of the sitting rooms making out post cards in our jeans and boots. These were not the proper attire for this exquisite place. It lent us an appetite for the better life.

"Let's go, I don't think I can stand all this opulence," I sighed.

On through the Ozarks. So hilly and curvy. It was fun riding on the two lane road of Highway 7. The tediousness of the fast lane returned when we joined I-30, staying on it through Texarkana and to the nights hotel, a KOA camp again. This wasn't the elegant hotel. It was flat and hard but far enough off the freeway to have silence except for a cow mooing in the meadow. We lounged around trying to make a semblance of our gear, cleaning us and it. I tried fixing my whisperlight stove again. The pressure pump didn't work. A drop of oil from the bike dipstick went a long way. It worked and dinner was prepared. No pool here so we took our time in the shower and watched some television in the recreation room.

One of our neighbors brought fresh baked muffins to us once we were out of bed in the morning. It was nice and we thanked her for her thoughtfulness. We packed them up to take with us and ate breakfast out. We weren't supposed to, as we ate in last night. With the temperature hovering around the 42 degree mark we didn't feel the need to shiver our way through oatmeal and instant coffee.

Chapter 2   Texas and Louisiana

I always wanted to go to Texas. It was here, all my western movie idols lived and breathed. We were not going to just ride through the panhandle to another state. This time we would drive into the heart of the state.

"Let's try to see Texas from the little roads, Shirley," I implored. "Have you seen more of this state than just where we went last year?"

"I've been to Dallas and Wichita Falls, but that's about all."

"The best I can say for me is the fly-in to Dallas-Fort Worth airport on our way to the Grand Canyon."

"Good. Let's see the state the old way."

We shifted into gear out of Texarcana south on 69, west on 77, south again on 259, to 155, to Tyler, home of the roses. Acres of roses in every color and style imaginable. The air wafted of roses. We walked the gardens for a few hours, snacking on a sweet treat and coffee again.

Back on the road it was uneventful on Highway 31 to Waco. We talked to a trucker with the name of Daddy Rabbit. Every radio handle carried some sort of connotation to it and this one was not any different. I asked if he had a lot of kids.

"Yea, I've got a couple kids in the wings," he explained, "Probably some more around the country I don't know about, too."

"Are you bragging or complaining?" I asked.

"Maybe a little bit of both, Pony Express." We rode on not seeing him for awhile and then we'd hear it over the radio, "Pony Express? You still there?"

"Yes, I'm here."

"I've gotta get off here in Waco. You two have yourself a safe ride, ya' hear? None of that fooling around down here with all these cowboys."

"Rest assured, we'll look after each other. You have a safe ride yourself. Look us up if you ever get to Michigan.

"Ten-four, see ya'." Ten miles down the road I asked Granny to switch to our own channel we pre-planned before we left.

"He was a good looking son-of-a-gun, wasn't he?" I asked.

"Yea, we should have asked him to stop for a coffee break."

225

"I didn't see any place to stop or I would have suggested it. Oh, well, let's get on the freeway to Austin. It's getting late in the afternoon. Our park is still to the south of town and you know how we hate driving through towns."

The chatter began now we were back on the interstate. We were talking to another mild-mannered trucker by the name of "Smilin' Joe". He had a sweet way of talking and we ate it up like candy. He asked us to stop for a break before we got to Austin and this time we took him on.

"We have to get gas pretty soon. Why don't we go on to the next gas place?" I suggested. "How far is it to the next truck stop?"

"Just about 20 miles. I don't know if I can wait that long to sit with you two. You're just too good looking to be watchin' in my mirror."

We stopped to get our gas while he parked his rig and said he'd see us inside.

"This is a fine kettle of fish. We don't even know if he's worth stopping for," said Shirley, a little exasperated.

"We don't have to marry him, we're only going to have something to eat. He's buying. He sounds good, doesn't he?"

"Yea, let's hope he isn't like the "potato man" we drove with last year up north. Remember him?"

"Oh, yes, he had the larynx of a Latin lover with the looks of a Gila monster." Our fears were put to rest inside the truck stop restaurant. We looked all over for our handsome prince and then met the frog. He wasn't much to look at for looks, and weighed a hefty 250 pounds or more. He was nice and polite to talk with but hard to look at. Soon we were back on the road to Austin, whizzing through the town with hardly a problem. As dusk settled in the campground, we set ourselves up and walked to a deli for our supper.

For breakfast, I tried to make pancakes on my repaired whisperlight stove only to find it still not wanting to cooperate. "I'm glad I brought along some sterno. What a waste of money," I reiterated to Shirley.

Making good time to San Antonio, it afforded us the rest of the day to tour the Alamo. No matter how many pictures of famous places one sees, it never quite looks like the pictures when you see it first hand. It looked so big in the pictures and so small in reality. Such a small fortress among these large office buildings. It is hard to put it in perspective. There was nothing here in the days of the battle to save our democracy. To visualize this I needed to get inside and feel the struggle in the walls.

The walls had been decaying and they have been repaired. It reminded me of our American flag and how it has been torn, burnt and broken. But with diligence has been repaired and returned to its glory.

The thick wooden doors welcomed us to the inner sanctum. Inside, a diorama gave me the perspective I needed to explain in minute detail how the long battle began and ended. Artifacts were displayed from the period. A tour was given to explain the entire building and the battle, and I went away with a greater understanding.

After a quiet lunch in a Woolworth store and stroll to peek into the storefronts, we returned to our bikes parked in a parking garage for more safety and began our trek to the east by way of Houston. The wind picked up furiously from the east. We headed straight into it making our gas mileage deteriorate. We forgot to check our gas gauges again and were running near empty when another trucker spied one down the highway for us and we were saved. There wasn't much of anything to look at while we drove along I-10. We would be on this road all the way to Florida. Where were the cowboys? Where were the horses?

It was a sunny day. Our faces had the beginnings of the raccoon image again. The wind blew us into the KOA for the night. The pool was too cold even though the air felt warm. The road dirt on my bike was getting to me and a fellow camper in a motor home loaned me the use of his hose and water to make it shine like new. We had a serene setting and should've slept well.

We didn't sleep all that well and were up early to make another batch of pancakes. Soon this batter would be gone and I wouldn't have to carry it or the maple syrup to go with it.

Stopping for coffee at a McDonalds' introduced us to a fellow biker riding his Honda from South America. He was interesting to talk to. He wasn't going our way but had to show us his chrome plated bike. It was pretty but needed a lot of care to keep it that way. It was more of a show bike.

My radio gave me some trouble as before. The coaxial cable came out and I didn't know it and then the wires connecting the radio to the battery came loose. This was not my trip for keeping the bike in perfect condition. It wasn't as time consuming as the dead battery of the California trip but just as annoying.

We stayed on I-10 talking to "Polar Bear" and "Puppy Dog", stopping to have coffee with them at one point. Another sang to us the lyrics of "Ode to Loose Wheel" to the tune of "Lucille" that is usually sung by Kenny Rogers, country-western singer.

After LaFayette I asked Shirley if she'd like to take some back roads into New Orleans for a change of pace and received a resounding, "Yes". Riding through the cane fields and bayous made us realize how lucky we were. Outside of New Orleans, a KOA advertised good prices and had tours available of the town. That was for us. We would rather someone else showed us their way through town than trying to find things ourselves. We signed up for a day and a night tour.

Another night of no sleep. Boats, trains, planes, fire sirens, kids yelling and dogs barking were enough to keep everyone awake all night. Making the usual pancake breakfast, we noticed a neighbor's car window broken during the night. Was it a prankster? Nobody knew.

Our bus was late, making our date with the tour bus late resulting in a couple angry tour people and passengers. We rode around all morning looking at the town, and had a riverboat tour. We snuck into the captains quarters and were given a quick look at it and in the kitchen or galley they welcomed our inquisitiveness. I read a book of a woman who tried to make it on a fishing boat in the gulf as a regular hand. Being a woman, they always thought she ought to be in the galley and she had a difficult time making her way into the system. She made it but at dire cost to her ego. She resigned after many years of indifference toward her.

There was no need to go back to the camp until after we finished our night tour. We didn't get enough walking in the day tour so we ventured on our own. We sampled many things we never had before. Alligator meat tasted more like chicken. We had to have jambalaya for lunch. It was delicious. Sampled fudge and had coffee auLait and bennaits. We were told they were coffee with cream and donuts fried in grease. Found a terrific etched buffalo horn and had it sent home. Where was I to carry a buffalo horn?

The tour bus was late for the evening. Tour people didn't know anything and more angry tourists showed up. We stayed together with a couple from our camp, Dennis and Stephanie Ephraim from New Zealand and another, Jack and Lillian Padden from Australia and one from San Francisco. We were aboard at long last and dropped off at several different night spots to see floor shows, drink, enjoy the revelry and for a final coffee AuLait and Bennaits. Other tid-bits of food were purchased for the next day. All in all we enjoyed the town. A great place to visit but not to live there. It was so busy. During the day we stood listening to the many vendors, panhandlers and musicians on the sidewalks. Music everywhere. At night it emitted from the many night spots out onto the streets.

Chapter 3

Mississippi, Alabama Florida, Georgia and South Carolina

The next day we got ourselves turned around somehow while getting on the freeway in town. We were heading to the west rather than the east. I exited the first exit and we were heading the right way.

Crossing over the border into Mississippi put us back on I-10 with beautiful white beaches of white sand to our right. On the left we passed many luxury homes and now and again some poverty stricken homes.

In Biloxi, our lunch would be at the Fishermans' Wharf for gumbo. I was gaining a taste for the spicy foods of this Cajun country. After a picture taking session, Shirley found her camera was not working. We were beginning to get a long list of broken items.

Because we stayed on I-10, the travel time was cut to a minimum. We passed along at a good speed with no trouble from the Hondas. Everything was in good working order. My mirror was no longer dangling, the headlight shone bright, the radios worked well. Something was amiss. The camera didn't matter as much. I still had mine. The air was not hot and sticky here in the south. Our timing might have been right. It wasn't warm enough to swim in the ocean, the winds were cool.

We rode on through Alabama without a hitch. We didn't stop to see anything but hummed along admiring the things we did see. Hardly did we notice crossing over Mobile Bay. If it wasn't on the map I wouldn't have known. The bridges were long as we went from island to island. Fishing and pleasure boats lined the waters' edges.

In Pensicola, we dropped down to four lane 98 to ride along the water. The beaches would have been much more inviting if it weren't so cool. Gulf winds penetrated our leather jackets while the sun continued to shine. A KOA camp was located in Destin. It was a nice camp with all the amenities most KOA's have. We took a walk to the beach across the busy highway at sundown to beachcomb and stretch our tired legs.

229

"How can our legs be so tired when we sit all day on those bikes?"

"I don't know. Maybe it's because we are used to more activity and they're used to getting more."

"My butt is getting the activity. Doesn't yours get sore sitting in that same position all the time?"

"Yea, I try to move around a little but there isn't any place to go."

"Remember how we say that about the bicycles?"

"But we get off them more often."

"Are you saying we need to get off more often on these, too?"

"It wouldn't hurt. Is that a pun?" she laughed.

"We have a lot of territory to cover. If we do that I will need more time off work. We'll be gone three weeks as it is."

"When are you going to retire so we don't have to plan around this all the time?"

"Not soon enough. When Walt retires you probably won't be going as much."

"Not with you. I hope he wants to travel in the car. He travels now but it's all business. I don't know that he enjoys the country like we do."

"I hope he does for your sake. What will you do if he just sits around the house?"

"He won't just sit around. The house needs to be finished. We've been living in it for a long time in its half finished state. I've got many things for him to do."

The beach was empty of people. The water lapped at the sand so quietly it was hard for us to believe it was ocean. A father and young son played with their dog at one end of the beach. Some larger motels were at the other with their lights blinking in the impending dark. The sun was setting on the far end over land turning the sky and sand into a brilliant orange, than violet and purple before the darkness was totally on us. We could just faintly make out the small surf along the sand as we trudged across the dunes and across the road to our home away from home.

We slept very well away from the road noises. The dunes must have been a good sound barrier. We noticed that as we walked back from the beach. We could hear a bird or two as we left to find breakfast the next morning. They flittered through the short scrubby bushes along the sand road to the highway. The temperatures were in the 50's as we departed Destin. Breakfast in a Cajun Country restaurant was fine. Some of the customers looked at us on the wary side. We could feel them talking about us. They saw us drive up on the Hondas. I felt we were still in Cajun country from all the rumors I'd heard. But we were in Florida now and there must not be a border with these people except on the maps. We

230

still enjoyed a good grits and eggs breakfast and admired their cherished row upon row of caps on the ceiling. Every cap that has been made must be on that ceiling. This was a truck stop of a sort. It was not on the interstate but must be frequented by truckers and they donated their caps to the cause.

Near Panama City Shirley called out, "I didn't call home today like I was suppose to, Pony Express."

"Does that mean we better stop, Granny?"

"Whenever you want, I just have to do it while Sheri is in the office, you know."

We turned into a Waffle House restaurant and I sat with a cup of coffee in front of me between some folks going off to the salt mines of work. The lady on my left started up the conversation, continuing to talk until Shirley got off the phone.

"You girls sure are brave."

"What do you mean," Shirley asked even though she knew her answer.

"To go off like that across the country with just the two of you, and on a motorcycle. You're so brave!"

"I don't know. Maybe we're just stupid."

"Whatever you call it, I admire anyone with the guts to do it. And you're having fun, too."

"You could do it, too, you know. It doesn't take that much thought to ride one of those."

"Not me. I wouldn't trust them. I don't even like driving the car." She wouldn't let us go until she could give us a hug and wish us a safe and happy journey. People like her are what this whole trip was about. It was seeing the country we lived in but the people were what made it what it was and these are people that will always be remembered in our thoughts. I wished I had obtained her name and address.

We continued on our way around the gulf on Alternate 27. The radio reported Hurricane Floyd was brewing in that gulf and we could see by the wind that we were going to be in it, if we didn't hurry and get inland to mom's house before it hit. We didn't linger long. Stopping in a swamp rest area for a quick lunch gave Shirley her first look at an armadillo. "I've always wanted to see one of those things," she said as she tried to get a picture of the scared animal. It retreated back into the weeds as she approached. It wandered off into the cabbage palm grove.

As the cloud cover was turning into a mean black, we pushed on. Mom lived in the Zephyrhills area and was waiting for us. It sprinkled slightly. We stayed two nights with her before we began our adventure up the eastern coast. We spent the time replenishing our supplies out of her kitchen and getting an oil change in both bikes. Some time in Tampa shopping gave us the walking we desperately needed. Time went fast and she bade us good-by again. We were on our way to Sea World in Orlando.

We had been to the "mecca of the south" before so neither of us wanted to return to the hubbub of Disney World. A good portion of our day was spent watching the fish and mammals of the sea and photographing the tropical floral groves.

We both visited Daytona Beach before and just scurried through the area to Flager Beach for the night. It was turning colder. It did not have the usual feel of warm Florida. The KOA had its own pub in the upper floor of the recreation hall where we indulged not only in a cold beer and hamburger but conversation with Dennis and Gertrude Bowers of Daytona Beach. They were motorcyclists going somewhere to pick up a larger Gold Wing they purchased in the north. They sat and watched us fix dinner, eat, read the map and fill out journals and post cards all the while talking. We were told we were next to a canal that was stocked with alligators. Before dark we wandered around the canal but didn't see anything that looked like alligators and went to bed.

They didn't come out of the canal to eat us up during the night either. Everything was still intact. We stayed along the ocean road till we reached Jacksonville. Many new condominiums were being erected along this road and the beaches would no longer be visible by the casual tourist. Stopping at one open beach, we examined the treasures in its sand. It was too cold to stay long. The beach was virtually deserted. The water was dark and angry as it crashed into the shallower water far out from the beach. The tide was out at this time of day. The sky mirrored the water in its' anger. The wind remained brisk, blowing fine white sand at us and scouring the finish on the bikes. We didn't like what it was doing and turned west to go further inland and ride the freeway again.

Shirley had not been to Savanna. This was a city one of us had not been to and it would provide another tour. I was here a few years before and enjoyed the old city on the water. I showed her the old cotton warehouses that were now businesses for the tourists on Bay Street and River Street. Introduced her to pralines and caramel apples.

When I was here before I took time out during the day to walk alone along the streets. I examined the old architecture. Many beautiful old buildings were being preserved. Stone stepping blocks were still in place next to hitching posts for the carriages of old. Some streets still had the old paving stones and gutters were bricked in red with the manufacturer's name enbedded in them. I visited Lee's headquarters, the pioneer Boy Scouter Powell's

232

house and the Daughters of the Revolution cemetery. It was a hot, humid August when I walked these streets. It was much cooler this October. We walked several miles and then had to depart to go to the next night's rest stop in South Carolina.

The temperature was dropping each morning as we drove north. It was only 48 degrees and it reminded us of our cold time in the north two years before. We had a long way to go before we finished our northern drive but hoped the weather would change for the better. It was still only October and there were many good days left before the snows fell.

One of our camp mates emerged from his tent in the morning. We didn't even hear him drive in during the night. He was driving a big Gold Wing and was from Quebec. Jacques Lemay could only speak French so we couldn't communicate as well as we would have liked. He pointed out on the map where he was from and where he was going. We pointed out our travels and he put on a big smile for our benefit. He was young and good looking. He wouldn't have any trouble getting around with that. We were traveling in opposite directions. It would have been interesting to be going the same way together. I don't know how we would have communicated on the bikes. He had a radio but we couldn't understand French.

Chapter 4   North Carolina and Virginia

We continued to ride in the cold through the border. Stopping for gas, Shirley ate some pie a la mode while I indulged in some hot chili to warm me up.

"You know, Marion, they say you should eat or drink cold things if you're cold and hot things if you're hot."

"I don't care. That ice cream makes me shiver just looking at it. This chili will last a long time in my stomach and it will feel good when it comes back up."

"My pie is warm," she teased.

She had some friends from back home who moved to Fayetteville. She had an address and phone number. She gave them a call when we were nearer the town and we had a welcome time with them. Ron and Betty LaMirand have lived in a town near us at home. A couple of their children came over and we tried to identify who knew who but failed. We watched a movie with them and then went to bed in a real bed. It was nice to be in one. We only had a few of those on this trip. One of our goals was to do a whole adventure like this without the use of a bed but when one was available I sure didn't say no to it!

We were up at our usual early hour and Ron knew a place where we could get a big breakfast for real cheap and we followed the two of them in their car to the restaurant. It was cheap and it was good and plentiful. We said our farewells again to some fine friends. I've met them again when they returned to our state and wouldn't you know, it would be in the restaurant that had the biggest and cheapest breakfast in town.

My radio needed a quick repair again and we were off to Goldboro. No longer were we on the freeway, but the smaller roads, to see scenery. U.S. 13 took us north, passing many peanut and cotton fields. Some were picked and some not. U.S. 70 and 13 would place us farther north past Greenville. "I recall many a truck driver saying they were heading for that town but to look at it, I can't understand why. What do you suppose they would have to truck here?"

234

"I don't know but there sure are a lot of tarpaper shacks. It looks like this is still slave country. It doesn't look like the sort of place we should want to stop in for long." On State 64, we were back to an easterly direction. In Plymouth, we looked at the map and checked the time. A KOA was located in Virginia Beach. We wanted to go to Cape Hateras and Nags Head out on the little spit of land. As late as it was getting and not knowing the availability of accommodations we opted to not go out there.

We crossed some toll bridges to get to Virginia Beach. One for five cents and one for ten cents. It was hardly worth the collection. Exact change was requested. Riding a motorcycle in main stream traffic of rat race pace is not fun when you have to dig for change.

The KOA was a very large park arranged in sections. We were put in the farthest-from-everything section next to the highway. "I think we are second class citizens here, don't you?"

"Why can't we park up there where the johns, water and electrical outlets are?" she asked.

"I know, it's not like they have a full house. It's half empty." To our right, an older couple was living out of their station wagon. They must be living there, perhaps homeless. Enough junk around the car showed it. They had two cats they fed and piles of possessions that indicated the same. On the other side, a some young boys were being noisy, blaring their radio above the maximum noise levels. That didn't bother us since the highway noises were louder.

Ear plugs worked well to drown out the noises for my sleep. Upon wakening, I heard the dreaded sound on the top of the tent. Shirley, waking, rolled over asking, "Are those acorns dropping?"

"I don't know, but I don't think I want to look outside."

She unzipped her warm bag, unzipped the tent door, zipped it back up and plopped back down in her bag.

"Does that mean it's sunny and warm out there and you can't wait to get up and out?"

"No, it means it's so foggy I can't see the acorns that aren't dropping on our tent."

I looked out the other open window myself and she was right. Nothing could be seen past our bikes sitting at the ready covered in moisture. The street lights were still burning up on the hill away from us with halos of light surrounding them. All was quiet except the noise on the road and the plopping of the water dropping on the tent from the trees. I laid back down in the warm, dry bed. We planned on making it to Washington, D.C. today where Shirley's husband worked. We planned on going to Delaware and Maryland before getting to McLean. I never saw Valley Forge. Even the dismal day was not going to shortstep our desire to see all. We needed to pass through these little states on our odyssey and were determined to do it today.

Chapter 5

Delaware, Maryland, Pennsylvania, D.C., W. Virginia and Ohio

Before we could do that we needed to pay the $9 fee to cross the Chesapeake Bay Bridge. I read the novel, *Chesapeake* by James Mitchner last winter and the thoughts of seeing for myself the spots I read about was exciting even if we didn't dwell on time there. The bridge was not only a bridge but a tunnel in two places. It was flat against the water. I felt more like on a boat crossing above the water and then a mole in the tunnels.

The long spit of land connecting what looks like two Virginias looked like the Nova Scotia territory we passed through the year before. Many estuaries on either side of the road. It was Sunday. Churches were everywhere; people were coming and going from them. Highway 13 carried us all the way up the penninsula to Maryland and into Wilmington. A flea market in Delaware containing anything one could possibly want to buy gave us a reprieve from sitting on the seats.

Just outside of Wilmington we got "misplaced" again but with diligence in map and sign reading we made our way through the afternoon Sunday traffic to the West Chester KOA camp.

We were allowed to pick any site we wanted in the tent section. We drove in the hilly camp and could not find a suitable spot.

"You know, I'm getting tired of being treated like a second class citizen, Shirley."

"What are you gonna do?" she asked as I rode back to the office.

"I'm gonna tell 'em so."

Back at the desk I implored them to give us a better place. They were very helpful and said we could take any place we wanted. It was the off season.

"Thank you," I said, "we've traveled all over this country and every KOA or other place treats us like second class citizens. I'm getting a little tired of it. We have just about all the things the big motor homes have. We have our living room, kitchen, bedroom and

237

even a vestibule when we use my smaller tent. The only thing we don't have is a bathroom and you have them here for our use the same as anyone elses'. You have the running water and the electricity if we need it."

The owner agreed. "Why don't you go up on the hill there with those other motor homes? The places are bigger and you'll be closer to the rest rooms!"

"Thank you, again, I surely appreciate your consideration."

With that we plunked ourselves between two bus sized motor homes. We were now part of the elite group but garnered no favors from anyone. We were sheltered from the wind.

The temperatures in the morning lowered to the thirties making a very cold night. We put all the clothing we could over us, using the space blanket over and under us. We were toasty inside. There was a good covering of frost on the tent when we awoke. We chipped it off and packed it up like it was nothing, taking a longer time than usual. Frost on the windshields could not be scraped off and we hoped by the time we made some pancakes and had a couple cups of coffee the frost would be wipeable. Shirley was trying to get a cold. We couldn't imagine why with the weather we have endured for the past two weeks. It took a long time to find Valley Forge. Roads weren't marked very well and we stopped to find some *Contact* for the cold. She was becoming a basket case before long. I reminded her of the deplorable cold the troops endured during the Valley Forge campaign. It didn't phase her at all.

We only stayed at the memorial a couple hours, walking the intended paths, absorbing as much sun and history as possible. The trees were changing color presenting us with a nice background for the many pictures I took. We didn't always get the fall colors since we usually toured in the summer months.

With the time change almost upon us the days didn't last as long as summer. We sped as best we could to get to Walt's before dark.

We put on our best duds and Walt took us and the owner of the house out to dinner by cab. In one of Kathryn's bedrooms, I could not sleep. I was given so many blankets I kept pushing them to the side but found no real relief. I probably should have just slept on the floor. I was too warm.

We were up early with Walt to catch the bus to the subway to go to D.C. We had breakfast with him and left him to his work to run around town. We toured the Bureau of Engraving and saw how our money was made. We were disappointed when they didn't give samples. The Washington monument attracted our attention. It was

238

a warm day at last and the sun was out in all its glory. Many joggers ran around the sidewalks as we walked to the Viet Nam memorial to pay our respects. Message bicyclists and document runners were everywhere. Traffic was as busy as usual in this government city.

After lunch in the L'Enhant Plaza near the postal headquarters with Walt, we viewed the Smithsonian Institute. I didn't like any of the display today. When a fire was reported I thought the whole thing could burn for all I cared but there was minimal damage to a kitchen in the building.

Union Station was closed for renovation but the Capital was open for tours. It was a lot of walking but we were in a deficit and didn't mind if we were hurting. We met up with Walt in late afternoon, taking the subway back and supper in another mall. We talked with Kathryn who was in her 80's before retiring for the night and then it was to bed. I opened the window and threw off a ton of blankets.

We were back to reality in the morning when I saw the ugliness I didn't want to see out the window. Drizzly rain. Walt had already gone to work and we had a light breakfast with Kathryn before leaving. It was still dark and dismal. I called my union headquarters in Alexandria, the day before, for directions to their offices and we made tracks for it. It was too early for business even though it took us a long time to find the right building. It was tucked away among the other buildings the same design and on a one way street. A restaurant where we spent some of that extra time was just around the corner.

Dressed in our warm extra clothes with yellow rain suits we were a sight to behold when our then vice-president, Vern Myers, opened the locked door. I knew most of the board members on sight and we were welcomed into their beautiful quarters. I met with Dallas Fields, our labor relations person. Scotty Hicks was present and a secretary, Mary Louis, showed us around as the board went about their tasks. A long talk with Mr. Miller, a past president, gave me some insight in the upcoming contract talks. He was an advisor to the board. Dallas invited us to sit in on a board meeting held that morning on our car allowance. Everyone was here for the meeting and I took home much good will from it.

As much as I enjoyed being with these fellows I knew my riding partner didn't want to stay too long. I didn't want to overstay the visit myself. We donned our cumbersome yellow rainsuits and continued to find our way out of Washington.

On to Manassas to see the memorial of the battle there during the Civil War. We were still touring on my history lesson. Lunch of Greek Gyros were good but kept returning to us as we rode along to U.S. 50. Shirley said she used this road many times in her drives

239

to and from D.C. and found it a welcome change from the freeway. The sun was out but it was cold and windy.

The temperatures dropped dramatically in the next three hours. The sun did not offer the warmth as it did earlier as we wound through the mountains of West Virginia. Crossing the Potomac river at Romney surprised me.

"Wasn't that the Potomac River sign back there, Granny?"

"I think so."

"Are we going the wrong way?"

"You have the map."

"I can't see it. It must be too small."

"Let's take a break so you can look," she suggested. We pulled off to the side of the road to check, finding it was the same river. "This must be where it begins, here in the mountains."

"Thank God. I don't want to do these miles again. It's too cold," I said as I tucked them under my armpits to try to warm them. Stamping my feet on the ground should bring back some circulation to them.

"Are you that cold?" she asked.

"My hands feel like they are going to fall off any minute. My gosh, you only have your summer gloves on. Aren't you freezing? The thermometer reads 34 degrees."

"No, I'm all right."

"You sure have a different comfort level than I. We'd better go before I freeze in this spot." I was wearing a pair of wool gloves under some leather gloves. They might have been too tight and cut off the circulation. She did put on the warmer ones she got from Armond.

The sun hit us in places when rounding hills or riding up them, warming us slightly. More often, we were in the shadows where it was colder. The sun was so brilliant in our faces it made it difficult to see well. A truck driver behind us on the curvy two lane road tried to talk us into being warm. It didn't work.

An hour later we stopped again.

"Granny, let's get a cup of coffee. I want to put on some warmer socks. My feet have lost their usefullness. What are we doing here, anyhow?"

"O.K., Pony Express. My cold isn't getting any better any way."

I changed all my wearing apparell. At 34 degrees and traveling at a speed of around 60 miles per hour, our wind chill factor was zero degrees or less. Just the thought made me feel cold.

We stopped for the night in the mountains. We could smell the coal in the air. Mines were everywhere. It was too cold to sleep out.

"If I see a motel somewhere, do you want to stop?"

240

"Yea, Walt told me to stay inside. He heard the weather report before he left."

"Fine, I see one ahead. Doesn't look like much."

"As long as it has heat and a bed, that's all that matters."

We filled up the tanks, ate supper,snuggled into a warm bed and watched television until we both fell asleep.

In the morning, the first thing that hit our nostrils was the coal smell in the cold air. We thought we could see particles flying around. No doubt, with all this coal, the furnaces here were coal furnaces. I expected there must be a lot of lung disease among the above ground residents. Breakfast would not be pancakes cooked on that stubborn Whisper-Light stove. It would be inside in the warm restaurant.

We bundled up like we did the day before, chipped off the frost on our seats to lay the sheepskin on it and were off. I fastened a water bottle to my handlebar some years ago to have it handy along the way. It had frozen water in it this morning. The sun barely peeped out over the trees as we tentatively ventured out into the below freezing air.

We only stopped long enough to get another tank of gas and use a bathroom. It was hard to unfold the hands from the grips. Our hip joints did not want to straighten up. We became rigid from the tenseness of keeping warm. We would hug the gas tank with our legs fighting the cold.

In Columbus, we stopped a longer period to sufficiently warm our insides in a restaurant. We dreaded going back out but knew there was no recourse. Almost dark and the temperatures falling again, we had to make another decision.

"Pony Express?

""Yea, Granny."

"Are you wanting to go all the way home tonight?"

"I don't know. It's still a long way and it's getting colder. What do you want to do?"

"I don't mind stopping another night in a motel."

"O.K. The next town is Findley. Can you make it that far?"

"Sure, no problem." With that we took another room. My hip hurt with a fury as I tried to swing it over the seat. I had a hard time getting off the bike. I didn't think I could get that tense with cold. A power head on the shower made it feel better. I was getting thawed out. A good meal at a Rax restaurant and we were set for the night.

We slept well on our final night. In the morning, it wasn't as cold but still only in the forties for the rest of our ride home. We ate breakfast at Bob Evans and arrived home in time for lunch. We

241

traveled 5050 miles on this adventure in the cold. This added 15 more states to our list plus Washington D.C. We would only need to go through the center three states of the country to get all 48 states on these bikes. No doubt, we would do many states several times.

....
"You should have gone along the gulf. It's nice along there," reminded Fred.

"I've heard that but we had no real desire to do it. Maybe if I talked to you before we went, we would have."

"You had a good time, anyway, that's all that counts. You're sure you don't want me to take you into Traverse City? I'm going that way. You can put your bike in the back of my bus."

"Now, if I did that I won't be able to say I did the whole adventure, would I?"

"No, I guess not."

"I won't be able to say I got to Traverse City if I don't get going."

"Show me what all this stuff is you have on your bike," he ordered when I reached for my helmet. I went through the details of my equipment as he watched in amazement. The spedometer, tool kit, tire pump. My wet sock wrapped water bottles, my funny looking handlebar wraps. I didn't get into the contents of my bags. I would never get into town if I did. Putting on my helmet and saying good-bye, he wished me luck and said he would pray for me.

Adventure #8

Calgary Stampede

Chapter 1   Michigan, Wisconsin Minnesota, North Dakota

.................I left Fred to wonder after me. I was riding along minding my business when I heard the familiar "bang" known by many bikers. It was hot and steamy as I rolled the bike to the grass, looking around to see if there were any resident to chase me off or worse, a dog. Nothing in sight, I relieved my Schwinn of its heavy load and took the wheel off in preparation of changing the tube. I repaired the old tube and reattached everything. Just as I prepared to get back on, the tire went flat again. I repeated the episode with some disappointment till I got it right and was off again, hotter than when I stopped. I wished Fred was there now.

I had my directions to Betty Boswells' house. She knew I was coming when I called her from the Upper Peninsula. She had a sense of humor that needed defining when I followed the directions up a steep hill. Pedaling down to my lowest granny gear, I stood in the stirrups for a few last pushes on the pedals before the bike stood still. I needed to push the bike to my consternation. The sweat was pouring down my back and under my helmet when I reached the top.

CALGARY STAMPEDE

"I have to tell everybody to come that way because they get lost the other way," she explained.

"But, Betty, I was riding a bike. I could have found the less hilly if you directed me." She only laughed at that and I was welcomed into her new farm house. We enjoyed a long two day visit, eating out at a marina one evening, harvesting her bountiful garden and even making jam from fresh apricots and berries. Betty lived with her nephew, Kurt, each doing their own thing in the vegetable and fruit growing business. We stayed up late into the night talking about old times and bringing each other up to date on the news of the day.

"Where did you go last year on your vacation?"

"Well, we had already been to all the states but Kansas, South Dakota and Nebraska. But it seemed like such an ordinary few states with nothing exciting to see, we extended the trip and went by way of Calgary. The stampede was held every year in July. The Olympics were held there last winter and I stuck my eyes to the television set every chance I got.   Shirley was anxious to be there. She loved horses. I just loved the scenery."

"How long were you gone?"

"Two weeks. It was one of our more disastrous trips. It almost severed our relationship."

"Why is that?"

"Well, let me tell you about the trip."

We left home with the same instructions, to send a post card a day and call every other day. That was not a problem. We did as we were told. The bikes were in perfect condition; everything worked. It was 104 degrees when we left. We were thankful for that, thinking it would be warm for the whole trip and we would be going north soon. Even though we carried a drinking bottle attached to the bike, the sun was so hot, the water was always tepid or warm. We stopped at every opportunity to get fresh water as we headed north to the upper peninsula of Michigan.

It was 360 miles to Newberry at my friends house. It was the place I usually stopped. It was almost dark when we arrived. No matter. Vina Gaunt was waiting for us. She was getting used to my late arrivals. She put us up in the Ponderosa again and we slept well. She was always astonished by what I was doing when I came up there.

We quickly dressed in the morning and ran over the driveway to her house where she had breakfast waiting. Vina believed in feeding her guests and it was appreciated. It didn't look like it was going to be as nice a day as yesterday.

It rained on and off for the day, but not enough for rain gear. It was still warm and stormy skies did not show much blue. We were

244

fortunate not to have anything serious happen and in no time were through Wisconsin and into Bimidji, Minnesota.

All the good thoughts we had about it being warmer on this trip were dashed with this storm front. It didn't get any cooler than 50 degrees and it wasn't supposed to get any warmer than 73 today. It was sunny, so that was in our favor. In Bimidji, we stayed at our first KOA, now becoming our most familiar place to stay.

The storm was still not over and threatened us the following day. I put on the long underwear in a restaurant rest room and felt much better. In North Dakota, we zipped across the interstate and had a hard time keeping awake on the treeless prairie. I reminisced over my solo trip on this very same road and found it much more alive then. We saw many dried up watering holes from the drought of '88. The bareness was still evident but I noticed the grasses were not there. They were shriveled and dead.

We elected to get as many provinces as we could on this trip and to do so would mean getting up to Manitoba. We turned north at Rugby so we could see the Peace Gardens at the border. The trucker conversations would be gone and we would have ourselves for company until we got on Canada's Provincial One.

Chapter 2   Manitoba, Saskatchewan
Alberta and
British Columbia

The Peace Gardens are on both sides of the border, laid out in a profusion of color. We relaxed in the sun and slight breeze for an hour or more, visited the gift shop. We were on Highway One, just a few miles to the north. We passed fields of blue and chartreuse carpets. I knew one of them was supposed to be flax but I couldn't identify the other. They lay in alternating patterns as far as the eye could see on both sides of the road absorbing the mid-day sunshine. I recalled as a child in geograpy class, we would do projects on what products different states and countries produced. I always had a hard finding something to represent flax.

The terrain didn't change at the border. It was still rolling and treeless. Now and again a farm house and their buildings were caught in crevices of fields surrounded by tall pines pointing to the light blue sky and shorter shrubs.

Meadowlark Camp on this One was so close to the main highway it would mean ear plugs for sleeping. Nearby was a camper outlet. It was closed. For something to do for the evening we fantasized over which one we could live in if someone would buy it for us as we peered through the high windows.

Edwin and Murial Bott shared a cup of instant coffee with us on our return. They were Canadians and gave us a short course on the farm products of the area.

Perhaps my thoughts of traveling alone were beginning to identify themselves on this adventure. It bothered me more and more to see the unorganized things my partner did. I thought I was organized and I would look on with dismay when she would remove everything from her bags and have them strewn all over the picnic tables in the name of order. Everything fit back into the bags every day, amazing me again. We were getting to be more like a married couple heading for divorce court. I had to try not to let it bother me.

We wandered west to Elkton. Today was Monday, a day of business. Changing our American money into Canadian currency was our utmost concern. The bank in this little town wouldn't open for more than an hour. The town reminded us of some place in the old days out in the prairie. No trees in the vicinity, wide streets and the only places of business were the bank, a feed store, restaurant and the city offices with a few lesser buildings, like homes. The street needed to have dirt with horses and wagons tied up to the rails with water troughs on the corners. Women in long dresses, men in cowboy hats and guns.

We ate another breakfast in the restaurant amid scutiny of the local people who didn't talk to us. We felt like we were strangers. We were.

We put on many miles across One. It was flat and the road was only two lanes. Traffic was not heavy but the wind picked up about 30-45 miles an hour. It was hard for us at first to convert American speeds and gallons to the Canadian wind speeds and liters. Sometimes the broadcasters on my radio would offer wind speeds and Celsius readings in both terms. We were close enough to the border for an intermingling of countries.

The miles ticked away while we sat out the endurance. It was not cold but not warm either. The bikes were running well. A few times it became touchy when we were about out of gas. Running against such a strong wind we could never tell when the time would come. Sometimes we only got 100 miles on a tank and sometimes 150 miles.

We marked all the camps along the road. Then waited to see how long it would be before we would be too tired to battle the wind before making a decision on how far to go for the day. Tonight would be Swift Current named after a river and what looked like a dammed lake south of town. We did not investigate. The wind made us too tired to do much of anything once we settled. We could not relax on the bikes as usual.

Some Canadian drivers drove terribly fast, faster than posted speeds by quite a margin. We saw many patrol cars but they also traveled at a high rate of speed. We couldn't figure why they bothered to post the speed.

Prices were cheaper in Canada. We took in to account the difference in currency, liters versus gallons and it was still cheaper than in the states. We parked next to a couple from Oregon going east.

"At least you're going with the wind," I said to them as they tried to put up their tent in the wind.

"Yea, it's been pretty good. We had some rain and a bad thunderstorm a couple days ago," returned Marv Otterson.

"Have you been sitting here long?" asked his wife, Dee.

"No, we just got in ourselves. You must have been in the storm we were in the other day."

247

"Was it bad?"

"No, it rained a little but nothing we couldn't handle. Hard to believe it was 104 degrees the day we left."

"It was pretty warm for us, too. Where are you going to eat?"

"We ate at that place down there around the corner before we came in. I can't remember the name now. "

"We still have to find something."

"You don't eat in camp, then?"

"Not if I can help it. This is my vacation, too."

"Can't blame you there," replied Shirley, "We seem to have kept that part of our wifely duties. Actually, I don't mind eating out in camp. It's different from eating at home and cooking over a hot stove."

"Yea," I said, "here you get to warm something someone else cooked and hope the bugs and rain don't get in to it." We all laughed at the luxury of camp life.

They went to get their dinner and when they returned we sat around talking long into the night.

It wasn't a good night for sleeping. We were in early enough yesterday to find a good spot to put up the tent. We chose a shady spot behind a windbreak of spruce trees, tying the clothes line for our laundry between them. With the wind, the clothes were dry in short order. But during the night a thunderstorm roiled up and we were awakened to thunder and lightning. There was little rain but the wind was incessant.

Breakfast was where we ate dinner the night before. We couldn't beat the all-you-can-eat price.

Terrain ran from this farmland to more prairie and then to mountains as we approached the formidable Northern Rockies. The wind picked up and the sky was partly cloudy. Rain was not in the forecast but I never knew a forecaster who could forecast correctly.

Suddenly, the bike began to falter and it wasn't from the wind. I looked at the gas gage and had only gone 95 miles. It couldn't be the gas, I thought. I didn't see Granny in my mirror and hadn't seen her for a long time.

"How 'bout ya Granny?" I hollered in the microphone over the wind and engine noises. I could only hear her in bits and pieces.

"Granny? Can you hear me?" I asked. She said something that sounded like she could.

"Something is wrong with my bike, it doesn't want to go very well."

"You're pro-ba-bly -out of g-as aga-in," she said brokenly. I flipped over to the reserve tank and it picked up again. I wondered

248

what I would do without her foresight. There might be an extra gallon or just a drop. It still was sputtering when she came back.

"I th-ink I've ru-n out-,t-oo". She was getting closer. Her voice was getting louder in my headphones. Just then a trucker who was listening to our conversation spotted me in front of him on the side of the road crawling at a slower pace.

"Pony Express?"

"Yea?" I came back.

"You're girl friend is behind me."

"Is she mobile or sitting," I asked.

"She's mobile. There's a truck stop ahead of you about eight miles. If you can get behind me and hold in nice and tight I'll shield you from the wind. You might make it that far."

"Where are you?" I asked.

"Comin' up right behind you."

"In that green 18?"

"You got it."

"Slow down a bit so I can match your speed."

"10-4."

I slipped in place behind him. It was one of the things I said I'd never do. Now he was my eyes and ears. "Granny?"

"Yes?"

"Can you get to the truck stop?"

"I think so."

"Can you go any faster and catch up to us?"

"No, I'm all right." We left it at that and the trucker kept telling me what was ahead. Slowing down behind a slower car, speeding up when the coast was clear. In the vacuum of the truck, I used very little gas. Sounds were diminished. It was as if my engine was not running. The wind was nowhere to be found. I was being held in suspension.

"I can see the station ahead, Pony Express. It's on your right. When I tell you, pull out and coast in."

"O.K. I'm putting a lot of trust in you."

"I know. In this wind you will have to fill up at every place you can. It's always like that up here. Mileage drops fast this direction. Stations aren't very frequent, neither."

"They are really. We aren't used to having to stop every 100 miles for it."

"O.K. Here we come, only a few hundred feet. I'll slow down some and when I tell you, turn out. Nnnnnnoooooowww." I left the road and turned nicely on the exit and was in the truck stop. I thanked him and he went on his way. Shirley pulled in shortly behind me and thanked him also as he went down the road.

"Thanks, Big Daddy."

"You got it, Granny. You two have a good trip."

"I'm sure we will." I filled up the tank. It was dry as a bone in a hot sun. I never had to fill up that much before. Shirley was the same.

We blew into Medicine Hat more for rest than for coffee. It was strenuous trying to keep the bike up against the wind. Running out of gas almost twice today we were happy to ride into Calgary where we planned on spending two nights.

Some fifty miles from Calgary the hills became hillier and were covered with the blue flowers of flax, if that was what it was, or green velvet carpet. With the farm houses tucked into their nitches of pines and huge white fluffy clouds in the deep blue sky, it presented quite a picture for my mobile camera. I wanted to say something to Granny about it but her radio wasn't working now. I hoped it was something we could fix ourselves. She gets upset when she can't and has to spend more money. I can't blame her, I don't like to spend money if I don't have to either.

Calgary is nestled in a long valley. Above, on the hills were a multitude of houses. All along the stretch coming into town were the remains of the Olympics. Signs, flags, advertisements. Bright colors of Canadian and foreign countries.

The KOA camp was right next to the high jump. I was so excited. I wished I was here during the winter months to be around the international people and felt all the pomp and circumstance. Flags of all nations were flown in a circle around one of the complexes making a perfect setting.

Many other campers were on motorcycles. They were here for the stampede starting tomorrow. We, as part of them, were having our own stampede. We walked to the pavilion once we were set up for the night in this big camp. Walking around examining the remnants of the bobsled run and the high jump. Inside, a sled sat for those who never saw one close up. It is the one sport we never seem to hear about. Only during the Olympics. Sitting inside, I could not believe they raced down at such high speeds in such a tiny sled and in such a cramped position.

It didn't get dark until almost 11 a.m. My Therm-o-rest mattress had sprung a leak and I couldn't find it. The ground was hard. Maybe I can find a new one in town tomorrow. When it did get dark, the town that we could see lit up the area like shimmering gold. It was light at 4:30 a.m. Short night. In town, in the morning, we searched out the stampede grounds. Taking the tram to the stampede grounds enabled us to parked in a unprotected parking lot. Our fears were with us the remainder of the day, wondering if we would have bikes when we returned. Calgary, we were sure, was not immune from crime. It was a bustling city.

250

The parade grounds were in the center of the fair grounds. We walked around the usual fair trappings of booths, food and wares finding our gate for the stampede.

The stampede itself was more a rodeo with broncho riding, barrel racing and all the pomp that goes with rodeos. One of the things that impressed us was the happy way the teen-agers conducted their ushering duties. They were all so clean and polished with immaculate uniforms. Most people dressed in western wear. Cowboy hats, boots and vests. Fancy belt buckles were on everyone.

We never saw a chuckwagon race before so it held our interest as we made bets on the winning wagon. If it was not first explained we would never have known what they were doing.

Before it turned dark, hot air balloons were filled and started filling the sky on a far hill on the opposite side of the stands. One brontosaurus was having trouble getting up with the high winds. It would pick up its head and start to rise and then fall back. It started again and was full of air and almost looked like it was too heavy to get up off the ground. The crowd all cheered when it finally made it to the sky without falling back. Night settled in.

Entertainment continued for several more hours. A musical variety show was filled with circus acts, singing and dancing and some acting. It was delightful. We were entertained well.

On the return we were enchanted with the whole city alight with millions of sparkling lights. Finding our bikes were still where we left them, we found our way to the campground in the dark. It was too hard to read the map in the dark and I relied on my sense of direction. The hills surrounding our camp were still lit as well. We were living in a fairy land.

We had a desire to go to Alaska. "Would you want to go if we could find the time, Shirley?"

"Sure, I'd like to go but you can't get off long enough."

"I know that. I don't think I would want to go on these bikes unless we had a male companion or two."

"What's the matter, you afraid of the bears?"

"Yes, for one thing. I think I would like to have them along to help fix our aging bikes, too. Don't you?"

"Of course, but who would we get?"

"I don't know. Maybe we'll have to go the conventional way. Think about it anyway." We would be getting as close as we could to Alaska today. Banff wasn't far off high in the mountains. We would have to cross the continental divide again and get into the Rockies. It was one place I loved to ride.

It was dark and cloudy when we left Calgary and looked like a thunderstorm coming over the mountains. The temperature dropped from 63 to 52 while we ate our breakfast. We would be going into the mountains. We could see them in the distance with their peaks reaching toward the sky. Some with snow on their tips. These peaks were sharper than the ones on the American side.

My camera became the target for breakage this time. Again we were down to only one. With the loss of Shirleys' radio and now my camera we were falling into the usual pattern.

After a rest for coffee on our drive to Banff we put all the clothes we brought with us on our cold bodies. Arriving early in the day, we located our camp for the night and were back in town to see the sights.

Chinese dinner was the fare for dinner with left-overs for the next meal. Using a telescope at a tourist stop, we could see high up into the mountains and across a deep valley. The sun was shining, the white fluffy clouds added to the pictorial assembling in the camera lens. Tiring of the resort town, we went looking for a larger hotel on the outskirts. We took a side road to locate it but were on the wrong side of the river. "It looks great from here, Shirley, like a chateau. Why don't you just take a picture of it from here and we can go back and find a trail to hike or something?"

"O.K. I don't think I care to go way over there. Isn't this river pretty? It reminds me of the Colorado."

"You know, I think every river we see has some remembrance to it of that bigger river," I reiterated. "Look how fast it's running. I sure wouldn't want to be in the raft in that rapid."

The temperature dropped to 40 degrees during the night. Neither of us were cold. We had enough warm sleeping apparel and I brought my winter bag. The mattress still insulated me from the ground.

It was a pretty day even if the clouds were overhead and threatened rain. It remained mildly cool. We sat through a cold breakfast and checked the local map for trail heads. Locating the Wannemuka Lake Trail of 13.6 km, not far from our camp, we elected to hike it as far as it went.

The trail was laid out along the river. On the other side, the mountain looked like it was laid out in layers horizontally. At one point, the trail narrowed over a rock slide.

"Marion, look what's come to see us."

"Oh, great!"

"Are we on their trail or are they on ours?"

"I don't know, but I don't want to ask."

"Why don't we deviate up the side here and see if they will walk by?"

"Sounds good. Did you get their portrait?"

252

"No, but I will," she said as she raised her camera. We scampered up the loose rocks above the trail and watched the mountain sheep take their time to continue down the trail. Those horns were made for butting and the ram looked like he was ready to butt anything that got in his way. He and his ewes moved on, stopping occasionally to give us the eye.

Walking in the wooded area, we saw many wild flowers of reds, yellows and blue colors. Sitting in a clearing for a short rest, we had a good view of the mountain across the river. Among the greenery were large areas of orange trees and then some of black. Fires were apparent. It was the first I had ever seen. "I wonder if they were started by lightning?" I asked.

"I don't know."

"Sad, isn't it though. But then they say lightning is a natural cause. Some seeds can't open unless they are heated. Pine seeds need heat."

"You ready?"

"Yea." We walked on down the level trail meandering in the coolness of the shady trees in places and into the warmer sun in others. Stopping to examine the flowers and odd shaped rock or tree formations. Confronting a fork in the trail turned us to the left for 5.6K uphill.

"It didn't look uphill when we started this fork. Maybe we should have taken the other one. It would have kept us closer to the waters edge."

"Well, it's too late now. Do you want to turn back?"

"No, this is all right." We walked up. The sky didn't look too good to go too much farther. The wind started and it was getting cooler again. After 3 hours, we called an end to the hike and turned back. The sun was playing games with the rain clouds. It would sprinkle a little and then the sun would come out to dry it. We sat on a stony beach by the river after the hike down the mountain. Shirley did her beachcombing. I sat and wrote in my journal and watched a boat or two go past, waving at the captains.

Time seemed to go on and on as we returned. With the threat of rain and no rain gear, we picked up the pace. It didn't seem to get us back any sooner. My hands were somewhat swollen. I carried a day pack. It might have had something to do with it. It wasn't tight or heavy but they can sometimes cut off circulation. Perhaps my age had something to do with it.

On a foot bridge across the river we encountered a herd of sheep. A ram stood in the center. We didn't quite know what he was going to do. He just stood there as if he was challenging us. Another couple on our side were frightened of them. We waited a long time for him to make his move to no avail. Once in awhile he came to our end of the bridge. We all scrambled for some form of safety. A tree, the other side of the barricade, a rock.

Then, without warning a herd of fifty or so ewes and babies came thundering through the brush on the hill behind us and ran across the wooden bridge to the other side where they stopped to nibble at the vegetation. The ram didn't move from his place of honor.

"What are we going to do? Should we just walk toward him and hope he moves along?"

"Not me," said the fellow.

"Not me, either," said Shirley.

"I guess we just wait him out." It wasn't long. I swear he heard and understood everything we were saying, and just moved along. In the picnic area, another herd was mooching off the tourists. Some were bold enough and tame enough to come up to the tables and help themselves. Some even jumped on the tables. A ranger was shooing them away and asking for everyone to not feed them.

The rain continued to threaten us as we rode home. Making dinner in a storm had us scurrying to get into our tent shelter to finish. It was warmer in the tent anyway and the food was mostly heated enough to eat. She beat me at a couple hands of cards when the rain quit. It was back into town to find a sinful dessert to catch our eye, see some falls that were more rapid than falls and then to bed. We walked a total of 12 miles on the trail and were not even tired. For once I didn't get sick.

The temperature hovered around 42 degrees as we packed up our wet tent to get moving. "I'm wearing my snow suit today, Shirley."

"I think I will, too."

I was trying out a pair of neopreme gloves made for bicycling in hopes of warmth. No luck. A tram ride was scheduled at Lake Louise if we could get there in time. It was a breakfast ride, they said on the brochures we picked up somewhere. We found it easily in the crisp mountain air. We could see the tram rise up the mountain, disappear and continue higher. It should be good.

"Don't forget the expedition camera, Shirl."

"I've got it. Do you think we should wear something warm?"

"I think I'll just wear my leather jacket and take the snow suit off."

It was a beautiful ride up. We saw all the mountains we ever wanted to see. It was so quiet in the gondola. If it wasn't for the bumping and grinding of the cable I would have thought we were flying up that mountain. The fog that lay on the ground was all but burned off by the sun now and the view was stupendous. Many of the peaks were covered in snow. Some new, some old. The hotel on the lake grew smaller and smaller as we ascended the mountain for breakfast of McDonald-like fare.

It was freezing up here. The doors of the ski lodge were open and the winds blew in. We couldn't find a warm corner anywhere while we ate. Some people went for a hike on a trail in the snow. The others sat shivering like us and then we had enough and returned. The lake in front of the hotel was of deep emerald green. The foothills were carpeted in pines as far as they could survive up the mountain and then the grey rock formations took over. The tips covered in snow and glaciers met the fluffy white clouds, catching them in their grasp. I had seen this picture on many calendars. I didn't believe it could be that intense and now I had the reality of it. The gondola lowered itself and us to the valley floor. We dipped between the trees and then were raised above again.

We mingled with the wealthier folk around the hotel awhile with a hot cup of coffee in the cafe outside in the sun. It was much warmer there but we felt out of place and wandered out.

Golden looked like a good place to spend the rest of our day. We passed over the Kicking Horse River, stopping long enough to watch some rafters and kayakers paddle. Canada named so many of their towns and rivers with such odd names, it invited us to visit just to see what was there. Was there really a Kicking Horse? Was that an Indian name? How about Medicine Hat? Dead Man's Flats? Another good one to the south of here, Skoocumchuck.

Jeanette Odea and Sue Reeb parked next to our site. They were on their way to Alaska from Florida. They were to meet other people from a Baptist Church on a boat to cruise up the inland passage.

They gave us their itinerary and what they expected to see and do. It only assuaged our interest. We would get there one day, I thought. Shirley lived there when she was younger and met and married her Navy husband there. She'd like to return.

We started out to walk to town but found it was going to be too far with having to stay on the road. There was no way to cross-country walk. We put in two and a half miles before we realized it and turned back uphill to retrieve our bikes from the mosquitos.

Chapter 3   Montana the
                              Fourth Time

We couldn't see going any farther west or north at this time. I would have liked to go to Jasper but the weather conditions were not right nor was the time. We met John Webbers from Sarnia, Ontario again in town after breakfast. John flew himself and his three speed old bike out to ride the roads in the mountains and to stay in the provincial parks. He reminded us of the Europeans. He wore no helmet or riding shoes. He wore sandals, Chinos and dress shirt. He smoked a pipe and was dressed like he was out for a Sunday drive, very casual. He didn't seem to be going very fast but we ran into him several times and we were all going the same way. Sometimes he would be in a campground before us. He was about 65 years old.

"I ride about 60 miles a day," he said when we inquired.

"This will be the last time we will see you," I told him when we turned around to talk to him. He was going the other way. He didn't stop and we rode next to him in this sleepy town with no traffic. "Maybe we will look you up some time back home."

"That would be fine. Did you get up to Jasper?"

"No, we don't have the time. We still have a lot of territory to cover."

"You have my address, don't you?"

"Yes, you gave it to me in my journal the other night, remember?"

"O.K. You have a safe trip back. God bless." We returned in the direction we started and watched him chug up the long hill ahead of him.

"He was a nice fellow," offered Shirley.

"Yea. Who did he remind you of?"

"Walt."

"That's what I thought, too." We turned the accelerator and headed south. We couldn't talk by radio. Hers was still useless. We were hoping it would warm up if we got to Montana today. It was uncomfortable riding with snow suits on so much of the time and still not warm enough. Mostly just the feet and hands were cold.

256

We hoped to see all of Glacier National Park if the weather held out. There was nothing much to see before going through customs or after for many miles. The mountains were to the left of us off in the distance. It was getting past lunch time when we entered a small town with nothing to offer but a tavern. I thought Shirley wouldn't mind going in for a hamburger. I stopped out front and was ready to park.

"You go on in there and I'll go find a park or something and eat out of my bags," she said.

"What do you mean?"

"I'm not eating in there."

"O.K. Is there any reason?"

"I can eat out of my bags, that's all." She started off without me, no discussion. I wasn't going to go in there and have her go down the road. I wondered what was on her mind now. I didn't have anything palatable in my bag. She must have something good that I don't know about, I thought. I took off, a little steamed for not understanding what was the problem. We rode all the way to Glacier without hand signals or speaking of any sort while I tried to figure out what was going on and came up with no answers.

We were passing many good picture taking spots. I wanted to get as many as I could but since my camera was broken, relied on her to take shots. She couldn't take them while driving and didn't stop for any either. That little thing played on my mind, too. We didn't make it to the park until after 5 p.m. when it is harder to find a campsite.

We took the "Going to the Sun" road through the mountains and saw the glacier we only saw through the fog and snow the time before. We stopped at the ranger station but this time it was too late for an interpretation as it was after 6 p.m. But we stood at the top and looked over the mountains and gazed in awe at the glaciers. They sparkled in the late sun but didn't look like they were melting any. It wasn't that warm up here.

The sun was out and it was warm. We unpacked again at our site and were sitting around doing whatever needed to be done and just putzing around. I studied the maps and asked her to look at them with me. I thought we still had time to spend another day here. Hike tomorrow and then leave the next day.

"You go ahead and hike. I'll just stay here till you get back," she said.

"Why? That wouldn't be any fun."

"Well, I don't want to hike."

"Are you hurting somewhere? What's the matter? You usually like to do these things."

"I just don't want to." I sat there for awhile trying to sort out what was going on but still came up with no answers.

257

"Well, I'm not going to leave you here while I go traipsing through the trails." We both moped around the rest of the night. "What's bothering you anyway?" I finally asked.

"Nothing. I would like to go to South Dakota to see the Fischbecks and then I'd like to see my cousin in Kansas and my brothers-in-law in Missouri." Now we were getting somewhere.

"Remember a long time ago when we first started doing these trips? You said, "this is your vacation. You go where you want to go and I'll go with you. Remember that?"

"Yes, but we do go where ever you want to go."

"And didn't I always ask you where you would like to go? Didn't I always include you in the planning? Didn't I always ask you to spend time with me looking over the maps and plan the trip with me?"

"Yea."

"Well, why are you acting this way now? If you wanted to go to some of these places, why didn't you say so before?"

"Because it was your vacation, I guess."

"Well, I didn't want to visit your relatives, I can tell you that. Didn't we visit with your sister and parents? And didn't we visit with some friends in the Carolinas? I didn't have too much of a hassle with any of those, did I? We've shared those visits pretty good. I just didn't like staying for days on end. We only stayed with my mother for two nights.

Let's look at the map. Where do they live? Let's see if we can plan a new route. We don't really have one here anyway, you know." We studied it together again and she seemed happier. Gads, what was I doing here? I felt like I was married. But then that's what happens in relationships. You must have the ability to fight and recoup from the fight.

The camp had been very quiet during the night. We didn't eat breakfast in camp but sought out an eating establishment some 30 miles away.

Browning was host to a greasy spoon with good greasy food. Next door a museum opened its doors. It was also a bronze sculptors' place of business. The artist, an older man, was in the building and was in the process of sculpting a work several feet high. He was busy shuffling through some junk in his shop. We peeked in and he asked us to come in and help. He was busy looking for the head of his work. "It's here somewhere. Darn fool thing. I just laid it down a few weeks ago and off it's walked," he said as he looked through boxes of stuff. We looked around without really looking into everything and came up with nothing. The body stood about eight feet tall in the middle of the floor.

"You here to see my museum?"

"Well, yes," answered Shirley.

258

"Well, what'er ya standin there for? Go on in and look at it."

We turned on our heels and went inside. "Kinda gruff, isn't he?" He had rows and rows of mostly western bronzes of all sizes and prices. It was not only a museum but a retail shop.

"Aren't these beautiful?" I asked Shirley. "I'd sure like to add one or two to my collection of pewter". In the museum there were many dioramas of battles with the Indians all created and displayed by this one man. When we went back to the shop he gave us a history of the making of bronze work. It gave me a better appreciation of the work.

"I collect pewter myself," I told him.

"Pewter, huh? Do you know how they make that?"

"I've read about it in the papers I get from time to time but I've forgotten the right process for now." He went into detail about it.

"Whose do you collect?"

"I have some Bill Pollack. Do you know him?"

"Know him, why he's the best damned dancer there is here in the west. Just saw him a few weeks ago. He does some darn good work, too."

"Oh, yea,? Tell me more."

"Well, I don't like to tell tales on nobody," he said.

"I'll let it go at that then," I said. "We've got to get going anyway. Sure do want to thank you for the time you spent with us. Let you get back to work."

"Time doesn't mean anything to a man my age. I like to bring in some of them younguns to teach them the art. I have a student around all the time. I teach them all I know. I don't know how else anyone will learn the trade these days. Most people can't afford to go to European schools and they don't teach it around here unless I do," he explained.

"You are doing a good thing. I like your philosophy. I wish I lived closer. I'd be here so much you'd pay to have me removed."

"I hardly believe that." We said our good-byes and steered east to the next town to find a radio repair shop.

For $10 it was fixed for another short time. We could hear each other if we were close. But close enough to talk over the noise of the engines was too close.

I suffered with cluster headaches for the past year or so. They were caused by dilating blood vessels in the brain. In the night, I would wake with a feeling that a sharp knife was stabbed through my left eye. I could not open the eye or move it without excruciating pain. I took medication designed for high blood pressure that would shrink the vessels and let the blood flow naturally. I was out of medication. We stopped at the K-Mart store to renew my medication. No pharmacy but the Best store next door sold radios. She bought a new one.

259

The wind was picking up and the rain was intermittent. The KOA at Great Falls, Montana afforded us the pie shaped shelter sites made of logs.

I didn't know what was wrong again but things were not right. No matter what I did, it was wrong. I shouldn't have wanted to put the tent that way, I shouldn't have wanted to put my stuff on the only picnic table. I shouldn't try to do anything to help her affix the radio on her bike before it rained. "Go make up your bed, why don't you" she commanded.

"Well, excuse me, my bed doesn't need making."

"Leave me alone." I could see I wasn't wanted for any help. Feeling hurt and not knowing what was going on, I put on my gear again, jumped on my bike and sped out of there in the drizzle that was setting in. I tried to block out my feelings. I can't get this upset. What was I doing here anyway? Maybe I shouldn't plan on riding with her anymore. I knew it was a long way from home and something was bothering her that I wasn't allowed to know. I found a pharmacy that could fill my prescription and returned.

She still didn't have it fixed when I returned and I wasn't going to help her. She couldn't fix it and left it. She was ready for dinner. We were going to eat out. I didn't say anything on the ride there but we did talk with a strain between us. I found a cheap camera and we replenished our scanty provisions and headed back to camp. She continued to work on it and we packed a box we found to send home some of our unneeded items.

Randy Taylor, a good looking lone biker from Vancouver came over to talk to us while we set up the tent. Nice fellow. He was going south to New Mexico and wanted some advice on things to see and what not to miss. I needed to get some space between her and I. While she was working on her radio, I went over to his table and we looked at maps and I advised him of some National Parks he wouldn't want to miss seeing.

"I've never traveled this way before, I mean on a motorcycle."

"You're kidding."

"No. You two are the first ones I've really talked to since I left home."

"You're not that far, you know, and have a long way to go yet."

"I know. Do you use your radios?"

"Well, we will tomorrow if she gets hers installed tonight. Her other one broke and we had an accident a couple years ago because we couldn't communicate."

"I've never used mine. I don't know what to say."

"Just listen to the others. You'll find out how it works soon enough."

"I have. They don't say anything important."

260

"Wait till you get into traffic situations. You'll hear all kinds of things. Bears are cop cars. You'll hear a lot of bantering. It's their way of keeping their sanity on those long drives."

Shirley asked Randy if he could help her do something with the radio when I walked back. I left them to find something else to do in the office.

Since we had so much friction the night before, we did not do the laundry that needed to be done. We got moving first thing in the morning and while the clothes were washing, Shirley made me a stack of pancakes to get some of her load of foodstuffs down to a manageable level. It might have been a peace offering for all I knew. Laundry done, we were off to the post office to mail the packages and then the tent came down. It was dry by this time. It was one of the few times we packed it this way.

We wandered into Sulphur White Springs for a rest stop. A city park was a good place for our lunch. It included a gaggle of geese we had not invited. Lunch was short.

We planned on staying at the same park in Hardin near Custers Battlefield. Along the road we encountered a wagon train. It looked like it would be fun to partake. When we asked about it in Hardin, we found it was something they do with kids who are on their way to becoming society drop-outs. It taught them self-reliance and team work.

It was another hot day and we were down to t-shirts rather than the heavy clothing we wore earlier. It felt so much better. The pool felt good this year and so did the hot tub. It was working.

Chapter 4

Return to Wyoming, South Dakota, Nebraska, 48th State-Kansas, Missouri, Indiana and Home

It was such a beautiful morning I suggested we go south to Wyoming and wing through the mountains one last time before we go for our next stop in South Dakota. I had an affinity for the Big Horns; they were my first mountains to cross on my solo trip. We wandered around them admiring the colors of the rocks and vegetation. Every color of the rainbow could be seen with each change in curves or hills. Formations changed frequently. I snapped countless pictures with my cheap camera hoping they would not be a waste of film. I didn't stop for all but shot them while moving. I would probably get many mirrors and windshields in the picture so I tried to shoot out the side.

Lunch was in a sheltered place in Worland. Between here and Ten Sleeps we spotted beiges, greens, rusts, yellows and occasional cattle among the oil rigs dotting the countryside.

"Do you know why they call this place, Ten Sleeps, Granny?"

"No. Why?"

"I thought you'd never ask. It took ten days for the Indians to get here from Buffalo, I think."

It was prettier in Shell canyon than on this road but it was the only one to swing us to Buffalo where we enjoyed an ice cream sundae. The land was barren between Buffalo and Gillette. The roads were long black ribbons strung out in barren land. I remembered this as the place I thought my skin would fall off from the burn I received. It was dry air that peeled most of my skin and it was trying to do it again. Shirley bought a comedy magazine for her daughter and we laughed over the contents for awhile smothering the bad feelings we had between us the past few days.

262

We lingered over a long breakfast in the morning. It amazed us that our bikes were working so well. We did nothing to change that but it was always on our mind to check them each night or morning.

"Marion, see those two bicyclists up there," she asked while we read a tourist information board at Devils' Tower. I looked where she pointed and saw one fellow riding a bicycle far ahead on a downhill and the other just leaving the parking area. "What about them?"

"Remember me telling you about these two guys who were riding across the country. I saw them in Howell at the melon festival last month."

"Yea, what about them?"

"I think that's them."

"You're kidding."

"No, let's see where they are going and find out."

"O.K."

They were stopped again at the entrance to the park and Shirley all but fell off her bike trying to stop out of traffic lanes to see them. It must be them I thought. She was getting off her bike and approaching them. I sat on the other side of the road until I knew for sure. Walking up, she introduced me to David Buchanan, from North Carolina and his buddy. They were the ones in Howell, a city not far from home. They were on a sabbatical from teaching, I think.They were carrying everything they owned. They encouraged us to try it. I noticed the worn shirt on one and the sunburn on the other. One had raccoon eyes from wearing sunglasses.

It sure looked like work, riding with all your belongings. It wasn't long before I changed my ideas on that score.

We had both been to Mount Rushmore and hadn't any desire to go back now. A biker worth his salt knows tha Sturgis is the mecca for motorcyclists. We wanted to see what was there to attract them. The map showed where to find Cheyenne Crossing, Lead and Deadwood.

"Let's go down this road. I've never been to these places," I said, pointing to the map.

"It's O.K. with me. I never was there either.

The Black Hills are or were loaded with gold. The Indians all but gave it away back in the 1800's. This is a special place for them. It has nothing to do with gold."

We meandered south of Spearfish, and the other towns and found nothing special to attract the bikers. Nice towns, nevertheless. Back to the north, a river provided a good place to have lunch. I was carrying my peanut butter and jelly in tubes now like toothpaste. They kept the food fresh but didn't hold enough for a long trip.

263

We sat along the banks, taking off our boots and socks to soak in the tumbling waters with other people. A trail led along the side where we walked, taking pictures of the falls in varying heights. It was a warm day and the coolness was restful. The Black Hills were much more vegetated than the places we had been visiting on this trip. The lushness was refreshing to the soul.

We still had a few miles to go to get to Faith. I remembered her talking about her sister and she leased land to a rancher out there. What we call farms are ranches out there. I didn't know that yet. I pictured an older man standing out there with pitchfork in hand in front of his well used barn out in the middle of nowhere. I remembered my grandfather looked this way and expected the farmers were all the same. Weathered from years of this work. I didn't expect what I saw.

First of all, I saw a rancher herding his cattle on an ATV. Where were the horses? Ranches were huge. Barns were non-existant. Fences were long. Hay was rolled laying in many different ways. Some in ditches along the road edge. They cut every speck of grass, between the freeway stretches as well.

She hadn't seen the Fischbachs in years and years. We found the nice suburban home hoping we could persuade them to let us pitch the tent in their backyard.

We were treated like old friends. We needn't have worried about accommodations tonight. They asked us to stay in their childrens' rooms. They let us clean up and took us out for a steak dinner and then a tour of the ranch. We drove around the town and saw a couple young men out back of a store practicing their rope expertises. A rodeo would be coming to town in a few days and they would be roping for cash prizes.

We exchanged stories. We went into detail about all the places we'd been and the people we saw. They marveled at the two little ladies traveling so far for so long on those two little motorcycles. Andrew gave us the whole story on the ranching in this area.

"How many acres do you have here on the ranch?" I asked.

"We don't measure in acres but in miles or sections."

"O.K. Why do they roll up hay and leave it where they do? There doesn't seem to be any rhyme nor reason to it."

"You can usually tell a good rancher from a bad one. Hay is usually stacked on top of hills to stay dry. Once in awhile they might put a couple bales in the low spots to absorb water. If they put it haphazard, it won't last long.

We drove down a long dirt road or cow path to the consternation of Yvette.

"You don't want to go down here with this car, Andy."

264

"Oh, it'll be all right," he said as he tried to reassure her. We just sat in the back seat grateful we weren't on our bikes as we bounced along.

"Wells are dug in sections about 100 feet down to water the cattle that are herded from section to section as the grass gets shorter. See those over there?" he pointed to a small herd. "Those were brought over here by my son the other day. When they have fed off here long enough, we move them to that other section and bring in the sheep to clean it all off. It grows back.

"I thought ranchers and sheparders were fueding all the time."

"There are no border wars any more with the sheep people. They have found that the sheep will eat what the cattle don't. We have miles and miles of 5-strand wire out there to keep them where they all belong.

"Now the seasons are what govern what our year is. In May, we brand."

"How do you do that? Some modern technology?"

"We do it the old fashioned way. One at a time."

"No kidding?"

"In July, we do the hay and in October, its roundup time. We have three ATV's here but use mostly horses for roundup. Horses react faster and turn sharper than any ATV can around a cow bent on breaking out. We'll have six or eight riders working to get them. We rope and brand each calf just like you see in the rodeos."

Looking out over the prairie we watched the sun setting, creating a soft orange sky and millions of stars overhead.

"I've always thought the prairie as being so barren. It really has a life of its own, doesn't it?"

We had a wonderful experience here; one I would never forget. I liked getting first hand explanations of how things are.

We had a long breakfast with these warm-hearted folks. I never felt the stranger like I have in other places and situations. We had a long way to go now to get to the next place on our new list. Hardington, Nebraska was next. Shirley lived there as a child and hadn't been back in a long time either. We said good-bye again.

All across South Dakota the roads were low rolling or flat. I am always amazed at the stability of our earlier pioneers trudging across this immense land. The winds picked up substantially as we trudged along on our powerful motorcycles. So much easier and faster than walking.

Arriving in Hardington, we looked everywhere for Shirleys' memories. They weren't found anywhere.

"We might just as well find a place to stay. It's getting late."

She was so intent in finding the things she remembered, I might just have talked to my water bottle. I sat it out on a doorstep

265

while she went wandering off somewhere. She returned, jumped on the bike and I followed her as she recollected places. I looked for signs for camping. I saw a police officer who said we could stay in the city park.We looked around for something else.She was in front of me when I saw the car behind with the blinking lights. Oh, oh! I didn't have a chance to say anything to Granny as she sped down the residential street. I was busy gearing down.

The officer who said we could stay in the park just wanted to know if we were lost. I talked to him awhile until Shirley returned. I told him she was looking for her past. Then she pulled up. He knew of her family but he said his wife would know more about them. He said we'd better get settled before it got dark.

"I'll be around all night to check on you. It will be safe for you with me on the job."

"Thanks, we appreciate that."

"I'll see if my wife, Karlyn will come out to talk to you."

"Oh, that would be nice but you don't have to do that," Shirley reassured him.

"No, I want to. She'd want to, too."

We went about the job of finding the park and setting up camp. We still had to fix supper and darkness would be on us in a short time. We drove around finding the best place after Office Lewis left us and found one on nicely mowed lawn soft enough I wouldn't need to blow up my confounded mattress.

No sooner had we prepared supper when another car came along and Karlyn jumped out. She and Shirley talked about people I never heard of, who was related to whom and who married who and stuff. I went about writing in my journal, swatting the hordes of mosquitos that found us again and she left us to cope. Shirley was ecstatic. It was like a real find. She wanted to see the museum. Her Grandpa Nelson had left some articles there. We found the museum when we went for a walk in the dark and she got her bearings. She couldn't sleep anyway. I was tired and by eleven o'clock we were back to the tent to try to get some sleep. We spent a very protected night in the city.

In the morning, we walked back downtown for a donut and coffee at one of the few places open on this Saturday. She gathered some more information from the locals and we went back, packed and found the museum where a grandfather donated some of his personal tools. We were off to Topeka, Kansas.

She called her cousins, Jim and Sue Boughn so they could expect us later in the day. Jim rode out to meet us on his motorcycle in case we should get lost with the directions he gave us.

We had a nice stay with them, sleeping on the carpeted basement recreation room floor. Pizza was brought in and their daughter was busy making cookies for us to eat. Jim gave us some pointers on his camping equipment and clothing. His Kawasaki foul weather gear was something we both could have used in those dark days of cold, wind and rain. A new version of headgear might prompt us to search out BMW.

"Do you know, this is the last state to get in our quest to ride through all 48? We have been to 8 provinces, too."

"That's exciting. How long has it taken?"

"Well, more like four years in all. The first year, Marion, rode herself so she went through many of them before I came along."

"And then I had to repeat them once she finally got that bike."

"I wish I was with you. We've been to a few different states, too, but not nearly what you guys have done."

Jim rode with us to breakfast on his usual Sunday morning ride. He expressed a desire to go to Alaska with another fellow. We asked if he'd let us ride with them and we were all going to think about it for the next year. Little did we know he would have an accident with his bike and break a leg. It ended our hopes of the next years Alaskan adventure. Jim gave the bikes a last minute check for us, tightening up a few things and tucking in others. We left and continued east to Perryville, Missouri.

We bumped into an elderly couple at a gas station. They drove two old motorcycles. They pulled trailers. In her trailer were usually dozens of cookies. She was known around that part of the state as the "Cooky Lady." That was her handle. She gave them out to the police patrolling the highways. She said she was always making cookies for them. He carried camping gear.

It would be another long pull across this state by the looks of the map. Perryville was off the beaten path but she wanted to go there, too. Two brothers-in-law lived there. She prepared me for what to expect when we got there on the radio to fill the time between truck chatter.

We took the Mark Twain National Forest to 67 double highway. This wasn't bad. We were low on fuel again when we entered the little twisty, curvy roads of DD, and T. There was no place to stop if we ran out of fuel. No gas stations. No commercial anything. No shoulder. The trees butted up to the road. We said our prayers while we tried to enjoy the woods where we found ourselves. It was wonderful to see town lit up when we emerged from the dark.

We visited with both brothers, ate out and had a generally quiet time with them. To get to the farm of one brother-in-law, we had to drive uphill on a long loose gravel road. Shirley went first, wobbling as far as I could see and then I went up. Scary. We returned the same way. My hands turned to sweaty palms in my gloves. It was easier to slide going down but the brakes were in good working order. I squeezed mine tight all the way down and breathed a sigh of relief.

We visited the farm where we were welcomed into the storage of a lifetime. Yes, she was right, Herb was the more roustabout. I thought he was going to take off with my bike if he got the chance. I took out the key before I got off just in case. He jumped on and bounced it a few times and listened to my squeaks. He removed Shirley's radio and commenced to fix the problem. It was a simple thing but needed soldering. She would hear again. He took us to town to get some equipment in his old beat up pick up truck, taking a look at the hay field on the way to see if it was dry enough to cut and then we were on our final jaunt home.

The rest of that trip was uneventful as we made the final leg though Indianapolis and beyond. It rained off and on. In Gloverdale, we stayed at our last KOA. Met Steve Crowell from Maine. He came in after we did and explained his straight across the states route. He left Maine one morning, putting on 1328 miles to get to his sisters house in just 26 hours. That was too much riding. He only stopped for gas and nature. His wife was having a high school reunion and said he couldn't stand being around all those over 40 women. He had an old 21 year old bike that he kept fixing and riding. Once he arrived he slept all night, drank the whole next afternoon and the next day headed back hime. From here he still had another 1000 miles to go. He thought he could qualify for the "Iron Butt" award after this week-end! I remembered how sore I was after spending just 500 miles in the saddle at one time.

Another young rider was in a hurry to get where he was going. He was due at an Army base but wanted to have his bike with him. He'd make it if he was careful.

We packed the tent wet in the morning fog. The dampness felt more like rain. I got that homing pigeon feel as we approached Michigan. It was always good to get home but on the other hand, the adventure would have to end. I would like to go home for a few days to touch base and be off somewhere else on a different adventure. But it would have to wait. I only was allowed so much time off per year and at the rate I'm going I wouldn't ever save enough time to go to Alaska. This became the last motorcycling adventure for awhile.

"Are we still friends?" I asked over the radio before we parted for home.

"Yea, why wouldn't we be?" she came back.

"I don't know. We've been pretty bitey this trip. I thought I'd better check to make sure."

"Don't be silly."

"Give me a call when you get home so I'll know you're there. O.K.?"

"O.K., Pony Express. Talk to you in a little while." We parted, she going home to Walt and I, to my always worried mother. I was the dutiful child and sent my daily post cards to her as usual. She was happy when I returned. I don't think she worries as much as that first time.

.............."Are you going on any other trips together?" asked Betty sitting with her legs curled under her drinking a fresh cup of coffee.

"Probably. Now it's time to go back to all the places we didn't have enough time to spend. I'd like to go back to the Grand Canyon or Bryce. Mt. Rainier had a lot of trails. I want to do some backpacking. I don't know if I can get her to do that. I may have some problem there."

Well, it's getting late."

"Yep, my gosh, it's after midnight. Where has the time gone?"

I went to sleep and slept very cozily. I would be leaving tomorrow for my final jaunt on my bicycle alone.

Adventure # 9

Failure Into
Accomplishment

Chapter 1   Cadillacs vs.
                               Volkswagons

I stretched as I looked at my watch. The sun was having a problem coming up over the horizon. I could hear noises in the kitchen. Betty must be up. I slid out of bed and remade it neatly, dressed and met her in the kitchen.

"How about some breakfast before you go?"

"A cup of coffee sounds good."

"It's already made. Kurt left you this." She handed me a plastic bag of some dark stuff.

"What is it?"

"That's those dried cherries I told you about." I opened the bag and sampled the fruit. It felt like raisins but looked more like tobacco.

"These are kinda tasty, aren't they?"

"I don't care for them. He'll dry just about anything."

"I'll munch on them on the way home. They'll give me an energy boost."

I packed my panniers with my belongings and a few other things she gave me to eat and pushed off into the damp morning.

ONTONAGON

PORKYS

NEGAUNEE

PARADISE

SAULTE STE.MARIE

CRYSTAL FALLS

NEWBERRY

BIG MAC

TRAVERSE CITY

FAILURE TURNED ACCOMPLISHMENT

DOTTED LINES RIDDEN ALONE

Brighton

The sun was to shine today and it was supposed to be warm. It was 70 degrees already as I coasted down the hills to town. After a few stops the wind picked up. I wasn't motivated much today. I made my stops last far too long and the sky began to hint of rain. The hills were long but they didn't bother me. I had nobody to complain to anyway. I stayed mostly on M-37 to M-115. That was the best part of my route today. It had a decent shoulder all the way to Cadillac State Park. Best of all, it was mostly on a downhill and I was receiving a tail wind all the way. It was too early to be staying in camp but there were no other camp grounds in the near distance. I rode 72 miles already.

I wandered around the city camp. I was bored. I read, I rode to a restaurant for pie and ice cream and called my best friend, Gary. On this trip I called him every day. He worried about me like a mother hen and wanted to know I was all right. It sounded so good to hear his voice. We talked for a long time. I missed him. I was lonesome. I wished Shirley could be here. He tried to help me get over my blues. "After all," he said, "you asked for it. You didn't have to ride it by yourself."

"I know that. But I just wanted to know I could do it alone."

"Then quit your complaining and do it."

"I'll call you tomorrow." I hung up the phone and returned sullenly to camp.

I thought about the flat television we saw in Florida last year. This would be a good time to use it. I laid out on the picnic table to read and couldn't concentrate on what I was reading. I kept going back to how I got in this situation..........

We met those two fellows at Devils Tower. That's what did it. I thought we could do the same thing. Why not? And there were all those people we saw out in New Hampshire and Vermont riding up the mountains. Magazine articles of riders having such a good time. Friends around the state telling tales of their escapades.

I checked all the catalogs for the best buys for panniers, checked all the ads and made my choice. I bought them at a discontinued sale and mounted them on my bike. Wow! It looked like the bikes I'd see on the road. I filled them with gear to see how they would feel when riding and went for a short jaunt. I rode to my brother's house. He lived amid some tough hills. I thought they rode easier than without them. I couldn't believe it.

I called Shirley. "You've got to try them. I swear. It's easier than riding with no load. Com' on over and ride mine and see for yourself. It's like riding in a Cadillac after getting out of a Volkswagon."

271

She gave it a try and it wasn't long before we had her bikes loaded with gear and trying them out on short trips. "Do you want to plan a trip, then?" I asked hopefully.

"Let's go somewhere around here first to see if we can do it. Where do you think we could go if we like it?"

"We could have Walt drive us to his brothers in Perryville, Missouri and ride home."

"Yea, or we could ride around the state, stay close to home."

"We've already ridden around the state. I'd like to ride across the United States from coast to coast."

"Kinda biting off more than you can chew, aren't you? How about around the Upper Peninsula. We haven't done that. Let's look at the maps."

The miles looked feasible. We wouldn't be so far from home that we couldn't get picked up if needed.

"I'll see if Walt minds first." I checked all the maps I had to get an idea of how many miles we were talking and how much time I would have to take off work. It should only take three weeks and be 1000 miles. That would give us time for delays for bad weather and breakdowns.

It was planned. We would try a short overnighter up north next week to get ready for next year.

We drove to Presque Isle where I owned some land and left the car. It was a nice cool morning when we left fully loaded as for a long trip. Stopping to see the largest limestone quarry in the state just before town, I heard the familiar "bang" on my rear tire.

"Oh, darn it," I said. I think the expletive was a little stronger then that but not to worry. I still would have to change the tire.

"Too bad" was all I heard from my riding partner as we looked out over the miles of open expanse to see the layers of limestone. Looking back at the bike, it looked forlorn with its' rear wheel rim resting on the ground. It started to sprinkle. The clouds were moving in since we started but we were immune to rain after all the storms we experienced over the last several years. It was just another shower.

Out came the rain gear.
Out came the repair material.
Off came the tire.
In went the new tube.
Pump, pump, pump.
On went the tire.
Away went the repair tools.
Off we went in the rain.

It came down in buckets as we rode nearer to town. Having breakfast at a marina waiting for it to stop made us change our mind

272

on rain camping for this time. "Why don't we just go back the way we came and forget about going to the falls?"

"Sounds good to me. It sure doesn't look like it's going to quit soon." With that, we went back into the drizzle and returned.

"I just want to know one thing, Shirley. We've done a lot of crazy things up to now. Are we still friends?"

"Sure, don't be silly. I didn't have to do this, you know. Nobody was breaking my arm."

"Are you comfortable riding with this extra weight?"

"It's just like you said, 'It's like jumping from a Volkswagon to a Cadillac'."

"Do you still want to go next summer?"

"Yea, as far as I know now."

"Good. It's done."

Chapter 2   Headlights in the Night

"If we go to the east, we would be back in the Newberry area in four days. We should know by then if we can ride the rest. I chose the east for that reason. It is flatter there, too, so we can build up our muscles early and be prepared for the hills in the west. If we go in August, we can have the other two week long rides we usually do out of the way and be up for it by then."

"What do you have planned for us to see that we haven't seen before?" she asked.

"Have you been to Drummond Island?"

"No."

"Either have I. We have to take a ferry to get there but I see there are two campgrounds that we can choose. Have you been to Muskallunge Lake?"

"No, it doesn't sound familiar."

"You'll like it there, too. Across the road from Muskallunge is Lake Superior. The only place I've been where you can find the nicest looking agates in Michigan. I know you like to look for treasures."

"I thought Michigan had nothing but the Petosky stones."

"You thought wrong. My father-in-law used to go up there to get stones he used in making jewelry."

We waited all winter and into the summer to go on this adventure. Summer could not go fast enough. We had other plans for the first months and this three weeks fit into our schedules for August 12.

I began many escapades at Vina's in Newberry and this was not an exception. She was forewarned about our impending date with destiny months in advance. She took them all as calmly as she could, always amazed.

We left home in the afternoon as soon as I could get away from work. I know we both wondered how well we would do. We had a fistful of county maps and a designated route to follow. I planned as best I could to follow the edge of the peninsula. Some stretches were not known to be paved. Those decisions would be made as we went along.

She would ride her old blue Schwinn with 12 gears, I had my trusty black Schwinn with 15 gears. I was comfortable on mine. We talked about nothing else on the drive to Newberry. Contingency plans were in place. We had everything in order to keep us on the road for three weeks.

At 8 a.m., we were ready to go. It was foggy when we crossed over the driveway to Vina's from the Ponderosa cabin. She fixed us a light breakfast and we took our last pictures together and I asked the same old question.

"Will we still be friends when this is over and done?"

"I don't know. It's too early to speculate," she answered.

On U.S. 28 we would be riding into the morning sun. The shoulder was wide and we could ride side by side. With an uphill at the start, we were warmed up at the top. My camera needed batteries right from the start and we stopped to catch our breaths while I purchased them in the gas station.

The next 25 miles were flat with a small hill or two to make us feel right. There was no wind or none that we were aware of and the sun burned off the fog early. It was a perfect bike riding day. The bike felt comfortable. She said hers was good, also.

We stopped for pie and coffee for a morning snack. I shed another layer of clothes and found I lost a favorite charm I wore around my neck. It was an omen. I was sure of it. It was a bicycle charm I bought when we were riding our first tour in Iowa. I had good bike riding luck since I wore it on a gold chain around my neck. I looked everywhere. It was gone. Shirley pulled up wanting to know what I was looking for and she looked with me. It was not found.

It was only shortly after the loss that I detected a front wheel wobble. It happened at any speed so it had to be something in weight distribution or front fork. If it was only distribution, it would be taken care of once I started eating the food in the panniers.

On a hot stretch of straight road, I could hear my chain grinding. In the next town, I found a place in the shadow of the post office and put on the jelly grease I carried in my repair pocket. I got the first wind that Shirley was getting uncomfortable and had been almost from the start.

"Maybe you didn't adjust the seat right. Do you want to change it?"

"No, it isn't that. It just hurts all over."

She was using the seat we used on our first DALMAC ride. The vinyl man's seat. I couldn't believe she would do that. She must have forgotten the feel of that tragic four day agony we did to ourselves. She wanted to keep going. She thought she could

275

work her way out of it; it was something she would have to get used to.

We stopped at Moran to lay down on a cement porch of a closed building to rest our backs and her backside. Lunch would be pita bread and peanut butter and jelly for me. I don't know what she ate. It was something different. It would be a long day today. There was not a campground close enough to get to within the 50 mile a day allotment. It would be 65.5 miles before we stopped. I was tired myself and could hardly wait to get to bed that night. We camped in the forest camp with limited facilities, meaning no showers. We didn't care, rest was what we needed. It was wooded and shady and few campers in the camp.

She brought her trusty fishing line and a couple of lures just in case she found the opportunity to catch dinner. We were on the banks of the Carp River.

"If all there is is carp in this river, you can eat all the fish you catch."

"I probably won't catch anything. Do you want to go with me?"

"Yea, I'll go and sit around while you make yourself useful. I need to go for a walk anyway to stretch out these muscles."

It wasn't far to the river where we could skinny down an embankment. She found a long stick to tie her line and cast it to the waters. It was relaxing to sit here in the cool damp air, listening to the ripples in the fast flowing river gurgling over debris under the bridge where we sat.

"Do you think you will feel like riding tomorrow?"

"I hope so. It doesn't hurt when I'm off the bike."

After a time, she didn't think the river had any fish and we were back looking through our packs for something more substantial. "I brought some gorp I put together. Do you want some?"

"No, I think I'll just have some fruit and one of these Top Shelf meals. Did you ever try them?"

"No, are they good?"

"I tried one or two before we left to see if they would be and they aren't bad. This one is spaghetti, I think. I took off the cardboard so they wouldn't take up so much space." This time I did not pack my sterno to cook with nor did I pack my hateful Whisper-Light stove. I brought an old propane bottle with an attached stove burner. It has been the winner so far in all the methods of cooking. Shirley brought one of the newer versions. They lit easily, were fast, and canisters could be found almost everywhere. The only problem was their size.

We packed my two-man tent because of it was smaller and lighter. We split it in half for weight; one carried the poles and the other the fabric. It would be more cramped but we didn't have as many things to put in it. Most of our things were left on the bikes.

We knew enough not to put food in the tent from listening to bear stories. This was black bear country and we didn't relish the idea of sleeping with them.

I did have a vestibule we could use on nights it might be raining. Most of our stuff could then be put in it while out of our way inside. We did not use it tonight.

We were snug in our warm beds asleep, when I was awakened.

"There's someone outside the tent."

"What?"

"Something is outside. I can hear it." How anyone can snore and be aware of what's outside was beyond me. She was out of her bag and peering out the tent door.

"Get outa there," she whispered.

"What is it?"

"Coons."

I got up quick. We never had this happen before. She played her flashlight out into the night. There by her bike were a pair of yellow eyes looking back at her, eating the contents of her gorp.

"That little rascal. I saw him open my bag and dip that out just like he knew what he was doing."

"You're kidding."

"No, I'm not. I saw him. He'd have to unzip the pannier, dig inside and then open the zip-lock on that bag. There was a couple dollars of goodies in there."

"Maybe you should have put the plastic bag over the pannier like I did."

"He'd get through that plastic."

"Yea, but you'd hear him getting into the bag sooner. I don't have anything that a coon can get into, I don't think. My stuff is all in hard to open containers."

She got out and put the rest of the bags in the tent. I looked around and couldn't see any damage to mine and left them. We went back to bed and probably stayed awake the rest of the night listening for the little marauders.

In the morning fog, we could see the remains of the plastic bag just past the bike.

"That little bugger just sat there and had himself a feast, you know? There were yogurt covered raisins and peanuts in there."

"That's one way of getting the load down to a more manageable weight sooner."

"I didn't mean to do it that way. I guess I didn't need to eat them anyway."

We ate a light breakfast and headed out onto the highway. Since it was a two lane back road we were trying to stay as close to the edge of the lane as possible. The fog was still thick by 8:30 and

277

we didn't want to wait anymore. We wore our yellow rain jackets so we'd be seen better and to keep the morning dampness away from our bones. Our orange flags waved side to side.

"How's your bottom feeling this morning?

"It still hurts. It was o.k. before I sat on the seat."

I could see this was not going to be a long tour just by the sound in her voice. I prayed I was wrong.

We were now near the waters' edge. Lake Huron should be with us to Drummond Island. At Hassel, we stopped for a second breakfast in a marina. An antique boat show was somewhere in the vicinity prompting many boaters to be out and about. The marina was filled with diners. We settled for a seat outside with many others. It was warm in the sun and it felt good. The fog had dissipated ten miles ago and the sun shone on another perfect biking day. We watched yachts ply the calm waters of the inner harbor making their way into port.

Some folks were feeling the saddles on our bikes parked along the fence near the restaurant.

"How can you stand them? They are so hard," one asked.

"They aren't bad. You get used to them. We ride a lot and its' not any different from you sitting all day in the car."

"She can say that. I don't have my usual seat and my butt hurts," rebuked Shirley.

"Yea, she put on the wrong one," I relinquished.

The morning wore on and she hurt more. Being warm and humid only added to her discomfort. We stopped at a tavern at Cedarville for her to call home. She complained about the seat over the phone. I don't know what good it would do but I knew she needed some outside advise and comfort from home. I walked outside while I waited for her, drinking a cold glass of water. "If we get up to the Soo I'll buy you a new seat, Shirley. It's a college town. They should have a decent one."

"You don't want to go to the island?"

"Sure, I do, but not if I have to hear you complaining and having to stop every mile or so. What good would that be?"

"It just feels like my butt is being pulled apart when I sit on that seat."

"I don't know why you put that one on anyway. You've ridden that bike before with another seat, haven't you?"

"Yea, but I put it on the other bike."

"Well, I don't even know why you didn't put your panniers on your better bike."

"I couldn't get the racks to fit."

"I thought they fit any bike."

"Well, they wouldn't fit mine."

"Couldn't Walt get them to fit either?"

"I didn't even ask him."

"Let's go. We can turn up this road and head for the Soo. By the time we get there the stores should be open.

My chain jammed as we plied the first hill on our new road. Damn! Shirley rode ahead but heard me yell and came back. She thought I hurt myself. It took the two of us to fix the darn thing. It was so jammed in the derailier we had to pry it out with a screw driver. My hands were covered in black grease. Good thing I carried grease remover. The temperature in the air had nothing to do with my hot temper at this point.

It took some doing but we found a private camp on the map after only 48.5 miles. It was a reprieve from our 65 mile day the day before. We set up in a grove of trees and could see and hear water lapping at the beach between some of the other campers. It was quiet and serene. We should sleep well tonight. It looked like rain again. We heard thunder in the distance. The showers were wonderful. I could have stayed till the water ran out.

"Let's take a walk around and up the hill there to that little store we passed."

"O.K. and when we come back I'll beat you at a game of cards if you like."

"You brought them, too?"

"Sure, where have we ever gone that we didn't have our cards with us. We have to have something to do when there isn't anything else."

The walk did me a world of good. Stretching leg muscles is an important must after riding all day. We sat outside on the ground eating junk food and drinking pop.

Losing that charm on my necklace brought more grief for me. I lifted my packed bike by the seat in the morning to reposition it in camp. I broke the part that attached the seat frame to the seat. I was beginning to wonder if this was the way it was going to be for the whole three weeks. Was this what happened to the others that rode long distances unsagged? Maybe the ones I talked to never liked to talk about the bad things that happened. I rode on a lopsided seat for the rest of the day.

Shirley was dragging her brakes. Another minor adjustment.

You think we never took care of our bikes. Little things became monstrous.

The road was flat all day. We both appreciated that. Shirley would have appreciated it if they would have fixed the patchwork quilt of repairs better. The patches had patches. Many bumps multiplied in intensity when the butt hurt like I knew hers must be doing.

279

A large, black dog chased us into the sleepy village of Pickford. I had dog repellant but it must have dried up. It didn't work. You can push those pedals around so easily when danger is nipping at your heels. We had our second breakfast in a restaurant and I tried to get a new bottle from the postmaster across the street. Even though I showed her my identification, she would not relinquish any of her supply.

A wind came up out of Pickford where we turned north. It was going the same direction so we let it go with us. It stayed there all the way into the Soo.

A herd of buffalo attracted our cameras on the way. It was another reprieve from the seat and I knew it. The sky was cloudy but it didn't look like rain.

One bike shop in town was not equipped for the things we needed. He had only mens' seats and wasn't all that capable at fixing things. I asked if he could Crazy Glue mine. He poo-pooh'd the idea.

"Give me your glue and I'll fix it myself." I did. It lasted most of a year.

"Is there any other shop in town we can find a seat?" we asked.

"Not that I know. You might ask when you get down town. There might be one down there."

All our hopes were not dashed yet. We indulged in an ice cream sundae before getting back in the saddle and shot back into the increasing Soo traffic. No more quiet country roads here. I asked a police officer and he thought there might be one on the Canadian side of the Soo. That would mean crossing the bridge and going through customs and maybe not finding one. "Let's go find the place he told us about and get on with it, Shirley."

I spotted a phone booth on a busy corner. "Who are you going to call," she asked.

First I got mad. Then I said, "It would be better to call over there instead of riding over and finding they don't have any, wouldn't it?"

She didn't say anything.

"I'm going to make my call home first." It was my turn for comfort from home.

I called Gary and laid my complaint on the line. He never influenced me in my decisions but let me rant and rave when I needed to. He was a good sounding block.

She was looking disgusted when I got off the line and I asked "Do you really want to find a seat or what?"

"I don't know. We probably can't."

"Look, if you don't even want to try, there is no sense me calling Canada for nothing."

"I'll ride like this."

"O.K." I was getting hotter. "I'm going back the way we were going. You can either stay here or you can follow. Suit yourself."

I would have had Walt express mail us the seat she had on her other bike if it would fit. She said it wouldn't. Where the old seat she had went to was beyond me. I wasn't understanding anything. She wasn't telling me anything. I was out of there. I wasn't going to baby her for the next three weeks.

She followed.

Brimley was only 11 miles from where we were. I told her that was where I was going for the night. It was early. Instead of Brimley we saw a campground a mile out of town.

"Do you think you can make it eleven miles or do you want to stop here?"

"Let's stop here."

Tension was high for several hours. We couldn't agree on anything. We set up camp without hardly a word. She took a shower and I stayed to play solitaire. We ate some supper and both laid down inside to rest. It was still light by 8:30.

"I saw a sign that said they had tour buses pick people up here to tour the Soo. Do you want to go?" she asked.

"Sure, why not. We've rested long enough. It's almost a new day. As we raced down the slope to catch the bus, the driver said, "This is the last shuttle."

"What do you mean?"

"I can take you there but you'll have to find your own way back."

"That wouldn't be very good. It's a long walk." He was good looking. He said he was from Canada. A lot of good looking men seemed to come from there. What were they doing different?

"Tell you what. My shift ends. I have to go to town and come back here with the bus. My car is parked right around the corner. I'll take you to town as soon as I come back. Are you game?"

We looked at each other and I said "Yes."

"O.K. See you in a few minutes."

"What are you driving so we'll know what to look for?"

"A big white Oldsmobile."

He left and Shirley hesitated. "You really think he'll come back?"

"I don't know. If he does it will add a little color to our otherwise dull life, I'm sure."

"Are you going to go?"

"Sure, if you go. You want to, don't you?"

"I don't know. We don't even know him."

"Yea."

"I'm going to bed."

"I'll wait up. If he comes back I'll get us out of it. Maybe he'll just stop and visit here in camp." I waited only a few minutes when I saw

281

a big white Oldsmobile circling the camp. I sat on the table in plain sight in the dark.

"He's here, Shirley," I said in a low voice so she could hear through the tent walls.

"You're kidding. I'm going to bed anyway." He circled around again and I didn't make any effort to flag him down. If he was that blind I was going to bed, too. So much for our dull life.

We made our oatmeal and coffee breakfast and packed up in our usual early hour. No sooner did we get on the road when the rain began. I put on my rain jacket at the start. Shirley didn't think the thick dew was going to last and went without it for awhile. She had to relent sooner than she thought.

It was a nasty day and we were nasty to each other by late afternoon. Brimley was only ten miles away. I wore a poncho over my rain jacket but the sweat inside the jacket made my clothes wet anyway. We changed into dry at a restaurant after a second breakfast and pushed on. The temperature never rose above 60 degrees. We stopped at an Indian burial ground and a lighthouse. I had a friend that was innkeeper of the Big Bay Lighthouse west of here. This keeper knew my friend and we exchanged newsworthy information.

There was a brisk headwind the rest of the day. The rain didn't let up. It slowed to a drizzle and then poured. We thought a hatchery would be a good place to rest. Shirley, the fisherman, looked over the empty tubs while I found the best thing they offered in the restroom. An electric hand drier. I dried all my clothes again and warmed my body. I didn't want to leave but someone might've wanted to use the one-hole restroom.

We rode through trees and trees and trees. While riding behind Shirley, I was astonished to see a person emerge from the woods carrying a huge golfing umbrella in a multitude of color. It was so striking against the green I was surprised. She turned around and I saw it was a woman and she wore a pair of overalls and boots and a flannel shirt. She had long blond hair, was about in her thirties. I hollered out to my partner, "They said we'd see some wildlife but I didn't think they meant two-legged."

She couldn't hear me and I went on wondering how she got there. There were no houses, no cars.

We stopped over a river-crossing for a wet lunch of peanut butter and jelly sandwiches. One or two vehicles went by honking their horns and waving.

I made reservations at Tahquamenon Falls a month ago. As the day wore on and on, we were engrossed in our own thoughts. I asked myself, what am I doing here? I hadn't heard a word out of my partner in a long time. I knew she was there. I kept her in front of

282

me. She would lag behind, stop and I wouldn't see her. I hollered again to the lady up front of me, "If we run into a motel, do you want to take it?"

A firm "Yes" came back. We rode on for miles it seemed. The rain turned to a mist. We passed the gate for the park. There wasn't anyone there to cancel the prepaid night. We went on to Paradise. A neat little house on the right had a sign indicating it would only take "Only Women". It was a rest home. I pulled in and Shirley did, too.

"What do you think? You want to see if they will let us rest here?"

She looked around and said "No," and pedaled out.

In town, we chose a nice motel with a German woman running it. She was very nice. The rain stopped and sun came out but we were still bundled in our rain jackets trying to keep our warmth inside. She allowed us to put the bikes inside and use their laundry facility. We were cleaning up when she came to our room and said if we hurried we could get to the museum at Whitefish Point before they closed.

"Whitefish Point?" I asked. "Isn't that quite a way away?"

"It's only about ten miles," she answered.

"Naw, we don't want to go that far today. We've already gone 47 miles and that would be 67 miles if we go. We're too tired."

"Take the Broncho," she returned as if it was done all the time.

"Just take the Broncho," I said without believing her.

"Ya."

We looked at each other not thinking she really said that. "You want to go?" asked Shirley.

"Why not."

"Then you girls better hurry. They close at 6."

We finished what we were doing and went to get the keys. "They are in the ignition."

They surely trusted people around there. Leaving keys where we lived would be a definite loss of vehicle. We rode up to the museum. I felt much better sitting on this seat than the one we were on for the past couple days. Shirley was even smiling and acting like nothing was wrong with her backside.

The museum was a very good one at that. Many things to see, videos, items from the deep, sounds of underwater divers. Most of it was of the shipwrecks that have piled up at this point. Many storms plague the waters in Lake Superior. The museum gave one the feeling you were under water. There were little outside influences to make you feel differently. It felt somewhat eery.

Walking outside, the wind hit us coldly in the face. We devoured a delicious dinner back in town and returned the vehicle with many thanks.

283

I had a good nights' sleep. Shirley did not. She chose the plastic covered bed that must have been meant for the kids. We elected to have breakfast at the same restaurant we had dinner the night before. The sun was still shining this morning as we made our way to the falls. It was a delightful morning to ride. Shirley was still hurting but said little about it.

We had been to the falls many times and always enjoyed seeing them from time to time. We visited with a busload of senior citizens who invited us to help ourselves to their leftover sandwiches and watermelon. We sat with them a long time exchanging stories and telling them how much fun we were having. We had a concertina played for us and pictures taken with them.

The rest of the day was uneventful. I told Shirley I would let her know what I was going to do when we got back to Newberry. She wasn't going any farther than that. I thought about it all day.

"Would you want to go south and rent a canoe and do the Au Sable River?" I asked.

"I don't know." I pedaled on in thought.

We could have done that because we had everything we needed to go for a few days at least. Then I remembered we couldn't replenish our supplies as easy as on the road.

I could continue the adventure alone but was afraid of the hills in the west. I wouldn't have anyone to complain to if I couldn't make it up the hill or if I couldn't finish, what would I do? I tossed that around for a long time. I should be strong enough to handle this myself, I kept telling myself. It shouldn't be much different from the solo motorcycle excursion. But now I would be relying on my physical strength and not mechanical. Why didn't she use the right seat?

Pulling into the yard, she asked me what I was going to do. I picked up the keys, held them in my hand for awhile and then put them in her hand. "Here's the keys. I'll ride my bike home."

"From here?"

"Yes. It won't be much farther, if at all, and I know the territory much better than in the west. I've made up my mind."

We took Vina out for dinner and visited for awhile before going to bed. I called Gary to tell him what I was going to do. He didn't say much except to be careful. I asked him to call mom and tell her the news so she wouldn't worry.

We rearranged some of the items. I would have to carry the whole tent. I put all the maps save the state map in the car. Everything else would not be changed. That was how I got myself into this.

284

Cadillac was not my favorite place. I was still bored. I washed out more of my socks before it was dark and since I carried a long pole with a bike flag at the end for safety, I used it for a clothesline. In the morning it was damp and of course, they weren't dry. Leaving the camp with my socks hanging out to dry only added to the safety factor. I should be home in a few days, I thought. It should be flat country from here.

It was. But right out of Cadillac it started to rain. Oh, drats! Put on the sauna suit. It kept the body heat in at least. Just two miles on the road, the chain jammed in the derailier again. I worked at it on the side of the road with no shoulder. It would not budge. Why couldn't this happen yesterday in the sun? Trucks passed spraying me with dirty road water. I used everything I could get my hands on to free it. I could not push my bike anywhere with the chain jammed. It wasn't like having a flat tire. I wanted to have one of those instead. I could fix that. Where was Shirley? I needed her to help. I needed a second pair of hands. What was I doing here?

After a half hour of pulling and pushing and tugging, it let loose. I couldn't adjust anything any more than it was. I was just very careful when I changed gears the rest of the trip.

This end of M-15 had no shoulder. I wanted to write the road commission or something. Maybe, my senator. Trucks didn't move over much. I clung tightly to my handlebars as I kept to the edge.

On the corner of M-115 and M-66, I tried to get into a restaurant but it was full. A fellow came out offering me his seat. He was leaving. I didn't take his seat. I just slid back on the saddle and rode out. It was easy riding. Most of the miles were enjoyable. I went down the road and found another place for lunch. A bowl of soup tasted like a second bowl. I devoured both. A lady stopped me on my way out to ask where I was from. When I told her, she went into a long tale about her life in the town not far from me.

I counted off the miles to each town. Two miles to Farwell, five to Clare. Changing direction slightly in Clare, I was hit with a 10-15 mile per hour tail wind. I zig-zagged my way through the flat land to Mt. Pleasant just 61 miles away and took a motel room. I wanted to go no farther than Rosebush but there were no accommodations. I thought of asking to put my tent up in someones' yard but I wasn't that desperate yet.

A shower felt good. But with nothing to do, I missed my partner. The riding wasn't so bad. It was the stopping for the night. At least, I could watch television.

I spent a lousy night in bed. I should have slept on the floor. I didn't want to eat breakfast alone. The bike was packed and ready to go to the nearest McDonalds' down the road. I passed by the Central Michigan University. That was our first over-night stay on our very first ride. It was empty now of the thousands of tents I once saw.

The sun was shining and a slight breeze from the north, north-east pushed me between Alma and Ithica by 10:30 a.m. I was happy the miles sped by so swiftly. Happy there were no hills to contend with.

The wind didn't stay calm. I was zig-zagging across the state again and would get a terrific blow to the left when I would turn to the east. It slowed me down and tired me out. I made plans to get to Sleepy Hollow State Park. It would be a total of 75 miles or so if I did. I stopped every five miles just to rest from the onslaught. The sky looked threatening. Low, dark clouds skidded over the landscape in this flat country of farms. An occasional windbreak of trees slowed the blowing. Some 55 miles into the day, I called Gary to see if he would meet me in Owasso. It wasn't that far from where he was working that day. We had not seen each other for three weeks or more and he was as anxious as I to be together. There weren't many miles for me to go to finish this adventure and I expected to be home the next day.

Had I planned on going to the Park, I would not have had the head winds I encountered for the final twenty miles. They must have switched direction on me while I was calling from the phone booth. It was one of the hardest twenty miles I rode all day.

He insisted over a late dinner that he was driving me home the last forty miles.

"Gary, I didn't ride all this way to be driven the last few miles."

"You shouldn't even be out here by yourself."

"But I have had no real problems and now I'm almost in my back yard," I protested. I gave him the tent and sleeping bag to lighten the load.

He left for work much earlier than I left for the road. I took my time getting started, eating breakfast in Durand with the farmers from the area. They wondered where I was going. It was a nice conversation and then I just couldn't seem to pedal that bike like I had been. It was a nice sunny day, with yet a breeze. Stopping many times along the way to rest, I ate dried cherries. I didn't have much of any other food left. The cherries boosted my energy but weren't regarded as "comfort food". I was more tired today than I was the whole two weeks, but pulled into my drive with a feeling I had accomplished something I didn't know I could do again. It was only 650 miles but didn't feel like it once I was home.

It was another adventure I tried alone and found I could do. I never intended to do it alone. I'm sure Shirley never intended to quit mid-stream either. I still recalled the days of my *age of reason* 22`and my first two-wheeler. Mom waving good-bye as I left home

286

each time. My fears of traveling alone never matured. This ride alone only made me realize I could do that Upper Peninsula by myself. I didn't need to have someone with me and I would do it next year whether alone or with someone. I wanted to do it before I was 50. I would be 51 in the fall after I returned. I was going. Poor Mom!

Chapter 3   A Change of Plan

Since we did not continue with our ride around the Upper Peninsula of Michigan in 1989 together, I had expected I would be finishing it alone if I were ever going to do it at all. We were still friends. I was surprised just after the Christmas holidays when she let me know that she had a new seat for her old bike.

"Do you want to finish the ride this summer?" she asked.

"Well, of course I want to. I suppose I will have to do it alone." I returned.

"I have this new seat I received for Christmas. If you want, I will go with you," she countered.

"You're kidding!"

"No, Walt got it for me." I was estactic. Perhaps the second half of my life could start with this 700 mile bike ride to set it off right.

We would start where we left off the proceeding year but to the west of Newberry following the Lake Superior shoreline to the Wisconsin border. We could cut over to the Lake Michigan lakeshore via the Michigan-Wisconsin border to the beginning.

I made t-shirts commemorating our ride. They were light blue with purple lettering. They said U.P. Experience across the front with a little bicycle looking like it was speeding and 1990 behind it. On the back I imprinted a map of our adventure with the roads and towns where we stayed the night.

But midstream into our plans I had a medical diagnosis that would require surgery and 8 weeks of recovery. All the plans had to be altered. Fearful I may never do this ride I decided to plan it for the first activity of the season.We both had some reservations. My situation made me feel very drained and tired. My blood pressure had dropped dramatically. I began taking naps in the afternoon. I didn't feel like training on the bike for one reason or other; usually it was too cold, too windy or mainly I just didn't feel like it. I had also gained some weight I didn't need to gain.

I managed to get in a little time in the saddle even if it wasn't the kind I needed. Shirley wasn't getting the time either making us wonder if we could build up the strength as we went along. There would be no turning back once we started.

With perseverance I brought my blood pressure up some through diet and medication, slowly getting the adrenaline needed if only because the time approaching was filling me with anxiety. A snowstorm delayed our departure for May.

We watched the weather reports avidly every night. We saw the pillows of snow piling up on the television screen, the snow driven by fierce spring winds. It was gone in a short time but the temperatures didn't rise fast enough to suit us.

"Why don't we wait a few days," I begged as time came closer and closer for leaving.

"Sounds good to me." she replied. I don't want to sound like a wet blanket but it wouldn't be a bit of fun pushing through the snowbanks and camping on the wet ground for that long."

I packed and unpacked for weeks. Since the weather at this time of year was unpredictable we needed cold weather, warm weather clothing and rain gear. That can be a problem when you are limited to weight and space. We compared items so we were compatible.

We had different likes and dislikes in food. We chose the foods we wanted ourselves but they were identical to any other time we had packed light. Mostly survival snack energy foods in case we couldn't find restaurants close by when we needed them. Survival foods were coffee, oatmeal, dried fruit and dehydrated meals.

The longest I had ridden was only 50 miles when we decided to leave. It felt like 550. We would be averaging 50 miles a day for two weeks.

Chapter 4   Run Out of Town

But on May 30 we packed our gear in the van on a delightfully warm afternoon heading north for Newberry where we began the last year. The excitement was being built up as we drove along. We focused on old memories of other rides. A vision of the unknown filled our heads. Could we do it without really training? Would Shirleys' seat be more comfortable this time? Would I endure the anticipated pressures on my tired body? Would we still be friends?

The day of reckoning dawned with a temperature of only 40 degrees. The sun peered over the eastern horizon promising at least a bright day, I hoped a warm day. Our hostess, Vina, prepared breakfast, we unpacked our steeds from the van and made final calls to home bases. The temperatures had risen to 50 degrees.

My camera had dead batteries last year but now had a new set. In starting, my chain did not want to mesh making quick adjustments a last minute item we hoped would not become a daily routine. It now was 60 degrees. Pedaling up the grade into McMillan, Shirley discovered her brakes were dragging again as they were last year. She felt someone was squeezing the brakes on as she was going downhill. We opened the spacer on the handlebar so they wouldn't be quite so tight but still give her some use.

McMillans' restaurant advertised huge cinnamon rolls. It gave us that excuse needed to stop and investigate. We said we wouldn't have any because we just had breakfast until we saw them. They were 4" high and 8"x 8" square with gooey pecans and cinnamon sauce all over them. They were beautiful! We indulged by splitting one in half, taking yet half of each half wrapped in plastic with us for the next morning. For once we could not consume all we ordered.

We found ourselves stopping for coffee as often as possible while testing the taste of apple or raspberry pie almost every day. It was fruit, wasn't it?

Out on the road the day was warming up. It should be a good one, we were feeling good, we hoped it would last. We had only gone 10 miles when the sun was at its best but the wind was

290

beginning to show signs of strengthening. Sweat ran down our backs and black flies began to show themselves. U.S. 28 is a flat, long, boring road to travel. The headwinds we encountered for the whole day made us push so much harder without going very fast that this, our first day, was torture.

We had about 60 miles to go to our overnight stay in Munising. There was nothing spectacular to see here but short, scrubby trees a distance from the roadway, a railroad bed to our left with power lines running the same direction, an occasional road kill on the side and a few creeks. A two foot easement ran along the two lane road so we were not on the actual traffic lane. At times that two feet seemed much smaller as trucks going one way would create a turbulence that made us hang tight to our steeds so as not to be blown off. Those heading our way giving us a little draft. Sure felt like most of them were going the other way! We'd stop at creeks and rivers for breaks but found all the biting flies congregated here. By the end of the day I had several large lumps on my scalp from the black flies that came in the slots of my helmet to settle in for the ride.

This was deer country. We kept an eye open but only found a couple road kill with other night creatures.

Pulling into a roadside park we ate a snack and laid out on the tables to straighten our backs. We were just not used to the bent-over position and half pound helmets on our heads. No wind here. What's the idea? A few resting travelers inquired where we were heading. It was hard to explain why we were so tired and achy when we had only gone 20 miles or so. We posed for pictures in Seney with a couple large carved, wooden Indians.

"I suppose the only way we're going to get where we're going is to get going," we'd say after procrastinating, as we eased our bodies lightly onto our seats.

"How are you doin' up there," I called to her. We could not ride side by side.

"I'm fine. This seat is great!"

"I'm glad. I hope you keep saying that the whole two weeks we'll be gone."

"You could have done away with this wind," she hollered back.

"What did you say?" I could not make out the words with the wind blowing through my helmet and by my ears.

"Turn off this wind," she shouted again.

"I'd sure like to. I'm not having it any easier than you. We would have to pick this day to go west." After 45 miles we were so tired from the oncoming wind, our thighs became tight, our seats still not becoming accustomed to our bodies. At Shingleton we had a good dinner served with soft seats. As we waited for our dinner to arrive we examined the sanity of riding such long distances without pretraining. My hip gave me a little problem but after a couple days if went away. Shirley had a bit of a knee problem that plagued her on and off most of the trip. My seat never really felt much better. I was used to riding in running shorts rather than the padded shorts for bicyclists but wore the padded ones for this trip since it was so early in the season.

In Munising, we had a couple big hills after the long stretch of flats. As tired as we were, I'm surprised we made it up and over with such ease. Shirley seemed to get a new burst of energy that I lacked, even stopping to take pictures of the beautiful blue bay shimmering in the sunlight to our right. I was afraid if I stopped on the way up I wouldn't get started again keeping the slow pace in a low gear to the top.

The plan was originally to arrive early enough to take the boat trip to see Pictured Rocks area in this town of Munising. But times and energy didn't seem to warrant. This would be just another in a series of things "we'll do another time on a different transportation mode". We could have taken the ferry to Grand Island to ride around at our leisure. That, too, was filed away. We found a private camp for the night on the water. The only place we had to pay 50 cents for a shower. Behind us we could hear the occasional call of a crane in the swampy area but never found it.

The temperatures never dropped below 60 degrees but was in upper 70's during the day. We were quite pleased though we suffered some pain. We expected it and got it. Walking around the beach looking for collectables and eating an unhurried supper relaxed us. The wind never died down all night but we slept well.

The next day we rode through Christmas with not a restaurant in sight. All the way to Au Train without one. We had planned on going for a 2 mile walk on the Song Bird Trail. It would be several miles against the strong wind to get to it, so we passed it by. A coffee shop wasn't going to open for an hour. We went on.

The rest of our scenery for this day would be more varied with turns, hills and sandy beach along beautiful blue Lake Superior State Park where we encountered a couple from California, chatting with them for awhile and taking pictures of a traveler who was napping on a picnic table with his pillow.

The wind was really picking up now as we pulled into a tavern for something to eat. The proprietor was very friendly fixing us a sample of his famous fish fry they would be serving later that evening.

"I think I'll have a hamburger. I love bar hamburgers."

"I'm not really hungry yet." I couldn't believe I was saying that.

"Have some fresh fish," said Mean Gene. He made a basket of trout just for us.

292

His wife brought out a huge hamburger for Shirley.

"Gez, does that look good."

For once I wasn't hungry enough to eat but had a desire for one of those hamburgers the rest of the trip. Mean Gene had several autograph books for people to sign all arranged into states with wooden covers bound in brass. We were invited to sign it. We were the only ones in the place so far on this Friday afternoon. Upon leaving we noticed the sign by the road. "Sand Point Pop. 2"

Not especially wanting to get back on the road again we groaned as we sat on our seats and turned the pedals around again. Huge white clouds began to roll in with ominous dark ones behind them. The road was fairly flat for a long time since we came onto the shoreline. We arrived at a crossroad near Marquette that would take us south of the town. We knew town would be very busy and hilly.

"Lets not go that way. You know how the traffic is in town," I pleaded.

"You won't get any lip out of me. You know I don't like traffic. Let's go that way, " she conceded as she looked over the map with me.

"Yea, it will take us around Marquette and into Ishpeming. There are three campsites there. That's where I planned for us to go last year."

Crossing over, we discovered the head winds were much stronger than we thought. Most of today we had endured cross winds but with our own wind it made them seem more like head winds. Some 30 mph gusts felt like we were running straight into a wall going nowhere. Changing into one of our lowest gears was mandatory as soon as possible. But just as we thought we had the right gear a gust would come up into our faces making a gear change all but impossible on such short notice. We tried standing up in the stirrups that held our feet on the pedals to get the extra power needed and just then the wind would dissipate and we'd find we were now in too low a gear spinning our feet wildly.

Out of desperation we stopped at a fish hatchery along the road as a reprieve. Leaving, we had to go directly uphill with no shoulder to ride on a very narrow roadway. Turning the corner we were back into a cross wind but no shoulder and many hills in quick succession, with a stream of trucks. The maps I had brought indicated this road to be a bike route. Since they were made 5 years ago this road must have changed. A couple hills we just couldn't pedal up because of the danger. We crossed the road to push the bikes on the pavement as we walked in the deep sand shoulder hoping not to be run over by the lumbering trucks. Thank goodness this road was only about 5 miles in length.

293

A widening in the road for a section over a river gave us some leeway. On the other side it was back to taking our chances.

"I'm not going to ride on this side," said Shirley emphatically.

"Look, we've only got one more hill. As soon as these last few trucks go past, I'm heading out. Com'on, you can make it." I sped off as fast as I could. She followed.

The remainder of the roads into Negaunee were newly paved. A nice wide car width shoulder giving us plenty of room to ride up the long hills measuring something like 2-3 miles in length.

"Remember that what goes up usually goes down," Shirley yelled from behind me when I was having a little difficulty going up. She tried to boost my energy level. Sure enough, the hills did go down. But they passed all too fast.

We arrived at Negaunee, an old mining town with old brick buildings. There were suppose to be at least three campgrounds according to my map; we needed direction. Riding through town we came upon a city police officer as he was poking his head out of his office.

We followed him in inquiring where one of these camps would be. He looked at me quizzically saying he didn't know where there was anyplace like that in this town.

"This is not a town for two respectable women to be in anyway" he emphasized.

"What do you mean?"

"The miners here are all out of work, there are more bars than churches, and the atmosphere isn't very good for you two women to be here alone." We looked at each other not knowing quite what to do or where to go.

"Where would the closest campground be then?" I asked.

"About 23 miles down the road in Ishpheming. I wouldn't recommend it either." There was no way either of us wanted to go that far today. We had already gone 50 miles.

"Would you feel funny about staying in a church?" he asked.

"Heck, no," we echoed.

"Let me call around to see what I can get for you."

"O.K. Sounds good."

As he pushed a few buttons on the phone I got the impression he was not really dialing anything at all. He said he was getting answering services from all the places he called but never talked to them. Dialing a few others after he told us that could have been insurance for himself.

"How about a cell?" asked Shirley.

"Oh, no, we can't do that because of liability."

"So what if we make camp in one of your so-called parks and you picked us up for vagrancy. How would liability work then?"

He pointed his finger right at me saying, "You had better not do that or I will just run you out of town. Let me call the motel on the outskirts of town." He dialed another number waiting for the operator to redial on the busy signal several times. After about 10 minutes I just asked to be directed to the motel. I thought this only happened in the old west.

After a rather comfortable night in a room with a bed and shower we were quite refreshed when we started out into the sunny day. "Let's catch breakfast in town. There must be something open." The first hill was a killer giving us excuses to stop often for one thing or another. Had two breakfasts before 10:30.

Clarksburg contained only one house with road construction on a hill. We stopped to figure out some strategy for getting up without stopping too much traffic. We had nobody to direct traffic though there were construction workers just standing around. I thought they were just waiting to see how we managed it. Shirley was a little skeptical as there was no shoulder and thought she would walk up.

"Well, I'm going for it, there's a break in traffic," I decided as I eased myself onto the saddle starting off. She followed me. Just as we both got to the brink of the hill a semi-truck driver decided he would not wait for us. He passed where oncoming traffic in the two lane road could not even see him or us. We squeezed over as far as we could. That made the truck come so close we could reach out and grab hold, the oncoming cars had to hit the gravel, and there were all kinds of markers, speed limits. We breathed a sigh of relief that we were still standing up after that incident. We needed the next restaurant for a cool lemonade.

Turning north off US 28 on M41 we had our first real tail wind and less traffic. We started to really sail for the first time. Made uphills at 15-22 mph and down at 33 mph. What a treat that didn't last long enough.

Pulling into Canyon Falls sounded like something out of Arizona. A half hour walk proved quite relaxing along a river trail to a real canyon with shelve rock, waterfalls, moist green foliage everywhere and a real gorge with the water rushing through it. We jumped down onto the shelf rock, Shirley laying on it to straighten her back in its warmth; I climbing around investigating the coolness of the water. A good place to soak ones' hot feet. In the quiet cool of the walkway lined with wood chips we were able to see a grotto-like area leading down to a real canyon gorge lined with shady, dark rock, the water rushing through it in brilliant white splashes. We stayed awhile enjoying the cool beauty of the place and then reluctantly walked back. We saw the wind had not stopped any but we tried to dig through our food bags for a little road lunch of

295

peanut butter and jelly on pita bread without it blowing away. My bike fell over parked against the picnic table.

Back on the bike into Baraga was another treat. A long sweeping downhill road led us several miles through L'anse to a pay phone. I called one of my mothers' friends and was told to just turn at a building to go up a little hill after we got into Baraga just a short distance away.

"A hill?" I hollered into the phone. "Not another hill."

"It's just a little hill," she consoled. The hill was little but coming onto it at the last minute as we searched for the right building we had to walk. "Oh, I thought you were on motorcycles." She tried to explain away her confusion.

We had a very nice time with Idabell St. Germain. She was 85 years young. She lived a full life with her husband in this north country staying in places many wives would never have stayed. She had many tales to tell of her excursions with him who she called "Saint". She drove an old blue Volkswagen. She had to take us to all her points of interest and then to dinner at a nice inn where she refused to let us pay for prime rib, drinks and dessert. On to the only casino in town owned by the native Indians. It was not the Vegas gala affair but just a quiet club where gaming tables were set up in a two room building.

Before we left for our town tour we had washed out some of our clothes, hanging them to dry on a clothesline behind her house. Now it decided to rain, rinsing out our clothes. When we arrived back home we brought them inside discovering that the tree that hung over the line bled a blueberry color stain on everything. Our underwear and socks and a nice white shirt were now a lovely purple polka-dot.

"I can't understand that," she said, "I've been hanging clothes out there for years." Idabell couldn't be convinced it came from her tree. But it was no real disaster. After all, who was going to be inspecting our underwear anyway?

We found sleeping in her sons' bed would be another one of those experiences we would add to our list. We giggled for some time with the door closed, when finally Idabell couldn't stand it any more and knocked on the door.

"What are you doing?" She sounded like a stern mother trying to get her children to settle down. It was a double bed, very soft and we both kept rolling into the center all night. We didn't sleep very well as we tried to stay on the high side of the bed. Her son, David, must have slept for years in the center. He was away on business while we were there.

"You prayed it would keep raining, didn't you?" I accused Idabell in the morning.

296

"Who, Me?"

"Yes, you. You know how you are. You didn't want us to leave and you probably prayed so hard He felt sorry for you." We all laughed as we looked out the window at the rain, reading the thermometer outside.

"I wonder when it will turn to snow?"

"It's 28 degrees, much too cold to want to ride in this rain. I guess we will stay another day."

"I wanted you to as I bought all this food when I heard you were going to be here and we can't let it go rotten!" She put on the very innocent look of someone who really hoped wasn't going to be caught in any act.

"You're in luck. We already discussed what we were going to do before we got out of bed when we heard the rain. You get to keep us another day. We just won't go up to Houghton but cut across the peninsula the next day and still be on schedule. We've both been there anyway."

She gave us more tour this day stopping at the Bishop Baraga shrine. She bussed us around in her old Volkswagon bug like an old pro. Dinner that night was the pasties. We played cards for the second time and in the evening we watched her dance around the floor while watching Lawrence Welk on the television, one of her favorite programs. Idabell put me to shame for her vitality.

By the next morning the sun was visible across the bay in front of her house. "Saint and I would always make comment on whether we could see L'anse first thing every morning." she explained. The temperature wasn't rising as well as the sun but it could've been because the thermometer was in the shade. Looked like frost on the pumpkin. We said some fond farewells anyway and left Idabell, one of the most energetic 85 year old women I had ever met.

"Now you just go down that street and turn left. It will take you just up the hill there by the casino we were at last night," she directed. We were gone.

We had only 22 miles to go to Ontanogan. We thought we could take our time. Leaving Baraga "up that little hill" proved to warm us up quickly as it was only 2 1/2 miles long. When we arrived at the top of yet another hill in Nisula we had just begun to really feel our leg muscles screaming. The day of rest must have started to soften them already. A small grocery store might have had a coffee counter. I asked the lady just inside the window as I took off some of my heavier clothes, but she nodded a "no." Disappointed we went in anyway. This lady was Postmaster Ruth Morris in a closet sized post office. Since this was my occupation we got to talking quickly on postal affairs as she poured us coffee from her thermos into our cups. She had also been taught by Idabell when she was younger. We lingered here just long enough to regain our strength. Starting off in brilliant sunshine uphill we waved,"so-long."

At the cut-off road to Mass, we pulled off to the left side of the roadway to rest where it looked like there would be little traffic. It wasn't long before lunch came out of the bags. The asphalt paving was warm. With our helmets making a comfortable pillow we stretched out on that warm pavement for a few minutes. We had to continue an uphill grade after leaving and seemingly the hills never went down till we arrived near Ontanogan.

I felt the exhaustion begin to set in again as Shirley pedaled on ahead. We rode our own pace as each of us became tired and then regained our strength. I lost Shirley as I went around a curve on that hill so pulled over to the side of the road to wait for her. But as I sat there I became worried when she didn't show up. I walked back around the curve a little way leaving my bike in place with the wind blowing it hard enough again to make it fall over. She came up the hill easily, telling me some woman had stopped her on the road when she had stopped to rest a bit, preaching some religion to her. Just then this same woman spotted me and preached hell and brimstone to me. I said nothing, got on my bike and rode away not knowing how else to get out of the conversation. We didn't need that.

A big IGA grocery store was the first place we had seen along the 22 miles. Since we were assured of finding a park to camp here we thought we had better replenish anything we needed. This store being well equipped to handle a deli counter and tables for sit-down eating invited us to have our dinner here. The seats weren't cushioned but it made little difference as long as they were not saddle shaped. We must be getting used to our saddles! We took an awfully long time chosing what we wanted. We must not have been too hungry. We usually ate small portions of food all day to just keep the hungry edge away and keep the energy on an upper level.

My chain jammed in the sprocket as we slowly left for the park. The inconvenience was repaired in short order and we glided down a nice downhill into town.

All of a sudden we heard this "ping" sound like we had ridden over something. We both looked down without seeing anything and rode on. Just then I noticed Shirley's back wheel wavering as she felt something not quite right also.

"I think I must have popped a spoke," she said with that "I don't believe it" look.

"Stop a minute so we can take a look." Pulling into a parking spot we confirmed the unthinkable. Neither of us carried extra spokes. Even if we had a spoke we wouldn't know how to fix it.

Riding these hills with this load would not prove a wise thing to do on a missing spoke.

There was not a spoke in town. Time was playing against us. It was 4:30 in the afternoon. One store had many outdoor items as well as mountain bikes. The young lady tried to help us as much as possible for the next hour. No, the fellow who would know where the spokes were was out of town till tomorrow but he could fix it if he had any. If he didn't, the closest shop was 60 miles away. She made a couple phone calls there. They wanted us to just bring the bike up and it would be fixed in no time.

The young helper in the store then tried to get us a bus ride, but they only ran on other days. Another young man came in saying he might be able to fix it if he could find the spoke she needed but he didn't look like he knew what he was talking about. Shirley then tried calling home but her husband wasn't there. The young lady's mother came in to take her home saying she would drive us up tomorrow to Houghton 60 miles away if we couldn't fix it by then but didn't want to stay all day.

Just then Bob Axley stopped in to see who belonged to the bikes out front. This man was about 6 feet tall, 220 pounds and a big smile. After looking over the situation he offered to fix it in short order. He seemed to know more about how to do it naming the right parts and tools.

"You go on down to the camp there to get set up for the night. I'll get the tools and spokes and be right back. I'll find you."

We rode down to the campground locating the nicest one by the water and set up. It wasn't long before a little red car pulled up with his smiling face and he started working on the wheel. Finding he had to have some other tool he jumped back into his car to get it and returned before we were able to finish setting up.

During the repair time he informed us that he had ridden around Lake Superior for his 50th birthday and was leaving on his 60th birthday to do it again in a few days. Lake Superior has to be about 1000 miles around its perimeter. He tried to explain the things he had made for lightening his load, to provide himself with entertainment and things to make the ride more comfortable. Many were quite ingenious like a sewing kit inside a pen, a fist sized mattress, tv, wrist radio. Reminded us of the comic strip, Dick Tracy.

Finding the bearing grease was dried up in the hub we found Vasoline lip balm worked well and were able to get all the bearings back in without losing them. If we hadn't put a plastic bag under the wheel we would be out looking for bearings. We were parked in beach sand. Truing the wheel took quite a long time and while we were doing this I made us all a cup of coffee mocha. We went to sleep that night with the sound of Lake Superior waves washing up on the beach, a satisfied feeling luck was still on our side and we found a new friends.

Chapter 5 Climbing Porky

As the sun was lifting itself out of the deep blue water into a cloud bank the next morning we were still bleary eyed and stiff getting out of the tent.

"Do you feel as stiff as I feel? I can hardly move," I said.

"I don't think I will get up."

"Remember what they always say, "the second day is always the worse", I recalled to her.

"But this is not the second day."

"So they lied when they said that. Maybe it's the fifth day."

I popped my head up out of the sleeping bag.

"Do you hear that?"

"What?"

"Sounds like Bob out there." Neither of us knew quite what to say or do. Bob was on his packed bike.

We crawled out of the tent as best we could, trying to look cool, heading for the outhouse.

He thought he would like to show us his gear, while we spent time making breakfast, trying to wash our faces and break camp all at the same time. We invited him along on today's ride to the mountains that were only 16 miles away on flat land and he took us up on it. He said he needed practice anyway.

"It shouldn't be too bad, Shirley," I explained, "he doesn't have a tent or sleeping bag. His intentions must be all right. You know three people can't squeeze into a two man tent."

It was nice having a different companion. He and Shirley could be heard talking a blue streak behind me. I just pedaled along. I couldn't hear well with the wind whipping by my ears anyway but I could hear them conversing.

We rolled along at our own speed that seemed to be rather slow for his hyper-active self. We still stopped every five miles. He talked constantly while riding and never quit when we weren't. There were no hills on this part. Arriving at the foothills of the Porcupine mountains it started to rain. We didn't need this. We stopped at a restaurant for coffee and more conversation but the rain still looked ominous like it wasn't going to let up. It was fairly

301

early and the campground was nearby but the pansies opted for a motel. We already knew how to put up a tent in the rain and didn't like being on the wet side.

Bob rode home on his bike saying he'd be back later with his truck to take us up to the top of the mountains to see the Lake of the Clouds. We really didn't expect to see him back but after washing our clothes and showering we went out to the lobby to see what else there was to do on a rainy afternoon without dry transportation. There he was, walking into the lobby with his truck sitting at the front door.

What were we to do? Refuse to be driven up the one way road to the top of the Porky's?

"You'd never ride all the way up there on your bikes," he said as we rode along in the truck. "I used to run up here and as you will see it is quite steep just a little further up. It was tough for us to run that." As we wound around and through the trees in the mist we could see what he was saying. I'm so glad he happened along. Nice ride down but oh, so hard going up. We could view the lake as we had seen it in so many pictures from such a high vantage point. Lake of the Clouds was a long lake nestled in miles of trees and could be seen from the higher outcropping where we walked.

Saying good-bye to Bob later was a little more difficult since he had extended so many kindnesses to us. We would surely keep in contact with him to see if he made his venture safely.

Leaving the mountain the next morning, we headed south directly into the wind and still up another long hill. It will be a long pull to any town today.

White Pine was a quiet mining town offering one restaurant for breakfast. The only event of this day other than the uphills and headwind was seeing a sheriff's car riding the opposite side of the road for miles looking off into the weeds alongside. We followed each other as we'd catch up on a downhill, he catching up with us on the uphills. We finally ran into him coming out of a restaurant eating an ice cream cone.

"What are you looking for?" Shirley asked of him.

Seems there was a motorcyclist missing from Minnesota. They were expecting foul play. We were then alerted to the search but never found him ourselves. Later in the week we heard over the news that he was found shot to death with all his identification missing as well as the license plate alongside a road where he was run off. Scary. It was one of the roads we were on, too.

Still heading in a southern direction we seemed to run out of big hills for awhile. We had a 4 mile stretch of 30 mph constant wind. We could have done with that. Made a side trip into what we thought was a town for coffee but there was no town. A bar, a small

302

store. We did find the tallest Lupine wildflowers I had ever seen along the short dirt road we took for the shortcut.

Lake Gogebic is about 10 miles long. When we came into the state camp ground on this lake we asked for a site with some sort of barrier against the wind. The lady kindly laughed but understood.

"You don't have a sticker on you bikes, do you" she asked.

"No, since when do you have to have them?" I returned. "It's not a motor vehicle.

"That's right. I wonder how they charge you?" Looked like she was new.

"I wasn't charged in a camp down state," I offered. She wasn't sure what to do but directed us to pick any site until she found an answer. In other parks at other times I was told that anyone coming in on their own power was reserved a spot but charged a minimum fee of only a couple dollars. They charged us the usual fee minus the vehicle sticker.

The black flies didn't seem to be as thick here. I was told to use an *Avon* product to ward them off but I decided I must be drawing them to me and quit using it. Perhaps that was why they weren't here. Once we set up camp at the lake we decided to lay for awhile in the sun on the grass. It was cool most of the day even with the sun, but here in a little protected site we chose it felt quite warming.

"Com'on Marion, you know you'll feel better after a walk."

"I'm just so tired, Shirley, I feel like something the cat dragged in." There were all kinds of things to investigate here. I was a reluctant. I just didn't want to go. My blood count must be low. I checked my pulse rate, it was slow for this time of day. My leg muscles said they had enough torture for one week. I just dragged along with Shirley as we investigated the beach area. Every chance I got I sat of a park bench feeling overly tired to move much. I had eaten a large apple shortly before we walked. It felt like a good case of overfill or indigestion taking hold. I worried I was just pushing myself too much; afraid I may have a physical breakdown so far from home with still a week to ride. I wondered if it was worth it.

The more I walked, the better I felt. Still tired but not as stiff. The park had created a trail walk into the woods.

"Look, there's a trail there that's marked," I said. "You want to go for a walk there?"

"How long is it?" inguired Shrley.

"I don't know, let's look." On the post a brochure gave an explanation and map with about two dozen markers posted along the way.

"Do you feel like going? You probably should walk. We can walk slow, you know, like we've been doing."

Yea, but I don't want to go in there without covering up against the ticks. Lets go back to the house and get a jacket."

303

Since there was a tick scare, we covered our bodies as best we could with clothing, tucking our pant legs in our socks the way it was recommended and began the 2 mile walk, reading the self-guiding tour paper as we went along. The ticks weren't bad but the mosquitos were. We forgot all about them, never even splashing on the repellant we carried. Hurrying along the trail, it too, was mostly uphill. Heading down out of the walk we commented on the serenity of the woods when we came upon a pile of bear scat in the trail. Our pace quickened. It looked fairly fresh and still steaming. We would have liked to have seen a bear but not on these terms. We saw none.

Mostly on our bikes, the only wildlife we saw on the road, were deer, dead and alive, possum, ground hogs, a lot of hummingbirds but only one oriole.

The wind died down. Back at our tent we found the black flies and mosquitos followed us home. We zipped ourselves into the tent to play cards. Sitting accombo, I noticed a small hard speck on my leg. "Look, what's this?"

"A wood tick."

"You're kidding! That's not the ones we aren't supposed to find, is it? I've never seen a wood or a deer tick."

We examined ourselves all over and picked several wood ticks off our legs. Examined all our clothes and bedding for the little buggers. We didn't find any of the tiny deer ticks that carried the lyme disease.

We could hardly wait to get on the road this morning. This M-64 should have taken us between any ridges of hills but we still met up with a couple steep ones. Most of the area around the lake was occupied by cottages.

On U.S. 2, we headed east hoping to have a tail wind for most of the distance back to Newberry. We found the area was devoid of any type of civilization. Nor was there any wind for some time. Just a continuously wooded area. There were plenty of horse flies. They would follow along with us, buzzing around as we pedaled, landing when we stopped.

"Get outta here," I yelled at them when they landed on my map case.

"Aren't they awful? I wonder why they are here anyway. What useful purpose do they serve?"

"Let's go, I can't stand them."

We didn't stop long when we did. Our water and any edible food was getting down to a minimum. We limited the water as best we could. Shirley still had an apple that sufficed for water. After 35 miles of the nothingness we entered Watersmeet. Stepping into an air conditioned cafe we cooled off very rapidly. We had a difficult time getting the waitress to bring enough water to replenish our bottles and ourselves. It was warm but not so warm to the non-riders. When we stopped we would drip sweat and feel warmer than we really were. It was good to sit down without flies. We stayed as long as we dared and then we were on our way.

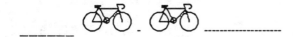

Chapter 6   The Challenge

At a roadside park, Shirley spoke to a kindly gentleman from Canada. Back on the road she had a black fly guest take hold of her eye.

"Can you see one in there?" she asked with tears running out of her eye. I poked around for a bit till she tried to do it herself in my mirror. The gentleman stopped whom she spoke with earlier and proceeded to remove it for her and made her wait till he dug through all his truck to get some kind of stuff to put in the eye. It was nice but really not necessary.

Now hills were so steep and long they required the lowest gear. Sometimes I would run up them at only 3 mph. So slow I could count the stones. I said to myself many times that if the speed would get to 2 mph I would have to get off and walk. But most of the time it would be 5 mph except on the really steep ones and it didn't last too long. Once up to the top we would gradually change into a higher gear. Sometimes we just stopped for a break. Then we'd race down at perhaps as high as 36 mph. It would be scary sometimes. When the road would narrow around a river overpass and we had to veer into the traffic lane.

The hills started coming on in more frequent succession. Our maps didn't indicate any real camping areas for quite a distance. When we came to Golden Lake we had already ridden 52 miles of frequent hills. A camp was on the end of a downhill. We pulled into it and made camp finally for the night. It was a pleasant little lake. The surface was so still you could see bottom. Every once in awhile a fish would jump making Shirley anxious to wet her meager supply line. It was a good thing we had some other food supply to rely on. She wasn't all that reliable.

It was here that I noticed my pack frame was minus a couple screws. I suppose they weren't put on as tight as they should. With the extra weight and rough roads we rode on occasion they must have worked loose. I salvaged one, borrowed the one tool to fit and taped and wired up another joint. It stayed together till arriving home. Duct tape has always saved my day.

Listening to the radio I brought along after retiring for the night it was predicted that our nice weather may come to an end tonight. There was a few times I thought I heard rain. I guess the pitter-patter I heard were varmints getting into Shirleys' bag of food she very carefully waterproofed and laid on the table outside our tent.

By morning she knew it was they that tore it all open, not getting to the little food left. We had a hurried breakfast of oatmeal and coffee. I would eat my breakfast while she rolled up her stuff and then we reversed the roles. We wanted to get on the road before it rained. We stayed ahead of it for a few miles. Just before riding into Iron River it sprinkled and then fell a bit harder. With only a couple miles to go we didn't stop to put on rain gear, hoping we could find a dry place before too long. It was a straight down hill roll into town. The cyclometer rang in at 36 mph but in the rain it took all I could to not pinch the brakes. It wouldn't have taken much to have made one little slip to be dead meat on the pavement.

It was a mile or two into the town that we happened onto a place that served breakfast. Inside there were few people as we stripped off some of our wet clothes and hung them to dry on other chairs while we relaxed and hoped the rain would quit. I made a quick call home as I did every day, settling in to the comfort of food right after. We waited till we thought we'd have to pay rent on the seats, donned our rain gear and headed out to the other side of town. On the advice of the waitress we continued on U.S. 2 rather than taking what could have been shorter route with less hills.

Just the other side of town we pulled into a shopping center for no reason at all except it was a different part of town and still a very heavy cold rain. We pulled our bikes between the double doors of a store going window shopping.

"I'm going to put on some diving wetsocks before leaving. It looks like it's going to be a long day in the cold rain. Temperatures were around 55 degrees," I told her when we came back to the forlorn looking bikes sitting between the doors. I had wanted to see if these would keep my feet warm in the rain. Now, having that chance, they worked well.

The rain let up as soon as we put rain gear on. It didn't rain till later that night. We made many clothes changes this day. The socks worked well even in the dry day.

What am I doing here? I thought as the hills came at us more frequently. We wished we would never see another but these were worse than any hills we encountered before. There seemed to be no end. We would get to the top of one hill only to see another in the distance. The hills of Iowa were not near as wicked as these. Those in southern Illinois might be close. We vowed a long

307

time ago never to go back. We vowed we would never ride there again. U.S. 2 got the same reputation.

A car going by with bikers in it (known because they were carrying them on the back of the car) yelled at us as we struggled up the hill to keep on biking! Cars automatically changed gears on the steepness of hills reminding us of the last granny gear we had and wishing we had more.

We found a motel in Crystal Falls that looked out over the valley below to the east. I could hardly wait to fill the tub with hot sudsy water and soak. The beds were hard enough to play ping-pong on them. We drove our bikes into the room leaving very little space for us. After washing out some clothes again hangers came in handy. I hung mine out behind the building out of sight of any incoming people. We took a short nap and when we awoke the sun was shining. Feeling rejuvenated we wondered what it was we could do since it was early afternoon yet.

"How about walking back into town? It can only be a mile or two."

"Sure, why not, we have nothing else to do and it will stretch our legs out." There was nothing to see in this town, but we did find a bakery to resupply some sweet rolls for morning. At the bottom of the hill a tavern was starting their Friday night fish fry. Sounded good though I was having trouble digesting greasy foods.

Rain was just beginning to fall as we left the tavern. With full stomachs we ran back up the hill to the motel. We were as soaked as our laundry. They did not get more of the purple polka-dots that fell in Baraga. As soon as we grabbed the clothes the rain quit and a double rainbow filled the sky. A good omen for tomorrow.

Shirley slept better than I did on the ping-pong beds. It wasn't much better than the ground. I thought the ground was softer. My indigestion didn't help matters. The morning sweet roll probably wasn't going to help.

Out in the cool morning we found we might just have a tail wind as soon as the wind started to blow harder. The road was much less hilly east of town. We earned this day. I could feel it. Crossing over the Wisconsin border was like turning the page of a book. Suddenly, the terrain and road surface changed. The vast amounts of trees were gone, now we were in farm country with barns, cows and plowed fields. The hoped for tail wind caught us making us fly down the road without hardly trying. We traveled at 22 mph on a flat road like it was a downhill.

"We're going to pay for this, you know that!" I hollered back to Shirley. She was enjoying the ride. The openness of the fields was such a contrast. Coming into Florence we had to stop for a real breakfast. We were doing so well we decided to tour the sport shop across the street for something to do. Questions were asnwered for several local people when they saw us and then we headed back to Michigan

At the "border" I called my friends, Jerry and Jody Kelly, in Norway to see if they were home. "Oh yes, but you only get me. I'm here. Jerry is out on the golf course." I expected that.

"OK, we'll be there in a little while. We may spend some time in Iron Mountain," I retorted.

On the advice of a waitress we did not go the back road around town. She only had to mention that it was more hilly than the town road. A mining museum was up the road.

"You want to go there?" hollered my companion when we were back on the road.

"I suppose. No, look, its up a hill." Too late. She had already turned in. "You really want to go up there?"

"Sure, why not?"

"I don't know. You are usually the one that doesn't want to go up hills." She was already up the hill when I found I was in the wrong gear and couldn't change. I walked the bike the distance.

Inside there were the usual trinkets to purchase. The saleslady started to talk to us. Before long she had two others in on the conversation. They were having a hard time believing we were on bikes. One of the ladies identified as Jean said she was a writer of the senior citizens column of the local paper.

"Would we mind being interviewed for the paper?" We didn't mind. While they talked to Shirley I wrote down a little expose` for them. "I've sent for my husband to bring a camera so we can get your picture. This will make the front page if we have a picture!" She was so excited. When he arrived we had a photo session with all of our cameras as well.

Just 10 miles down the road to Norway it started to sprinkle again. "We'll just stop in for a little bit, Shirley, if you don't care. Then we'll go find a motel." There weren't any campgrounds in the vicinity either. We didn't need to find a motel. We were invited to stay there. While we hadn't planned it, it was tempting and we didn't have to have our arms broken to be convinced.

They were the best of hosts. Jody had just made some rhubarb bread that we devoured like we hadn't eaten for a month. When Jerry arrived we finished all the rest. We changed into some more presentable clothing. While the steaks were thawing he took us for a drive to see all northern Wisconsin and southern Upper Peninsula. We saw the giant ski slide in their town that was used very little mostly for lack of snow. We walked up and around to view the area from the top and then off to see some deer feeding in the fields. Before long we were at the Mud Duck Inn for a drink and having dinner. The steaks he took out to thaw were forgotten. Jerry wouldn't have it that we pay without a floor fight so we let him do so.

They'd been telling us about the herds of deer they see everywhere in the fields, so back out we went. Just as we ran out of field we finally saw a herd. Their credibility was saved!

_____  ------------------

Chapter 7   Still Friends

While I didn't sleep well again, Shirley did. I'm glad one of us did. After lingering over breakfast long enough we all hugged and we started off. Stopped at a local grocery so I could get an antacid for my indigestion. The owner wouldn't cash a $20.00 check so I mentioned Jerry's name and he said it would be all right.

A mile out of town Shirley had a flat tire on the same tire that broke the spoke. That tire was beginning to get a bad name. Upon investigation we found a small bone fragment was the culprit. We had it fixed in less than half an hour. We were getting good! We just couldn't pump 90 pounds of pressure into it. We stopped down the road where a Department of Natural Resources fellow provided a few pumps, sending us off down the road only a few miles to Vulcan.

Vulcan had an underground train that took us into an abandoned mine, a living museum. We spent a cold half hour there and time looking at the trinkets and taking pictures of some interesting things outside.

It was here that we saw the real devastation of the tent worms. We had been riding along the side of the road where millions of the caterpillars would come out of the grass onto the roadway getting smashed by tires. We did our bit for humanity, ourselves, trying to run over as many as we could. But here at the mine they were crawling all over anything shiny as well making complete messes of themselves.

Our destination today was Escanaba. We dallied for a long time in Vulcan. Twenty miles down the road we found a nice truck stop to eat lunch. Talked to a few people explaining our destination and theirs and then off to a store to buy some goodies.

Oftentimes, there was a slight tail wind and one or two smaller hills, but nothing we couldn't handle. Riding into Bark River I stopped to call another friend who would not forgive me if I rode by without calling.

"Leo is out somewhere but I'm here. Come on back, just a mile or so," his wife pleaded.

"A mile or so against this insessant wind, I reminded her, was not something we would do for fun."

"I'll go get Leo and be right down." We sat out on the steps of the gas station and it wasn't long that a white car came roaring into the parking area blasting its horn. He jumped out of his car. "Marion, for god's sake, how are you," he said as he gave me a big hug. I knew Leo and Mary Knauf for ages as I knew Jerry and Jody. Still time was pressing on. They invited us back. He was even willing to bring a truck to bring us back but our schedule would really have been messed up if we didn't get as far as Escanaba, I explained. That was still 15-20 miles away and it was getting later than usual. We were tired.

After a short time we were off in the wind again. I was really getting exhausted. I even wondered if I could continue. Shirley rode up front of me as I took my time. I stopped for the five mile break, she kept on since we could see town from here. We had a nice dinner in Escanaba. It rejuvenated me. Stopping at a restaurant was better than being stuck eating the dregs of our survival foods! We knew we would have a good tail wind the rest of the way as we would be heading north. Thank goodness. It will be 52 miles again today. The park was good, fully equipped with bombarding biting flies and mosquitos. The showers were hot at least and the area was not yet overrun with happy campers.

Though we were still in sound of the busy highway we both slept good in the 60 degree night. It was sunny again as we finished off some more oatmeal. It was only 5 miles before we ran into an eatery. There is nothing better than starting out the day with a good breakfast but especially a good cup of coffee.

Heading out to the north was great but it only lasted to Rapid River where we turned east catching the south winds in the side again. It was beginning to do us in physically and mentally. For a long time I drafted Shirley, regaining some strength. A model of a beautiful log home on this road prompted us to stop. It was the same one I had seen in brochures I had sent for a couple years ago. We toured poking around into all the rooms wishing it was our house. When we found out the price of duplication of just the logs we lightly touched it as if it might break. Two floors, three bedrooms and three baths one with Jaccuzi, formal dining area and loft with porch around half of it ran a mere $95,000 for just the shell.

We rolled on, Shirley in front as I drafted her again. She got behind me as I regained some strength against the wind but she couldn't stay up with me. "Why don't you draft me when you're tired," I asked.

"I didn't think you wanted me to be that close," she answered. I didn't care if she drafted if she didn't touch wheels, making us fall.

312

We were heading for Indian Lakes, but with this wind decided we didn't need to go 20 miles out of our way just to say we were there. On to Manistique it would be 64 miles. We were along the coastline but the winds brought up by the expanse of Lake Michigan were rather cold. We stopped for lunch at a fishing access. It would still be a few miles to Manistique.

We came finally to a choice between two restaurants close together. I chose the one with the paved lot. I consumed another bowl of chicken soup and raspberry pie. We had almost completed our consumers test for the pie. The soup was the only thing I could ever find on the menu that wouldn't be fried in grease. Shirley tested the apple pies, I, the raspberry.

We got some more tips by a couple living in our next day's territory. What the roads were like, etc. They also told us about a trip they were about to make to the Artic circle.

"Why the Artic Circle?" I asked.

"Why not?" they came back. "We've never been there!"

We stopped at the Chamber of Commerce in Manistique to see if there were any other places besides this one at a Ramada Inn to no avail. So there we were--second class citizens again, making camp out back with the other tenters. We had access to the pool and Jaccuzi but we brought no suits with us and we were sure they would frown on skinny dipping.

Even the dining room was too elegant for our wrinkled biking clothes. We opted to take a walk on the beach, finding a secluded place away from the cool wind to lay on the sand and then back to camp to finish off survival food. It was a bittersweet last night in camp.

We slept pretty good but it didn't look too nice when we woke up, this being our last day of riding. We kept saying over and over-- only 52 more miles, only 52 more miles. It started to rain before we were packed up.

We lingered inside over a nice breakfast. (Not too many people showed up for breakfast in the elegant room at 7 am.) But just as we were ready to get on our steeds for the last leg it stopped raining. It didn't remain so for the whole day but it was cloudy and we did have some sporatic showers. As we were heading north part of the time we were thankful for the gentle push even on the less hilly roads if there were any.

Only ten miles out it started to rain again. I used to think how crazy bikers were when I saw them riding in the rain with their bikes all packed for traveling long distances, now I knew they were. Even if a biker is wearing the state of the art rain duds, I have yet to see one stay completely dry and comfortable. At best it holds in the warmth of the body. Rain doesn't get in much but it wouldn't get

313

into a zip-lock bag either. The bikers get wet from their own perspiration.

It was still raining as we arrived in Gulliver. We were directed by a grocery store owner to an incredible fine log resort. Complete with fire in the fireplace. We tried drying some of our clothes so they wouldn't feel so damp when we left. They had the best coffee and the warmest atmosphere for such a cold rainy morning.

We had quite a way to go so we didn't stay too long, heading into the wind and rain to the main highway again. As I rode along I kept warm just thinking of that fireplace. Blaney Park wasn't too far and we were going north. It didn't take us as long with the wind but there was nothing here to stop for. It was on a steep hill. Stopping at the top we glanced at the road in front of us. As far as we could see it was like a roller coaster.

"Well, we might as well keep on going. No one is going to iron them out," I sighed. We still stopped every 5 miles or so for a short rest. It proved to be a real needed affair sometimes.

At Germfask we were to take a turn to the east again but we weren't sure where. Conveniently there was an eatery on the corner. Chicken soup and pie time again. I elected to change into some dry clothes here. Taking off the wet ones I found not a dry spot. When we left I put my rain jacket back on but it wasn't raining now. It was only 5 miles down Ten Curves Road that I stopped to take it off stuffing it in my handlebar bag, hoping not to wear again that day. Shirley rode on ahead. She had a lot more energy that I now. She continued to wear her plastic rain jacket that made me sweat just looking at it. It wasn't before I caught up with her. She shed her sauna suit.

We only had 10 miles to go. As we pedaled our hearts out a car passed. It was the couple we saw in Thompson who were going to the Artic Circle. They honked and waved as they went by probably happy we took the road they recommended.

Back onto U.S. 28 it felt like we were almost to the end of our tour. I could see the van waiting to accept the bikes in its' back end. I could see our friend Vina making us a cup of coffee and I could see the rain come down. Getting to the gas station on the corner for a little reprieve we sat out this little shower not wanting to get any wetter. I had already worked up a sweat inside my sweatshirt and I could see hair dripping on Shirleys' forehead.

"Looks like we've almost got it made, gal, how do you feel about only four more miles?"

"I sure wouldn't be disappointed if someone wanted to shorten it more."

"If I remember, it was uphill when we left here 13 days ago. So it must be a slight downhill once we are over this next one."

314

"I remember how I had a hard time making it up this slight grade to McMillan," she laughed. U.S. 28 didn't have much of a shoulder so we had to very careful. We were on such smooth, wide shoulders for so long this one was rather disgusting. It was almost all downhill. It wasn't long before the blinker light became a beacon just a short way away. Vina's was just a stones throw from it and we made a B-line for it pulling into the yard thanking our lucky stars we made it safely. It was done. It was over. Another long 650 miles.

It took about two weeks for the muscles in my legs to relax back to their flabbiness. The soreness had gone out after the first four or five days of not riding and a tightness took over. The indigestion took several weeks to remove itself but I had dropped four pounds in weight even with the amount of food I put away. This may not be the end of long distance riding. It will just have to wait till I am back on my feet again.

If it hadn't been for my friend, Shirley, I don't think I could have sustained this whole trip. If it weren't for her, I would never have ventured past my front yard into the world around me. I never would have gained the confidence to go it alone. I would have had to rely on other friends telling me about the places they have seen. Best of all, we were still friends! Even though it sounded as if we were having tough times we rallied around each other and they became great experiences. We can still laugh at how miserable we felt in the cold rain on either bike or the night the 'coons ate her food bag. We sigh over the beautiful sights we saw.

I would not have experienced the Colorado River, Mt. Rainier, the bayous of Louisiana, the gold of the Feather River, the numbing cold of West Virginia, the winds of Saskatchewan, the forts in the west. I would not have seen the wagon ruts embedded in stone, the north-eastern seas, the glaciers, the mountains, the plains, the people, especially the people.

I loved those friendly Iowans, Mike Boyle, the Fischbachs', Dorothy Bacon, Bob Axley, and all the others I encountered along those few years. These experiences I share, in hopes that someone who may be afraid to venture past their front door, will learn to master that fear and enjoy our country and all it has to offer. Now it's time for me to slow the pace. I need to really get down and smell the roses in all those places I didn't have time. I want to hike the other roads in that crazy quilt. The small dotted lines that indicate trails rather than roads. Even the thin lines offer adventure.

I still want to ride my bicycle across the United States. I'm working on maps now to ride it to Florida. I want to pan for gold, backpack into the cracks and crevasses of canyons and mountains, make that trip to Alaska.

I'm only 51 years old, I tell myself. I have many years to complete what I set out to do. But there are so many things to do and not enough time to do them all. Look out, Mom, here it comes! Where do you want to go next year, Shirley?

EPILOG

The summer of 1991 was less active due to other items of interests for the two of us. We kept more to ourselves and tended to families. But time passed and yearnings to continue to do something different eroded our senses. By the end of summer we were found backpacking on Isle Royal National Park in Lake Superior.

We had a beautiful time learning to cope with 45 pound packs, some expected blisters and sore muscles. By the fourth day we felt we were old hands and could have gone more miles than planned. We were in touch with nature. The wildlife kept their distance to our displeasure but we knew they were there by their songs and droppings. Wildflowers were everywhere and we had several berry dishes to supplement our dehydrated food menu. The solitude was overwhelming. It gave us hours of time to think and talk of our own feelings about many personal things.

We discussed the ideas of volunteering our services, bringing our children to this place and everyone else we could capture. I still want to bicycle to Florida next spring. But who knows, we might have something else in mind by then.................